ESSENTIAL
ASTROLOGY

ABOUT THE AUTHOR

Amy Herring is a professional astrologer, writer, teacher, and speaker. She is a graduate of Steven Forrest's Evolutionary Astrology Apprenticeship Program and has studied with Jeffrey Wolf Green's Pluto School. Her articles have appeared in popular publications such as *Llewellyn's Moon Sign Book*, *Dell Horoscope Magazine*, and *WellBeing Astrology*. Amy offers a multitude of learning resources, articles, worksheets, and videos at her website, HeavenlyTruth.com, and her YouTube channel features her popular 10-Minute Astrology video learning series. Her first book, *Astrology of the Moon*, focusing on the natal and progressed Moon, was published in 2010.

Everything You Need to Know to
Interpret Your Natal Chart

ESSENTIAL

ASTROLOGY

AMY HERRING

Llewellyn Publications
Woodbury, Minnesota

FIRST EDITION
First Printing, 2016

Cover art: iStockphoto.com/31215554/©pixelparticle
         iStockphoto.com/59729414/©robertsrob
         iStockphoto.com/11782688/©omergenc
Cover design: Ellen Lawson
Interior illustrations: Llewellyn Art Department

Llewellyn is a registered trademark of Llewellyn Worldwide Ltd.

Library of Congress Cataloging-in-Publication Data
Names: Herring, Amy, 1974– author.
Title: Essential astrology : everything you need to know to interpret your natal chart / by Amy Herring.
Description: First Edition. | Woodbury : Llewellyn Worldwide, Ltd, 2016. | Includes bibliographical references.
Identifiers: LCCN 2015044363 (print) | LCCN 2015045329 (ebook) | ISBN 9780738735634 | ISBN 9780738747798 ()
Subjects: LCSH: Natal astrology. | Birth charts.
Classification: LCC BF1719 .H47 2016 (print) | LCC BF1719 (ebook) | DDC 133.5/4—dc23
LC record available at http://lccn.loc.gov/2015044363

Llewellyn Worldwide Ltd. does not participate in, endorse, or have any authority or responsibility concerning private business transactions between our authors and the public.

All mail addressed to the author is forwarded but the publisher cannot, unless specifically instructed by the author, give out an address or phone number.

Any Internet references contained in this work are current at publication time, but the publisher cannot guarantee that a specific location will continue to be maintained. Please refer to the publisher's website for links to authors' websites and other sources.

Llewellyn Publications
A Division of Llewellyn Worldwide Ltd.
2143 Wooddale Drive
Woodbury, MN 55125-2989
www.llewellyn.com

Printed in the United States of America

OTHER BOOKS BY AMY HERRING

Astrology of the Moon
(Llewellyn, 2010)

CONTENTS

SECTION THREE: CHART INTERPRETATION

FIGURES

ACKNOWLEDGMENTS

I gotta give the love to Capricorn for this book's existence.

Thank you to my Capricorn Sun husband for his deep, patient breaths when I told him I was going to write a second book and his stoic support of me before, during, and after. He makes me laugh every day—at him and with him.

Thank you to my Capricorn Moon best friend for nagging me to write a beginner's book for over ten years. Such persistence!

As always, thank you to Steven Forrest, my Capricorn Sun mentor, who gave me words for a kind of depth astrology I could only sense existed so many years ago.

Thank you to all my students (Capricorns and otherwise!) for re-breaking the seal on my sense of wonder every time I see *their* minds blown by astrology.

A special thank you to Melissa, who generously offered me her inspiring space to write uninterrupted not once, but twice; Christi, for allowing me to exploit her novice status to read and comment on the completed manuscript; and Oscar, for serving as my token authority on Leo.

INTRODUCTION
BETWEEN FATE AND FREE WILL

Astrology is able to reflect the living, changing reality that we are all living as real, multi-dimensional people, and that each component of a chart embodies a range of potential, not a set of one-dimensional behaviors. The natal chart, while it is fixed in *time*, reveals a path of infinite growth, not a set of finite personality stereotypes. All definitions and techniques in this book will be presented with this idea in mind.

You've heard the declarative statements and definitive personality traits of the Sun signs, such as Geminis are fickle, Cancers love children, and Virgos are fussy. Debunking and unpacking those stereotypes is at the heart of the purpose of this book. Astrology's best use is not to define and limit but to allow us to know and fulfill our potential, remove internal roadblocks, and even to heal our wounds. Inherent in human nature is the potential to evolve, and good astrology focuses on that potential, revealing the path toward evolution. A natal chart is less a set of definite personality traits and more a map to living life at your maximum potential, fulfilling the unique needs and gifts you bring to it.

This book approaches astrology from a psychological and symbolic point of view. You will learn to think more psychologically as you use the techniques and definitions in this book because you will have to think beyond stereotypical sign behaviors and think more about their motivations. Rather than assuming that all Geminis talk a lot or all Leos want to be the center of attention, you'll come to understand why that may or may *not* always be true.

Psychologist Carl Jung said that "when an inner situation is not made conscious, it appears outside, as fate." Many people reject astrology because they do not like the idea that their personality or future has been predetermined, robbing them of their free will to act. However, astrology can comfortably encompass both the ideas of fate and free will, and modern astrology looks much less favorably on the fateful, rigid definitions that ancient astrology favored.

Fate can be defined as something inevitable or set in stone, traits or circumstances that are beyond our control. The planetary motion of the heavens is predictable and happens on its own, which is fateful. That you were born while the Sun was in a certain place in the sky is permanent and unchangeable, yet understanding what that means about you and how you can respond to that energy flowing inside of you is in your control and you can act according to conscious choices and personal free will. In working within your natal chart, you can become more aware of your potential and therefore make choices that move you toward wholeness, keeping you in touch with your true self and making it less likely you'll feel a victim of fate. The standard astrological stereotypes may reflect your life less accurately the more you become conscious of and embody your true self, while learning to respond creatively to and with your natal chart.

Don't think of your natal chart as an instructional manual, but as your own personal myth—to work with, live through, and also live-beyond. Your natal chart can be thought of as your toolbox for this lifetime. In it are sturdy, reliable tools that you can use to build your life, but learning to use those tools properly and to their full potential is the key to building the life you want. A hammer is a tool, but you can use it to build a house or smash your own thumb. It is helpful to think of your natal chart as what you are becoming and creating, in addition to what you already are.

BEYOND SUN SIGNS AND HOROSCOPES

While there are many theories, no one can say definitively why astrology works. Astrologers tend to abide by the axiom "as above, so below," meaning that what we see reflected in the heavens, we also see symbolically on Earth. This book is written from the perspective that the movement of the heavens is reflective of or synchronous with events on Earth, not that planetary movement *causes* anything. Your natal chart does not cause you to behave the way you do or think the way you do, but simply provides insight into your inner workings.

You may have come to astrology by way of reading your horoscope now and then and having it pique your interest. A horoscope that you might read in a newspaper, magazine, or book or on a website is a short interpretation of what might happen in your life during a given time (typically a day, week, month, or year) based on your sign, or, to be more specific, your *Sun* sign. When you ask someone what their sign is, you are actually asking them what their Sun sign is, which is determined by the sign the Sun was traveling through on the date of your birth. If you are a Cancer, for instance, your birthday falls in late June or early to mid July, when the Sun travels through the sign of Cancer every year. All of the other planets were also in a particular sign when you were born, but Sun signs are the most widely known.

Most people don't realize that horoscopes are just one aspect of astrology, and are often a poor representation. The term *horoscope* has been popularized to mean the brief descriptive paragraphs that you find in a daily newspaper, monthly magazine, Sun sign almanac, or website that attempt to forecast what your day, week, month, or year will be like and what events will unfold. The actual definition of a horoscope, however, is an entire astrological chart that depicts the planets placed in signs and houses, and is what you will study in this book. To avoid confusion, the terms *chart* or *natal chart* will be used when discussing the entirety of an astrological chart.

Horoscopes vary as much as the people writing them. Astrological symbols have essential core meanings, but those meanings are open to interpretation depending on someone's point of view, experiences, and astrological knowledge. If you are a Cancer, you might get one message from one Cancer horoscope and a different message from another horoscope from a different source. Assuming that qualified astrologers wrote both horoscopes and both horoscopes were written for your sign, one is not necessarily more correct than the other, as each is an *interpretation* of a variety of celestial events that might be happening and relevant to Cancers.

Sun sign horoscopes can be a form of "diluted" astrology because they are based only on your Sun sign and make assumptions about (or ignore) the rest of your chart in order to make one size fit all. A criticism most people have about astrology is that it lumps everyone on the planet into twelve categories, which seems too limited to account for human diversity. What are the chances that every Cancer is having exactly the same experiences on a given day? Slim to none. The value of horoscopes lies mostly in attracting people to astrology due to their "entertainment value"—a disclaimer that is often used to excuse the all-too-likely possibility that a horoscope might not come true. These horoscopes are limited, and are more useful in their capacity as a thought for the day rather than something to live your life by. One could say they are astrology's poetry.

Popular astrology, such as canned sign definitions, computer-generated astrology reports, and Sun sign horoscopes, is often ineffective because they are one person's interpretation, fixed and unchanging, which many people unfamiliar with astrology's complexity will then read and consider to be *the* definitive statement about any particular component of astrology. Astrology *itself* is fluid. Just like a group of one hundred words could be used to make an infinite variety of sentences and stories, the keywords of astrology are not all there is to astrology; the sum is greater than its parts. As we dip our toe into the Cancer experience, for example, we interact with it; it is alive and we respond creatively to it and within it. All you can do with a rote interpretation is accept it or reject it because it doesn't reveal its essence;

it is pre-distilled and fed to you in short, shallow nuggets of interpretation. That is not self-knowledge or self-exploration, but self-definition and self-categorization.

Astrology is a *symbolic* language of life. Symbols lose their efficacy when their fluid, multifaceted, living nature is pinned down into one solid, unchanging form. When the symbolic is made literal, it becomes flat, dull, and lifeless. Mistaking a manifestation of a symbol for the symbol itself misses the point. The symbol is a rich, deep well from which manifestations of that symbol can be drawn. Its representations are each reflections of that essence, not the essence itself. Like Plato's Forms or Jung's archetypes, we draw from that well when we participate in and embody those energies, but when we try to make a symbol literal, it becomes flat, two-dimensional, and inflexible. Astrology as a fixed, literal tool of definition and prediction fails too often when applied to an individual who cannot be reduced to a collection of rigid personality traits.

Even if you had a natal chart that was identical to someone else's (and you very well may), that person would not necessarily live as you do, have the same experiences as you, or make the same choices as you in every case. Astrologer Elizabeth Rose Campbell said it well: "The car is the same, but the driver is different."

Instead, the natal chart is your constant companion, a guide to consult when you are feeling lost and when you want to remember who you are at the core. It doesn't reveal everything, but it reveals the important things: the creative building blocks of you. It is a symbol from which your life can spring, renewed, at any and every moment in which you draw breath.

A natal chart interpretation should facilitate soul-making and soul-expression, not replace it with definitions of the limitations of what a person is, as if astrology can even see that. Instead of defining the branches, we peer at and nurture the root, so the person can use it to grow.

HOW TO USE THIS BOOK

This book is not a smorgasbord of astrology. You will not find a single word about a sign's signature flower, gemstone, favorite color, or average shoe size in this book. Only the *essential* meanings of the signs, planets, houses, and aspects, simply but deeply defined, are present, not flaky keywords and stereotypes that contain no personalized meaning. You will also learn how to quickly get into the nitty-gritty of interpreting a chart with skill and insight. You will find out how to get to the deepest layers of a natal chart, and bring what is most essential and meaningful to the surface. Many valuable and interesting topics branch out from these essentials, such as the study of asteroids, comets, fixed stars, decanates, or transits and progressions. All of these topics are worthy of further study and can enrich your knowledge and application of astrology, but they all build off of an understanding of the essentials of natal astrology.

You'll want to have a copy of your birth chart on hand while you read this book. To have a complete and accurate calculation of your natal chart, you will need to know your birth date, place of birth, and the exact time of your birth. In most cases, the most challenging birth data to identify is the exact birth time. In the last few decades, birth times have been documented more regularly on the birth certificate, and your birth certificate will likely be the most reliable source for an accurate birth time. If you do not have a copy of your birth certificate, it's a good idea to obtain one! See the resources at the end of this book for suggestions on how to get a copy of your birth certificate and how to get a copy of your natal chart if you don't already have one.

If your birth certificate does not list your birth time, look for any other document on which it might have been recorded, such as an old family bible, family tree, baby book, or photo album. After searching documents, asking relatives is your next best bet. It's important to try to find the birth time documented first, since relatives, even Mom or Dad, can be mistaken.

If after all efforts you are unable to obtain your birth time, there is one other option known as chart rectification. This process involves gathering the dates of a number of significant experiences in your life and using them to trace backward, in a manner of speaking, to arrive at your likely birth time. It is not a simple process and has a margin of error, so it's not a good substitute for exhausting all other efforts to find your exact birth time. If you do pursue rectification, it can be very useful to have at least a vague idea of your birth time, such as "in the morning" or "after your dad got off work," or "in the wee hours." These statements can help narrow down the possibilities for an astrologer to rectify your natal chart.

Chart rectification must be performed by a highly skilled and experienced astrologer to yield the best results, as rectification is a very detailed and complicated process with a high margin for error in inexperienced hands. Because of this, not all astrologers offer chart rectification.

If you cannot find your birth time and rectification is not an option, don't despair. Your full birth date will map your planets and signs (without the houses) accurately enough, with the exception of the Moon. The Moon moves rapidly and changes signs roughly every two and a quarter days; therefore, the odds of the Moon having moved into another sign sometime on your birth date is higher than for the other planets.

When calculating your birth chart on a website or in a program, a default birth time will likely be required. Using noon is a good default if you don't know the exact time. The location of the planets in their signs will not change much, if at all, as long as you have the correct day of birth. The Moon is, again, the exception. If you calculate your chart using a default noon birth time and find that the Moon in the chart has just entered or is about to leave a sign, then it's impossible to know your natal Moon sign without a birth time.[1]

---

1. There are other methods (such as a solar chart) available that attempt to map the houses with no birth time. However, it is this astrologer's opinion that the inaccuracies inherent in such methods render these methods ineffective for placing the planets in their houses.

Chart calculation by hand is an interesting and admirable skill, but is not covered in this book. Accurate astrological software or websites can calculate your natal chart for you, but chart calculation is a process that has many opportunities for inaccuracies to creep in, so be sure to use a reliable program or website to calculate your natal chart. When in doubt, use more than one source to confirm the accuracy. Software and website suggestions are in the back of this book.

As you will soon see while reading this book, astrology is a powerful tool for insight into anyone's personality. Just as it has been deemed unethical for psychologists to talk about their private client sessions or doctors to reveal medical conditions of their patients without consent, it is also considered, in the astrological community, unethical to read a person's chart without their permission. The sensitive nature of what can be revealed, even with people who don't give credence to astrology, can be a violation of trust, especially in an age where information is becoming almost more valuable than money.

There are exceptions, of course, such as a parent reading their own child's chart, or reading the chart of a public figure, but it is always best to get permission before looking at another's chart, especially if you intend to share information about it with others.

SECTION ONE
THE HISTORY AND
ASTRONOMY OF ASTROLOGY

CHAPTER 1
THE HISTORY OF ASTROLOGY

WHAT IS ASTROLOGY?

Astrology is the study of the planets, stars, and other heavenly bodies based on the idea that they symbolically reflect (not cause) human personalities and affairs. Astrology has been called a language of symbols. Just like each letter of our alphabet has its own sound or set of sounds, each astrological symbol has a meaning or set of meanings. Just as we put letters of the alphabet together to form words, we can put astrological symbols together to form more nuanced and complex meanings.

Central to astrology is the concept of something or someone beginning. Whether it's an event, a country, or a person, it has a birth. Looking to the placement of certain planetary bodies at the moment of birth forms the astrology chart. A natal chart, or birth chart, usually refers specifically to the birth of an individual. Defining a distinct beginning can be difficult. When does something begin—when the idea was conceived or when the form took its final shape? While there is a branch of astrology that studies the prenatal condition, a natal chart is constructed based on the moment when something took independent form, as opposed to conception.

A BRIEF HISTORY

Astrology has been applied throughout the ages with different philosophical concepts driving it. Initially it was used as a form of divination, to determine the future and divine the will of the gods. Through further development and merging of different cultures, astrology developed into a more complex system. After a lengthy and prestigious reign, astrology's popularity died down and was looked on negatively in the seventeenth and eighteenth centuries, before it found its way back into the public's interest and imagination.

Theosophists like Alan Leo tried to simplify astrology to be more easily accessible and understood by the general public. The focus of astrology also shifted from divination to character interpretation (Leo's motto was "Character is destiny"). Astrologers such as Dane Rudhyar and Marc Edmund Jones carried it further into psychological interpretations as psychology gained popularity, and even the respected psychologist Carl Jung studied astrology, coining the term synchronicity as an expression of what astrology is built on: a correlation of seemingly unconnected events that happen simultaneously.

Popular Sun sign columns made astrology more accessible and are still what mainstream astrology focuses on today, although most people don't realize the depth contained within astrology because of this trend. Astrology is a system that has proven its ability to adapt to its users and to the current zeitgeist, with a long and diverse tradition to draw from.

CHAPTER 2
THE ASTRONOMY
OF ASTROLOGY

ASTRONOMY VS. ASTROLOGY

Both astronomy and astrology encompass the study of the stars and planets but for different purposes and with different methods. For most of history they were joined; astronomers were astrologers and vice versa. Much of what we know about astronomy today was discovered and studied by astrologers, because the two disciplines were relatively inseparable for much of history.

TROPICAL ASTROLOGY

Astrology is the broad heading for a diverse arena of systems and techniques that have developed over time all over the world. While the basic idea is the same, the methods in which this idea is carried out can vary. Tropical astrology, which is sometimes called Western astrology, is used widely and is the approach used in this book. Tropical astrology divides the sky into twelve equally sized signs, beginning with Aries as the first sign. Aries starts at the point of the March equinox, one of the two times of the year when the Sun is aligned with the earth's equator, and the earth's axial tilt is pointed neither away from or toward the Sun. The March equinox is one of the two dates each year when the day and night are of equal length. The two equinoxes mark the beginning point of Aries and the beginning point of its op-posite sign, Libra. The two solstices, when the Sun reaches its highest or lowest point relative to the equator, mark the points of Cancer and Capricorn, respectively.[2]

---

2. The tropical astrological system is based on the earth's relationship to the Sun as it moves through the sky, not the relatively fixed points of the constellation of the same name. The signs and constellations may share a name in Western culture, but they do not align perfectly with each other in the sky due to a phenomenon known as *axial precession*, more commonly referred to as the *precession of the equinoxes*. See the glossary for more information.

CHAPTER 3

THE NATAL CHART MAP

When you begin a journey, you need a map. In the case of your astrological journey, that map is your birth chart, or natal chart. A natal chart is essentially a simplified map of the heavens at the moment of your birth, as it would look from your birthplace, a sort of freeze-frame snapshot. The location of the Sun, Moon, and the planets are shown two-dimensionally in a chart. The earth is not placed in the chart because it is in the center. While it has been known for centuries that the planets revolve around the Sun and not the earth, astrology originated before this was common knowledge and is based on observation from the vantage point of Earth. Most astrological traditions operate from a geocentric (Earth-centered) point of view, perhaps because it is subjective experience, not detached observation, that makes astrology meaningful and personal. Even now, astrology is all about the observer, and at least from this perspective, the universe really does revolve around you!

The astronomy of a natal chart is fascinating and complex. The conveniences of accurate computer-program calculation of charts have made it easier than ever to create a natal chart in seconds. While you do not need to know how to perform the calculations to interpret a natal chart, knowing a few foundational concepts will help you understand the basics of how the three-dimensional sky is translated into a two-dimensional map.

THREE-DIMENSIONAL ASTROLOGY

Imagine looking out at the night sky. We know that the universe around us seems infinite in every direction and that the pinpoints of light we see are heavenly bodies that are tremendous and varied distances away from the earth. However, *visually* speaking, it appears that the velvet black backdrop that is the sky has been decorated with diamonds. This backdrop is referred to as the *celestial sphere*, and it is against this backdrop that we project the zodiac and other divisions of space used to organize an astrology chart (figure 1).

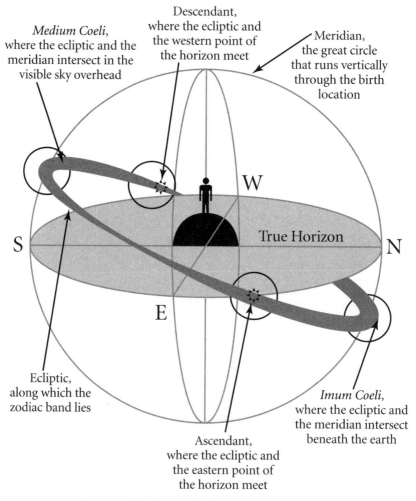

Figure 1: The Celestial Sphere and Great Circles

An imaginary line drawn through the earth is called a great circle. Rather than seeing this as a simple line, think of this division as a plane, slicing through the earth and out into space, like a magician's blade appears to slice through a trusting assistant when performing the illusion of cutting someone in half in the magic box.

To keep things simple, we'll focus on three great circles that are most relevant to the creation of the natal chart map: the *ecliptic*, the *horizon*, and the *meridian*. These planes run through the center of the earth and out into the celestial sphere at different angles.

The ecliptic marks the Sun's apparent path against the starry constellations through the year (just imagine that you could still see the stars despite the bright sunlight). The twelve signs encircle the earth along this path, known as the band of the zodiac. The zodiac band is made up of the twelve signs, sections of sky equally spaced around the circle, from Aries to Pisces in a fixed order.

The horizon divides the earth and heavens into the northern and southern hemispheres. The *true* or *rational* horizon runs through the center of the earth and is what is used in chart calculation.

While the horizon divides the earth horizontally, the meridian at your birth location divides the earth and sky vertically, dividing the earth and heavens into eastern and western hemispheres.

The intersections of these circles determine important points in the natal chart. Where the ecliptic and the horizon intersect determine the Ascendant and Descendant in a natal chart. The intersections of the ecliptic and the meridian determine the *Medium Coeli* and *Imum Coeli*. In astrological practice, these intersecting points are more commonly called the Midheaven and the Nadir.[3]

---

3. The *Medium Coeli* is commonly referred to by astrologers as the Midheaven and the *Imum Coeli* as the Nadir. However, this can get confusing when referencing astronomical designations, because the astronomical nadir is actually the point directly underneath the observer, whereas the astrological Nadir refers to the point under the earth where the ecliptic and the meridian meet. Likewise, the terms Midheaven and Zenith are sometimes used interchangeably, but this is incorrect; the astronomical zenith is the point directly above the observer, whereas the astrological Midheaven is the point above the earth where the ecliptic and the meridian meet.

Although it is the earth that spins, the signs of the zodiac appear to spin around us, each one rising and setting in succession. Because the earth spins on its axis roughly once every twenty-four-hour day, all twelve signs rise and set every day. The sign that was rising over the eastern horizon at the moment and location of your birth is known as your *rising sign*, or Ascendant,[4] and the sign that was setting at the same time and place is your Descendant. The planets, Sun, and Moon all appear to move around us in the same fashion, rising over the eastern horizon and setting over the western horizon throughout the day, carried along with the signs as they appear to rise and set in rotation.

TWO-DIMENSIONAL ASTROLOGY

An astrology chart is typically drawn as a circle (figure 2).

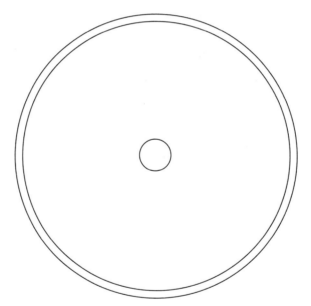

Figure 2: The Blank Astrology Chart

---

4. Although the terms *rising sign* and *Ascendant* are often used interchangeably, there is a specific difference between the two. The rising sign refers to the entire sign that was rising over the horizon in the place and time of your birth, whereas the Ascendant refers to the specific intersection at which that rising sign and the horizon meet.

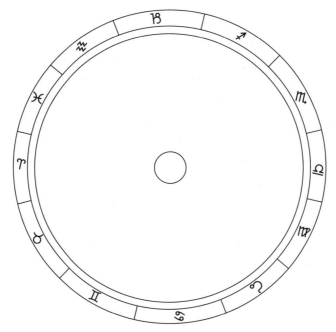

Figure 3: The Zodiac Band

SIGNS

The zodiac band containing the twelve signs is set around the outside of the circle, with the sign that was rising set at the left (figure 3).

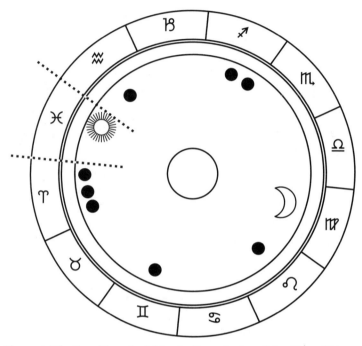

Figure 4: The Sun Placed within the Boundaries of the Sign of Pisces;
Planets, Yet Unlabeled, Dot the Circle

PLANETS

Planets may appear anywhere in this circle, according to the sign they were in at the time of your birth. The planets appear to move around the earth as they orbit the Sun and fall within the boundaries of a sign at any given point in their orbit. For instance, when you were born, perhaps the Sun could be seen when looking out into the section of sky we call Pisces. That means that the Sun would appear against the backdrop of the celestial sphere in the section of the ecliptic designated as Pisces (figure 4).

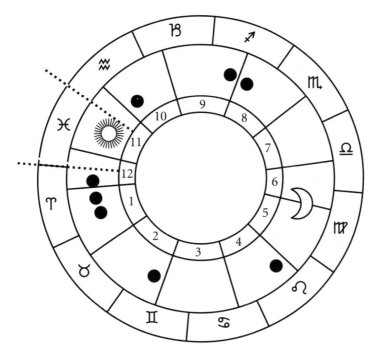

*Figure 5: The Sun Placed within the Boundaries of the Sign of Pisces
and also within the Boundaries of the Eleventh House*

HOUSES

A natal chart is divided through the center into twelve houses, like
pieces of a pie (figure 5). The houses are numbered 1–12, starting with
the first house on the left and ending with the twelfth house, and con-
secutively numbered in counterclockwise fashion around the chart.
House and sign boundaries are called *cusps*. As you can see, the planets
in figure 4 have not moved, but the houses have appeared over the top.
Houses *overlay* the circle of the chart and therefore "house" the planets
and signs within their boundaries.[5] Sign boundaries and house boundaries do not always align, so think of them independently.

---

5. It's important to note that in most styles of chart drawing, the sign boundaries
   are not marked all the way through the circle as the houses are, to avoid confusion. However, the sign boundaries, as well as the house boundaries, run all the way
   through a chart.

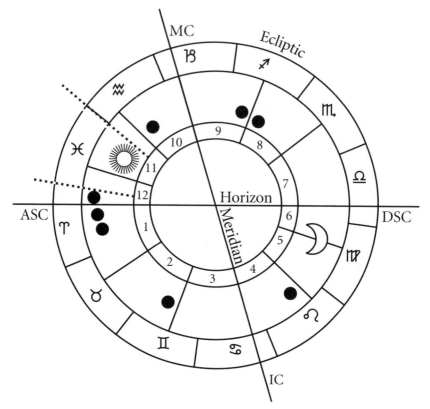

Figure 6: The Great Circles and Angles Represented in the Natal Chart

ANGLES

The house divisions stem from the meridian and horizon circles mentioned previously. The four points at which these two great circles intersect the ecliptic mark an angle (figure 6). The angle called the Ascendant (or ASC) is the first house cusp, the angle called the *Imum Coeli* (or IC) is the fourth house cusp, the angle called the Descendant (or DSC) is the seventh house cusp, and the angle called the *Medium Coeli* (or MC) is the tenth house cusp, with all other houses falling in between. Planets above the horizon in the chart are planets that were actually visible in the sky at a person's time of birth. Planets below the horizon in the chart are planets that were not visible and were beneath our viewpoint at the time and place of birth.

Unlike the signs, the houses are not all necessarily the same size; each house's beginning location is derived from the earthly time and location of your birth rather than distributed evenly across the sky. A chart is sometimes referred to as a "wheel" because it is round and the lines drawn through the center of the chart that mark the house boundaries are reminiscent of spokes.

The houses will always be in numerical order, but their individual size and the signs nearby will appear differently for someone born in a different location. If we see the Moon in Taurus in the fourth house in a natal chart, it tells us that at the time of this person's birth, the sign of Taurus was under the earth, and the Moon was in that Taurus section of sky—again, under the earth, as defined from our specific birth location. For someone born at the same moment elsewhere on the planet, Taurus, and the Moon, may be high in the sky, and in the tenth house of the natal chart of *that* person.

ASTROLOGY'S GLYPHS

If astrology is a language, then glyphs are its shorthand. Each planet and sign has its own symbol to represent it (as shown in the sign band in the previous examples). These symbols, called *glyphs*, are a convenient way to organize the names of all of astrology's components neatly into a chart wheel. Becoming familiar with and eventually memorizing the glyphs will help you sight-read any chart. Every planet, sign, and aspect has a glyph to represent it. The houses use glyphs you are already familiar with: the numbers 1–12. You will learn about aspects later.

Planets
⊙ Sun
☽ Moon
☿ Mercury
♀ Venus
♂ Mars
♃ Jupiter
♄ Saturn

♅ Uranus

♆ Neptune

♇ Pluto (or ♇)

Signs

♈ Aries

♉ Taurus

♊ Gemini

♋ Cancer

♌ Leo

♍ Virgo

♎ Libra

♏ Scorpio

♐ Sagittarius

♑ Capricorn

♒ Aquarius

♓ Pisces

Aspects

☌ Conjunction

✶ Sextile

□ Square

△ Trine

☍ Opposition

DEGREES

To more precisely note the location of a planet in a natal chart, degrees are used. Planets are not just placed in their signs in our natal chart map, but are also accompanied by notations that show at what degree a planet was located at the time of birth. It is not enough to know that Jupiter was traveling through Libra at the moment of birth, but *how far into* Libra? Beginning? Middle?

Since the sky is represented by a circle (the natal chart), and the signs lie along the edge of that circle, the degrees derive from the signs. A circle is measured as 360 degrees. Each sign is 30 degrees wide (or ¹⁄₁₂th of that circle), and there are 12 signs (12 signs x 30 degrees = 360 degrees). Planets and house cusps are assigned a numerical degree depending on where they fall within a sign.

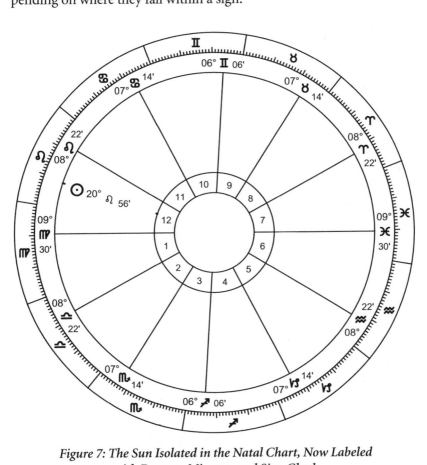

Figure 7: The Sun Isolated in the Natal Chart, Now Labeled with Degrees, Minutes, and Sign Glyph

In figure 7, we see that the Sun is 20 degrees into the sign of Leo. You can see the degree symbol (°) following the 20.

Just as a day is divided into hours, and hours into minutes, degrees are divided in the same way. There are 60 minutes in a degree, just as in an hour. The Sun's position at 20 degrees of Leo also shows a second number: 56. That means that the Sun was 20 degrees and 56 minutes into Leo, which is very near the end of that particular degree and almost into 21 degrees. Minutes are shown with a small apostrophe (') following them to distinguish them from degrees and to specify a planet's location within a sign with further precision.[6, 7]

The importance of degrees and minutes will become more relevant when learning about planetary aspects. For now, just become familiar with seeing degrees and minutes next to a planet's symbol and note how they help you further specify a planet's location within a sign and house.

---

6. Minutes in the context of an astrology chart aren't a measurement of time, but a measurement of distance.

7. Minutes can be divided into seconds. Just as there are 60 minutes in a degree, there are 60 seconds in a minute. The precision of seconds in a planet's position in an astrology chart is typically unnecessary, and it is not common to see them noted along with degrees and minutes in a chart.

CHAPTER 4
READING THE MAP

Now that you know how the map is constructed and what the components represent, you will be able to "read" the map to orient yourself to everything's location. Interpretation of the *meaning* of each planet's location will follow, but you must be able to orient yourself with a chart before you can probe into what it means. You can start anywhere, but for now, start with the Sun.

Using figure 7, locate the Sun by its glyph ($\odot$).

Next, note that the Sun is in the sign of Leo (Ω), as you can see by noticing that it falls within the edges of the Ω sign section as shown along the outside of the wheel, and also that the glyph for Leo lies next to the degree notation for the Sun. We can also see that the Sun is in Leo by tracing the sign boundaries and noting that the Sun falls within the boundaries of Leo. Note the degree and minute of the Sun's position within that sign, which is 20 degrees and 56 minutes.

Then note that the Sun is in the twelfth house, because the Sun's glyph falls within the lines that section off house number 12 on the natal chart map.

You now can state the location of a planet in a natal chart in an organized way. Put it all together like this:

The Sun is at 20 degrees 56 minutes of Leo, in the twelfth house.

Or use the shorthand version: $\odot 20°\Omega 56'$, 12th

HOUSES AND ANGLES

The planets are not the only objects on your natal chart map you'll want to be able to locate. Each house cusp falls within the boundaries of a sign, too, just as a planet does, and you'll need to know how to spot and note that as well.

Start with the first house cusp, also known as the Ascendant, in figure 7. It is the first "pie piece" section starting from the left side of the chart, simply labeled "1". The line just above it is where the first house *begins*, so it is the first house cusp. The line where the first house *ends* is actually also the beginning of the second house, so it is the second house cusp, and so on. Trace the first house cusp from the center out to the sign wheel along the outside of the chart, and you'll see what sign boundaries the line falls within—in this case, Virgo (♍), and more specifically, 9 degrees and 30 minutes of Virgo (9°♍30'). Drop your gaze to the line that divides the first house from the second house, and do the same thing, noting that in this example the second house cusp falls in Libra (♎), specifically beginning at 3 degrees and 42 minutes of Libra (3°♎42').

ASTROLOGICAL GRAMMAR

Astrology is like a language; it has defined components that can be put together to create whole sentences that can communicate something meaningful. Becoming intimately familiar with the depth of meaning in each component will take time and is discussed in later chapters. For now, here's a quick look at astrology's "grammar."

Planets represent different fundamental human needs and the various voices inside of us that clamor for our attention. Planets are like the nouns of a chart, defining the who or what.

Signs represent the different ways a planet can express its needs. Signs are like the adjectives of a chart that reveal the style in which we meet the needs of our planetary nouns.

Houses represent our various activities and behaviors in life and the context or situations in our lives that we might look to in order to most comfortably meet our planetary needs (nouns) in the style (adjectives) we find most fulfilling. The houses are the verbs of the chart.

To create an astrological sentence, start with the planet and put it *in* a sign and house—for example, "Venus in Pisces in the third house."

Aspects take things a step further, connecting whole sentences into the paragraphs and chapters that create our complex and intricate inner story.

SECTION TWO
ASTROLOGICAL MEANINGS

CHAPTER 5
THE PLANETS

THE ROLE PLANETS PLAY

The planets represent the basic, universal experiences of being human and can be expressed as a particular need or set of needs that we all have and are motivated to fulfill. How we go about fulfilling those needs and the way in which we prioritize them can vary among individuals, but we all have feelings and want to protect ourselves when we feel vulnerable (symbolized by the Moon), and we all have the need to learn and express our thoughts, opinions, and beliefs (symbolized by Mercury), and so on.

A planet represents a human desire or need but doesn't dictate how that need must be met. The characteristics, personality, and style of fulfilling and defining the planetary needs come mostly from the sign that a planet acts through. A planet represents a desire for some sort of action to be taken or a need to be fulfilled. *How* it goes about defining those needs and the style in which it takes those actions is governed by the sign the planet is in, and the types of behaviors through which those needs are expressed are governed by the house the planet resides in. Therefore, the planets themselves have a somewhat neutral, undiluted style, until placed in a sign and house, where the planet's motive is filled out with the hows and whys of fulfilling that agenda.

Picture a natal chart as a theater. Planets can be compared to actors, signs to wardrobe and props, and houses to the stage and scenery itself.

A pair of tights, a tunic, and a set of wings invoke the idea of a fairy, but until an actor steps into that fairy wardrobe, there is no action on stage. Everyone's theater is the same. The twelve signs and twelve houses are laid out, ready to be tried on and tell a story. As the planetary actors enter the theater, they decide which clothes, props, and sets will best tell the story they want to tell. Your natal chart holds the planets in particular signs and houses that help you tell and experience *your* story.

PLANETS DEFINED

The Sun and Moon are not planets. The Sun is a star and the Moon is an orbiting satellite for the earth.[8] The North and South Nodes of the Moon are not even actual objects at all, but are calculated points in space. As you'll see, there are many points in space and heavenly bodies that are referenced in an astrology chart that aren't technically planets but fall in the planet category because of their function in a chart and for ease of reference. Astrologically speaking, the word planet is often used as a catchall term that can include luminaries, asteroids, and mathematically defined points.

THE SUN

The Sun represents the need to create and sustain a coherent and consistent sense of self and a healthy self-image. While our family, friends, lovers, culture, and many other factors have an influence on our sense of self, the Sun represents the core traits and needs that we have internalized as being foundational to the person we are.

The Sun is the energy core that makes the machine of self run. When we express ourselves in the style of our Sun's requirements and we do the behaviors that are consistent with our Sun's needs (as defined by its sign and house placement in our chart), we keep our inner core fueled, providing us with the vitality to live and thrive, enlivening and sustaining us. The Sun's placement in your natal chart can tell you what behaviors are most self-affirming to you.

---

8. The Sun and Moon are sometimes referred to as the *luminaries*.

The way we express our core qualities of self and how we take what we are and create definitions and guidelines for sustaining that self can, and must, evolve as we grow, mature, and change through gained knowledge and life experience. However, we all sense that line that we cannot cross without deeply compromising the essence of who we are, the things we can't do or say because they would violate the very fiber of our being—and those things can often be traced back to the Sun in our chart.

The Sun is the center of our solar system and holds the planets in orbit around itself. Likewise, the Sun in our natal chart performs a similar task: it is the center of us, the core component of our inner solar system, and it holds all the varying parts of us in check. In essence, it provides cohesion to our internal makeup; it is the governing body in charge that keeps us from internal anarchy or endless chaos. Without a solid sense of self, we would all be crazier than we are, with our internal voices always shouting and conflicting, vying for the chance to use our body and soul to act according to their agenda. We all have conflicting "voices" in ourselves, and the Sun, our primary sense of self, hears and makes sense of them, integrating them as best it can into the core needs that govern us.

There is a psychological concept that somewhat illustrates the Sun's job in our chart, called the ego. In psychologist Sigmund Freud's three-part structure of the psyche, the ego acts as a kind of mediator, reconciling the demands of the id (our inner wild child) and the superego (essentially our conscience) with the reality of the outer world: what we can get from it versus what we want. Just as the ego has to manage and try to fulfill the range of our needs within the bounds of reality, so the Sun is tasked with maintaining a central base of operations in our personality and reining in our various internal voices to maintain our sense of sanity and a cohesive self. Essentially, the Sun is our conscious, central, directing self.

Undernourished Sun

Just as feeding our Sun keeps us vital and self-assured, when we don't take care of our Sun, we don't have enough energy to maintain a clear, central sense of self. We may find ourselves feeling a little insane from inner conflict and chronic self-doubt; certainly we all feel this way from time to time. Periodically as we change, we may find ourselves in an identity crisis, where the old self needs to be redefined. But constantly feeling like we don't know who we are or doubting ourselves can be the result of an undernourished Sun.

The distance between our yellow Sun and planet Earth is balanced in the cosmos. If it were bigger, we would burn up. If it were smaller, we would freeze. If the Sun in our natal chart is unhealthy, we may react in a variety of ways, but we typically do so in one of two ways: we try to make ourselves bigger or we try to make ourselves smaller.

Red Giant, White Dwarf

A healthy natal Sun fuels a healthy sense of confidence and self-appreciation—not too much and not too little. But if instead of being self-appreciative we are self-loathing, if instead of feeling confident we are chronically insecure, we may deal with that or combat that by trying to inflate our sense of importance. We may attempt to fool ourselves and others into thinking we are bigger or better than we feel inside by effectively trying to steal the energy from others to build ourselves up, which is not sustainable. Like a Red Giant star, burning up everything around it, this behavior can be consuming and exhausting to those around us. We can become egocentric, stealing energy from others in order to compensate for a lack of true confidence in who we are to sustain us.

The Red Giant Sun can show up in behaviors such as bragging, lying about or inflating one's abilities, excessive seeking of compliments and praise, cutting others down in order to appear superior, competitiveness that doesn't stem from wanting to do one's best but in being better than others, and so on.

If we know we can't fool ourselves or don't have the personality to try to inflate our sense of importance, we may succumb to chronic feelings of insecurity or worthlessness by deflating, becoming smaller and smaller and taking up as little space in our own lives as possible. Like the White Dwarf star, all that we are is compressed into a tiny space, with no way to express ourselves or to shine as bright as our capacity. We may shrink our presence and chronically defer to the energy and vitality of others, allowing them to take up the space that we should, effectively making ourselves invisible. Energy-depleting depression can set in as the result of chronically shrinking ourselves, leaving us figuratively lifeless.

The White Dwarf Sun can show up in behaviors such as a distinct lack of pride in ourselves and what we have to offer, being accommodating to others to an extreme and at great cost to our own needs, making efforts not to be noticed or stand out (that are not simply attributable to introversion), and so on.

When we participate in the behaviors that support our Sun's house and sign placement, we reinforce the sense of who we are and what we're about at our center, as well as our life force itself. When healthy, our Sun provides a sustainable level of confidence, energy, and pride in ourselves.

Keywords Clarified

Due to the popularity of the twelve signs of the zodiac, they are most vulnerable to stereotyping, but the planets and houses also have keywords assigned to them that can be misleading, incomplete, or difficult to relate to. It may be not that they are incorrect, but that they have been misunderstood when applied in this kind of depth astrology. By tracing some of the literal or less obvious keywords back to the planet, sign, or house they are associated with, it becomes more evident how those keywords became associated with the *essence* of the planet, sign, or house, rather than being literal or flat descriptions to be applied to a person.

For example, the Sun has been associated with the keyword ego, which you've already learned is not a reference to the popular implication of someone being egocentric or full of themselves, but instead refers to the psychological principle of ego as the conscious self and mediator of the personality. Individuality is another keyword that is not incorrect, but its meaning must be differentiated from its use in describing the planet Uranus. Individuality in reference to Uranus means specifically to be and set oneself apart, to recognize inherent qualities of self often in contrast to the status quo, whereas individuality in reference to the Sun is a more inclusive and general term for the idea of your overall sense of self and identity.

The Sun in Action

You'll learn more about the characteristics of the signs and houses later, but for now, here is an example to help you see the Sun's constant influence even through changing signs and houses. If the Sun resides in Taurus in the eighth house in a natal chart, it likely indicates a person whose sense of self centers on characteristics of calmness, common sense, and practicality (Taurus). They may identify themselves as a person with a stable, timeless personality at their core, and see themselves as dependable and loyal (Taurus). With the Sun in the eighth house, their Taurean need for quiet may accentuate an eighth house need for privacy and to be able to retreat from the world into themselves to recharge and regroup.

By contrast, if the Sun is in Sagittarius in the third house in a natal chart, such a person will likely identify with the characteristics of flexibility, adventurousness, and openness (Sagittarius), maybe even feeling themselves to be a seeker of truth through varied experiences. Experiencing foreign ideas and customs (Sagittarius) may enliven and energize them (Sun). Communicating and exchanging ideas may be the primary way they feed their core sense of self, reinforcing who they are (third house). Learning will likely be not just a pleasure, but a way of life for them, food for their very being.

By doing the behaviors suggested by our Sun's sign and house, we can maintain strength and confidence in who we are. A Taurus Sun will feel more confident and more like themselves when they have a healthy routine that provides them with a sense of stability and continuity, and will feel diminished and drained by a lifestyle that is constantly on the go, haphazard, or highly stressful and changeable. A Sagittarius Sun will be enlivened by the freedom to go wherever the wind takes them, in body or in spirit, and will be dulled or drained by a lifestyle that doesn't change or carries no potential for surprise.

Question Everything

Asking the right questions of the planets enables you to uncover the meaningful answers from a planet about its role in your natal chart. You can ask these questions and more of the Sun in your chart, getting answers from the sign and house in which it resides:

- What do you need to do in order to maintain a sense of self and overall wholeness?
- What are some major characteristics that you identify with strongly?
- What are your most central personality traits?
- What activities help you build and reinforce your sense of self?
- What behaviors are confidence-building and self-affirming for you?

THE MOON

The Moon represents the need to feel sheltered, safe, and nurtured. It is the most vulnerable and protected part of us. Simply stated, the Moon represents our heart. The Moon's placement in a natal chart according to sign and house can reveal the ways and means through which we seek emotional security and happiness. It represents the areas of life that we approach most subjectively and what form our temper tantrums may take when we need to air our emotional wounds.

We all have a need to feel safe, but beyond that we also have individual desires and emotional yearnings that are more specific to us, and the Moon in our natal chart can illustrate what those specific needs are. Astrologer Noel Tyl says the Moon represents our "reigning emotional needs," the things that are at the top of the list of what our heart craves to feel happy, safe, and comforted. Beyond the basic requirements of food and physical shelter, what makes you feel good? Do you feel happiest in a fast-paced environment or in a peaceful one? Does your heart continually draw you to worldly or spiritual pursuits? Do you feel sad and lonely without frequent social contact, or do you find respite in long periods of time spent alone? The Moon's position in your chart can provide some answers to these fundamental questions.

The Moon symbolizes the subjective, emotional ways we experience and react to life. Even when the Moon is placed in a rationally oriented air sign or a logically motivated earth sign, it is still motivated by *emotional need* (no matter how much it would like to think otherwise). A Virgo Moon *needs* to *feel* in control. A Sagittarius Moon *needs* to *feel* free. These needs are what underlie the actions taken or not taken, the words spoken or not spoken.

We often say things like "it doesn't make any sense" or "that's illogical" in order to refute or discount emotional reactions, and while questioning ourselves is often a good tool for clarification, it's also nonsensical, because reason and emotion run on two different tracks. Like science and religion, they answer different questions entirely and aren't in competition. It's true that "wars" between the head and the heart are certainly a common experience in life and can cause distress when we are trying to make a decision or come to a conclusion; however, it's like two different committee members weighing in on an issue, fighting for their cause in the best way they know how given their agendas and experience.

The Moon also symbolizes your instinctual self, a role it shares with other planetary symbols. While Mars governs the fight-or-flight instinct to act, the Moon corresponds to our instinctual emotional reactions to our environment. The Moon isn't about thinking, but simply feeling and responding. When we think about, verbalize, or act on our feelings, we are utilizing our Mercury (thought and speech) or Mars (action) functions, but the spontaneous emotional response that flows out of us is pure Moon symbolism. This is also why the Moon, along with Pluto, can symbolize the unconscious—the part of us that we are not aware of in a cognizant way but that still affects our behavior.

The Moon reveals the ways that we want to care for others and be cared for ourselves. Just as we have a vulnerable side that needs protection, we may also be moved to protect the vulnerable sides of others, especially those who cannot easily protect themselves. At the top of the list are the ones we love. Although we may have the instinct to nurture in the area of life that our Moon is most active in, the sign our Moon is in can illuminate the things we may do or say in an attempt to show love and care for others. Do we make them laugh? Bring them chicken soup? Give them tough love? By the same token, which of these methods bring you the most comfort? What gives you the warm fuzzies? Your Moon's position can tell you.

Feeling safe and cared for naturally inspires trust. We may have a sense of trust about a certain environment or situation that is having a positive effect on us. Most directly, trust is something that we extend to a person with whom we feel safe. When we trust, we let our guard down, whether by conscious choice or instinct. We are less likely to guard our behavior or withhold our opinions from someone when we trust them.

Trust is one of the most fundamental emotions ruled by the Moon, next to love. To a small degree, Venus may weigh in on what inspires us to trust another, because when we like someone we are somewhat more likely to let down our guard. However, real trust is not simply the belief that someone means us no harm or that they will be true to their word. Trust is a primal bond that is formed when we lay ourselves bare to someone, which is not just an act of will, but a letting down of our guard on the unconscious level too.

The Moon's position shows us not only what we need most but also what may bring us the most emotional pain when our needs go unmet. When we feel unsafe, we may feel anxious. When our trust is betrayed, we may feel hurt and angry. When we cannot find a way to meet our own needs, we may feel despondent.

The Moon Misapplied

We encounter the dark side of our Moon when we give too little or too much credence to our emotional needs alone. Although it is important to live a life that allows us to feel safe and nurtured, seeking out *only* safe and comfortable circumstances can prevent us from growing, as growth is inherently a risky and insecure venture. Stepping out of our emotional comfort zone is sometimes the best way to discover more of our whole selves.

As the Moon represents our inner child, so can engaging in the dark side of the Moon show our most childish and immature behavior. When our responses to life are purely emotional, we may be prone to tantrums when our needs are not immediately and totally met. Everyone needs a good tantrum now and then, but leading a life from a chronically emotional and unthinking standpoint can prevent us from growing. Learning how to satisfy our own needs, as well as learning to adapt, are both significant on the road to maturity.

We may also be in the shadow of the dark side of our Moon when our emotional selves are neglected, either by a lack of nurturing relationships in our lives or by being too chronically dismissive of our emotional needs.

Keywords Clarified

Mother is a common keyword associated with the Moon and is sometimes used in reference to your own mother and *her* influence in your life via the Moon's placement in *your* natal chart. This literal application is misleading because it sounds as though it's describing the personality or even mothering style of your mother, but your mother has her *own* chart! Instead, you must understand it in reference to your own ability to give and receive what the symbol of "mother" represents: nurturance, love, and trust. And what's a mother without a child? Your "inner child" is another Moon keyword that is not necessarily incorrect or misleading, but it has become a buzzword that has lost its ability to impact us. While the inner child can refer to a specific psychological concept, it works off of the symbolism of the concept of a child: innocent, trusting, and vulnerable; therefore, it is an appropriate symbol for the Moon.

Domesticity, or your domestic environment, is also referred to frequently when speaking of the Moon, perhaps symbolically because the home environment is where we are meant to feel most at ease, sheltered, and nurtured by the symbolic "womb" of home. Just as our home is our most private place set apart from the world, so is our heart a sacred, protected space. The Moon's connection with domestic life sometimes leads people to believe that the position of the Moon can tell you exactly what your current home life is like or even what your early home life may have looked like, but other areas of the chart, such as the fourth house and any planets or signs contained in it, contribute to the complexity of that picture. Also, as with any astrological symbol or combination, there are multiple ways that the essence of it can take form, and in this case, unless you raised yourself alone, there were multiple Moons shaping that environment!

The Moon in Action

If the Moon is in Libra in the fourth house, this would likely be a person who feels safe and nurtured when they are sheltered from the world, literally in their private home or bedroom or symbolically by not easily revealing how they feel. A sense of emotional equilibrium may be most comfortable, and conflict or even heated discussions could emotionally drain them. Being treated unfairly or seeing others treated unfairly or without respect may be deeply hurtful to them. They will likely feel most nurtured in calm and beautiful environments, and loved ones could build trust with them by drawing them out and considering their point of view. They could be at risk for hiding their feelings when they should be sharing them if they are afraid of hurting someone else or causing tension.

If the Moon is in Aries in the third house, this person may feel most comfortable when they speak their mind and they are free to express their opinions without hesitation or having to censor themselves. They will likely feel they can trust people who are straightforward and say what they mean. They will probably not be afraid of heated discussions and, in fact, may delight in an energetic discussion, even if it gets a little impassioned. They may feel happiest when they are heard. They may be at risk for assuming that others feel the same way they do and only having one point of view—theirs.

Question Everything

You can ask these questions of the Moon in your chart, and the sign and house of the Moon will reveal the answers:

- In what ways do you need to be cared for to feel protected?
- What behaviors might you participate in to reinforce your comfort zone?
- What kinds of things make you feel happy? Sad? Loved? Vulnerable?
- What things encourage or break your trust?
- What or whom do you most instinctively want to nurture and protect?

MERCURY

Mercury represents our need to exchange information, whether we are speaking, writing, singing, or whether we are listening, gathering, seeking, learning, or in any way expressing what we know and what we want to communicate. Mercury is our need to know, tell, and understand; broadly defined, it is our mind and our voice.

Mercury is our built-in data processor: it takes in information, processes it, and shares it. Mercury's sign and house placement can illustrate how we gather and organize information, the topics we like to study, and our approach to studying. Much can be learned about our learning style from Mercury's placement in our chart. Do you learn best with visual or verbal instruction? Do you prefer to study topics in an orderly and thorough fashion or do you skip around, filling in the blanks in a more haphazard fashion? These are all questions your Mercury placement can address.

Written or verbal communication is a frequent method in which we receive new information. Once we learn something new, whether formally in instruction or informally through casual conversation, we process it. We try to make sense of it by categorizing what we have learned and linking it to what we already know, expanding or sometimes changing our understanding of a topic entirely.

We take in information not only by listening and reading, but also simply by observing what is happening around us. Mercury is also at work through observation and perception. We learn, too, by observing nonverbal communication or simply watching an event unfold. The information we take in can be used in an immediate reaction and response or taken in for later integration, but in all cases Mercury is at work.

We can see this symbolism in Roman mythology. The god Mercury wore winged sandals so he could deliver information quickly as the "messenger of the gods." The rapid back-and-forth energy of any sort of exchange is Mercury's domain, which also includes commerce and the fast-paced barter and negotiation of the marketplace.

Once received, information regarding our own internal library of facts and opinions can be shared through communication. Mercury's placement in your chart can indicate your style of speaking and what you like to talk about. It can reveal what motivates you to share your knowledge or opinions with others at all and the style in which you like to do that. Are you talkative or do you prefer to share information only when necessary? Do you feel motivated to talk about the big issues or to keep it personal? Are you a storyteller or do you stick to the facts? Do you share what you know spontaneously or do you prefer to gather your thoughts and mull things over first? Mercury's chart placement can answer these questions and more.

Mercury Misapplied

In general, Mercury's vulnerability to going awry can be seen in things like premature judgments, excessive closed- or open-mindedness, and information overload leading to burnout or mental chaos and confusion.

Both the kind of information we take in and the sources to which we look for information shape the ideas and opinions we have. The less diverse the outlets, the more vulnerable we are to making assumptions about the knowledge we accumulate. Every time we acquire a nugget of knowledge, it's not just the concept but also its source that gives the information meaning or significance. Your Mercury placement can shed light on the nature of these blind spots that we all have.

Keywords Clarified

Because Mercury represents the mind, any idea that has been associated with the mind, from learning to consciousness itself, can be used as a keyword for Mercury. One keyword that is commonly used but can be misleading is intelligence. Mercury is appropriately associated with this idea, but it can lead one to believe that Mercury can indicate your *level* of intelligence, which isn't the case. Understanding the idea of intelligence through Mercury's placement in a chart will tell you more about the *kinds* of things someone is likely to be inherently knowledgeable about, perhaps partly because it can also tell you the kinds of subjects that someone is interested in and therefore is likely to study. There are many different ways to measure and define intelligence—someone may rank high in one method and low in another. Therefore, Mercury will reveal tendencies around intelligence, such as aptitude or inaptitude for certain subjects, preferred learning styles, and possible challenges to learning, rather than the measurement of intelligence itself.

The ability to reason is a Mercurial function, but that doesn't mean everyone's style of information processing is Spock-like. No one has a completely objective view because everyone's perspective is colored by their prior experiences, preconceived notions, and the tendency toward information bias (seeing what we want to see or what we wish was true). The sign and house in which Mercury is located will reveal specifics about the nature of those biases and perspectives.

Mercury in Action

If Mercury is placed in Capricorn in the sixth house, this person will likely express themselves in very matter-of-fact ways, with less of a tendency toward small talk and a desire to get to the point and communicate the facts at hand. They might primarily enjoy daily tasks and work that involve planning, precision, and practicality, such as jobs that involve technical writing or project management, both of which would have them using their mental and communication abilities to produce tangible, grounded results. They likely will communicate in a direct, objective, and formal way, and they may be at risk for being so focused on facts and practical information that they overlook or discount nuances of meaning.

If we move Mercury into the twelfth house in Cancer, this person will likely be less concerned with practical, mundane thoughts and more inclined toward an active fantasy life, with a bottomless imagination. They might write or otherwise express themselves and/or pursue information in symbolic, emotional ways, such as through poetry, music, or novels rich in metaphor or fantastical worlds and characters. Whether or not they write their thoughts down, they may be frequent daydreamers. They may not be comfortable readily revealing the raw truth of what they think or their opinions about things because their thoughts would be so interlaced with subjective impressions and emotions that they would want to be certain they were in company they could trust before allowing themselves to be so vulnerable. They may find it difficult to be understood or to communicate clearly if they get overwhelmed by emotion, preferring to withdraw into silence until they can calm down.

Question Everything

You can ask these questions of Mercury in your chart, and the sign and house in which this planet resides will automatically reveal the answers:

- What topics draw your attention most easily?
- What style of learning works best for you?
- When communicating, how do you express your ideas?
- In what ways might you be prone to miscommunication?
- What might be the nature of your mental blind spots, assumptions, or hang-ups?

VENUS

The primary need of Venus is to connect with something or someone. Venus is called the planet of relationship, although it's more specifically about the motivation behind relating itself: to feel connected to another person and not alone. To support and be supported in some way, either through shared experience or the validation that comes from feeling like someone really *gets* us, activates Venus in our chart.

Venus's primary domain is *relationships* of all kinds, though most obviously through relationships between people. While no relationship is congenial all of the time, Venus is the part of us that longs for harmony in relationship. Venus represents the desire and need to relate, and the sign and house placements reveal the methods that enable us to connect to someone or something. This desire for connection can prompt a wide range of behaviors under Venus's rule, such as the way we go about making ourselves attractive to others, or the style and intensity of the effort we undertake every time we want to forge a new connection or renew an existing one. Venus's placement in your

chart reveals what you want to offer in relationship, and having someone receive and appreciate that offering fosters a sense of connection.

The other domains of Venus share this common thread of connec-
tivity and relationship. As far as Venus is concerned, relationships can
be redefined to be not just between two people but also between you
and *anything*, such as art and how it can move you. When we appreciate a work of art, we know it's a completely subjective judgment as to
whether or not we like it—a matter of personal taste. When a work
of art, any art, moves us, we feel an affinity with it, a connection to it.
We could go so far as to say that we feel a part of us has been discovered, reflected, and understood. Who among us hasn't been moved by
a particular lyric from a song or piece of poetry that expresses something in us we may not have been able to otherwise express so precisely? Art's ability to mirror some part of ourselves back allows us to
connect with ourselves, to feel that somehow we are seen.

A third concept associated with Venus is value or worth. Value is
almost an extension of the love and beauty topics, for what we love or
find beautiful we may also consider to be of great worth. Someone we
love or something we're attracted to becomes more valuable and important to us. Worth, beauty, and likableness are all subjective—they
need a beholder. Your Venus placement by sign, house, and planetary
aspects can play a part in what kinds of things you find beautiful and
attractive, be they clothing, art, music, and so on. They say "beauty
is in the eye of the beholder," which reflects the reciprocal dynamic
inherent in relationship.

Venus Misapplied

When we misuse Venus energy, it will usually be revealed through
dysfunctional relating styles, either chronically in our intimate relationships or in our social habits in general. This can get out of hand
when we go to extremes to manipulate others to like us or trust us as
opposed to expressing a true and sincere desire to relate, authentically
and willingly. The methods we employ in these cases can be as varied
as the signs and houses in which Venus resides.

Keywords Clarified

One big concept that Venus is expected to encompass is love. While that's not inaccurate, Venus doesn't carry that weight alone. Love is a big idea that many planets can play a part in, such as the emotional trust that the Moon represents or the heat of passion of Mars, or even the commitment bonds and natural sense of obligation of Saturn that can arise in us, not to mention the role the houses play in the actualities of love. Venus has to do specifically with the part of love that is expressed in our affinity for someone and our desire to feel a sense of togetherness.

Often coupled with love is the concept of compatibility, which, while accurate, isn't completely managed by Venus. Compatibility is another one of those big ideas that can have a multifaceted definition. If it is defined simply by how well we get along with someone, then your Venus placement can tell you a lot about the characteristics you admire or relate to most in relationships—essentially, what you like about someone. However, almost every kind of relationship requires more than just getting along with someone, and again we can turn to Mars, the Moon, Saturn, and so on to help understand the needs of the other parts of us that are also significant in understanding our compatibility with someone.

Venus has long been associated with the feminine, and its definition has even been split between the genders. In traditional astrology, the principle of femininity has long been assigned to women and Venus has been seen as a feminine planet. In a woman's chart, Venus has been said to reveal her femininity and how she attracts a man, whereas in a man's chart, Venus reveals the qualities he looks for in a woman. Not only is this stereotyping at its worst, but it simply does not reflect a modern language or lifestyle; it has become outdated. The fact is, we all have Venus placed somewhere in our chart, regardless of what gender or style of sexual expression we identify with. To disown any planet or project it onto a certain gender dishonors the wholeness capable in any individual, not to mention reduces all of humanity to limited sexual or gender-based categories. A more apt term for Venus from the angle of femininity would be *receptivity*. To permit a feeling of relatedness and connection with another, we have to be open to receiving from them as one part of that equation.

Venus in Action

If Venus is found in the tenth house in a natal chart, it will likely represent someone whose sense of life path or career revolves around a Venus principle of relating or supporting, such as a counselor, a motivational speaker, or even someone who works in retail, a field that involves working with the public and could even incorporate the aspect of Venus and beauty. This person may enjoy relating to others in a professional setting and find value in relationships with those they consider colleagues. They may naturally gravitate toward romantic relationships with people they respect professionally.

If Venus is placed in Aquarius in the eighth house, this person might be attracted to intense people who have a depth about them (eighth) and are also intellectually stimulating (Aquarius). They likely will want to have a deep bond (eighth) but also maintain their freedom (Aquarius), finding that delicate balance between intimacy and individuality.

Question Everything

You can ask these questions of Venus in your chart, and the sign and house of in which this planet resides will reveal the answers:

- What kinds of people are you attracted to as friends or romantic partners?
- How do you initiate a relationship?
- What kinds of behaviors from others repel you?
- What do you find beautiful and how do you like to express your own sense of style and beauty?

MARS

Almost everything that Mars symbolizes can be traced back to the idea of our *will*. Will is a word that has found its way into many English words and phrases, such as willpower, willfulness, or the saying "Where there's a will, there's a way." Will is our ability to make a conscious choice and act on that choice—decision-making is not just an intellectual exercise. Although making a decision may be mostly intellectual if we are debating our choices or weighing the pros and cons in each potential choice, once we choose, we assert our will. When we say "I will," we are making a choice, expressing our intention, and committing our energy.

Willpower, which is a word often used in the context of either denying ourselves something or forcing ourselves to do something, is actually still an expression of desire, but having conflicting desires is a regular occurrence for those of us in the human race.

Mars is often called the "action planet." An action frequently begins with a desire, a *want*. This desire can build up a tension inside of us that *drives* us to then *pursue* what we want, to take an *action* toward getting the object of our desire. We use our Mars when we *initiate* anything. While it may be arguable that the Moon, symbolizing our emotions and heart, could have more to do with our wants and desires, with Mars simply being the heart's servant to go out and get what we want, there's a hunger and a possessing, conquering energy in the word desire that aligns more with the spirit of Mars.

Mars also has a hand in conflict, whether we internally thwart our own will or externally find ourselves blocked or thwarted by another. A conflict with someone is not merely a formal way to describe an argument; a conflict actually precedes the conflict. A conflict with someone is a clash of wills. One person wants one thing, another wants something else, and the two are then in conflict. *How* you deal with that conflict is revealed through Mars's placement by sign and house in your chart. Do you state your case and risk an argument? Do you avoid the situation and hope it resolves itself? These methods and more are among the possibilities. Anger is a sure sign we have entered into conflict, and is also governed by Mars, as it often arises as a defense mechanism, self-defense being Mars's domain.

Mars's placement in our chart can tell us what our passions are—not necessarily our casual interests and hobbies, but what we're willing to pursue because we feel motivated to capture, resolve, or even fight against something. In general, whatever makes your blood boil can be traced back to Mars, whether it's boiling because of anger and defense or excitement and desire. One of our most primal desires is expressed in our sex drive; what turns us on (and off) and how we go about pursuing the one we want to possess can all be traced back to Mars's position in our chart.

Astrology is commonly applied toward understanding matters of love and sex, often simplistically summed up by Venus (love) and Mars (sex). Mars does have a great deal to do with our sexual nature, not only in that sex is a physical act and our Mars placement can reveal a lot about our physical constitution and how we expel and replenish our physical energy, but also that Mars holds sway over how we express our passions and drive. In fact, our basic primal drives for fundamental things like food, shelter, and sex can often be traced back to Mars because Mars represents the most animal part of us—the part that understands the primal need to survive.

Mars symbolizes our sense of personal power when we consider power as an extension of our will. Using our will is exercising our personal power, and a strong will and confidence in our own powerfulness are closely related. When someone is willful, *full of will*, they are difficult to control because they have a power all their own that they will not relinquish.

Mars Misapplied

The misuse of Mars tends to show up in either the chronic overuse or underuse of our will and subsequent power. We may do this in an overt way by being too aggressive or attempting to overpower others, or we may subvert our own will too easily and allow others to force their will upon us. In either case, whether we are predator or prey, our will is at play.

Keywords Explained

Mars is often referred to as the "war planet," painting a picture that Mars is aggressive and conflict-seeking. But Mars is not inherently aggressive, as that is a *style* of expression that can vary given the sign in which Mars resides. When the potential for conflict arises, it is Mars that we call upon, so in that way it is the war planet, but not because Mars inherently wants to initiate war or loves war necessarily. Mars is built to defend and attack, but our reasons for engaging in conflict are as varied as the signs and houses in which Mars may reside. When what we want conflict with what another wants, Mars can settle the issue, but whether it does so by negotiation, aggressive attack, or surrender all depends on the sign through which it expresses. Even refusing to take an action is an action—it is an act of will.

Just as Venus has been stereotyped as a planet representing the feminine, Mars is often associated with the masculine. This has been interpreted in the past as a division, with Venus being synonymous with women and Mars with men, artificially dividing the two planets along with the two genders into tidy boxes. Older astrology texts often reflect the zeitgeist in which they were written, stating that "Venus in a man's chart will dictate the kind of woman he is sexually attracted to" and vice versa for women, essentially encouraging a given gender to disown the opposite one and project it onto someone of the opposite gender. The terms masculine and feminine can be useful in understanding the Mars-Venus planetary pair, but only if we understand the symbolism at work outside of the strict, literal definitions. The masculine energy represented by Mars, in this sense, is the pursuing, outgoing type of energy as the yang to the yin of the yielding, receptive energy of the feminine.

Mars in Action

When Mars is found in Scorpio in the natal chart, it often indicates a person who is intensely driven by their passions, who wants to take everything they do to its deepest potential and beyond. They will never be satisfied with half-efforts or careful actions; a person with this placement favors courageous, borderline-destructive, breaking-through-their-own-barriers action that makes them feel most alive. When they get angry, their reaction is strong and forceful, which can consume them, and they may sometimes take extreme actions fueled by the depth of their emotional response.

With Mars in Scorpio in the seventh house, this intensity is directed into relationships and an intense need to connect deeply, not superficially or casually, with one or two significant people in their lives that they can build trust with. They may be at risk for overwhelming significant others with their intensity and sometimes possessiveness, especially if the partner needs more breathing room in the relationship than Mars in Scorpio does. They give and require loyalty and transparency from those they love in order to trust (seventh house) them.

By contrast, if Mars is placed in Scorpio in the second house, that intensity and all-or-nothing approach will likely be directed into their achievements and building resources. Building a strong résumé, literally or metaphorically, can provide an important sense of personal power and strength. They may be at risk for pushing themselves or situations too far in order to combat any insecurity they may feel about their abilities or worth, to prove themselves to others and themselves.

Question Everything

You can ask these questions of Mars in your chart, and the sign and house in which it resides will reveal the answers:

- What motivates you to take action on something?
- In what way do you go after what you want?

- How do you express your passionate nature? What turns you on?
- In what ways do you defend yourself when hurt, scared, or angry?
- What kinds of things make you angry and how do you show it?
- How do you handle yourself in arguments or confrontations?
- How do you prefer to release pent-up energy?

JUPITER

The primary need of Jupiter is not to reach our potential, but to reach *toward* our potential, to expand beyond what we already are and what already is, beyond the possible or the known. Jupiter represents our ability and need to hope, to take leaps of faith, to try new things, and to do the impossible. It is hope that encourages us to try anything at all, especially for the first time, and we need it any time we say yes to something new. Jupiter represents our desire for bigger, better, more, in the best (and sometimes worst) sense. The nature of the things that give us this urge to hope and spark our enthusiasm lies with the sign in which our natal Jupiter resides.

Because Jupiter is about breaking your own glass ceiling, there is always an inherent element of risk when we embrace Jupiter in our chart. Sometimes we take that risk by letting go of one thing before we get hold of the next thing—we must let go of what we've got in order to have the freedom and ability to reach higher for something else. In that moment, we have nothing; we're caught between what we had and what we don't yet have. Other times we encounter that risk by betting on our future, whether it's in the case of reaching for something better, or something as simple as believing it'll all work out (faith), believing we can do it (confidence), or believing there's more on the other side (expansion). Jupiterian breakthroughs are about us reaching beyond our limits.

Jupiter assists this process by encouraging us to temporarily suspend our disbelief or negative thoughts. It encourages us not to be realists, but optimists. We're not going to risk a new experience if we are *sure* it will end badly, but if we're not sure, then we're free to hope it will end well. Gambling is a great example of Jupiter in action because it combines the thrill of risk and the possibility of striking it big with the unending wish for MORE. Gambling isn't necessarily a dirty word; we gamble when we "bet" on our future, and that's what Jupiter is all about: the promise that if you risk now, it will pay off later. Obviously that isn't always the case. Some gambles don't yield what we'd hoped they would and some fail entirely. Jupiter doesn't necessarily promise success, but you can't win if you don't play.

Expansion is a word frequently used when describing Jupiter. Embodying Jupiter energy can make us feel big in any number of ways. We may experience this as a swell of goodwill and generosity toward others, a sense of self-confidence and faith in ourselves, or a burst of enthusiasm in response to an exciting possibility. Jupiter encourages us to grow by leaps and bounds. Jupiter growth is meant to be effortless and simple, but that doesn't always mean it *is* that easy. We just have to be willing to try, to get out of our own way, and sometimes that's the hardest thing of all. Having confidence, or at least faking it till you make it, is also a favorite Jupiterian method.

Jupiter is the part of us that knows the reality we see today was just a fantasy in the distant past until someone decided to believe and try something new. Every invention that we may think as commonplace today and take for granted was once just an inventor's wild dream (or happy accident), created because someone was willing to risk failure in pursuit of something great. Jupiter is the part of us that knows that in some ways we are only as capable as we *believe* we are.

Jupiter Misapplied

The misuse of Jupiter's energy reveals itself when we overextend ourselves, metaphorically biting off more than we can chew. Whether it's overspending, overeating, committing to too many projects or activities, or even excessive optimism to the point of naiveté, the "yes" inherent in Jupiter can become a problem if we don't *ever* say no. Faith and hope without the balancing effect of reality and common sense can lead to a crash landing of epic proportions when the consequences of our overextension catch up with us. Our style and methods of overextension are described by the sign and house of our natal Jupiter.

Keywords Clarified

Jupiter is known as the "planet of luck," implying that the location of Jupiter in a natal chart is the area of life in which someone might be luckier than the next person. This doesn't usually manifest in obvious or literal ways, but instead, luckiness is the natural result of us taking advantage of an opportunity or opening ourselves up to possibilities that set things in motion, sometimes providing us with a lucky break seemingly out of nowhere.

Since Jupiter supposedly brings luck, and luck brings all manner of good things, Jupiter is often associated with abundance, wealth, prosperity, and success. But these things are never guaranteed with Jupiter if we say no to opportunity too often. Jupiter is the idea of the possible, and if we reach for the possible we might make it real. But the possible is just the promise of riches, not necessarily guaranteeing the *having*, and if the having does happen, it may not be in exactly the way we'd envisioned. Since Jupiter also represents the possibility of overdoing something, we can use up or spend our abundance just as quickly as we gain it and, in many cases, faster than we gain it. Nevertheless, Jupiter experiences often tend to bring positive things, even when it's too much of a good thing.

Jupiter in Action

Jupiter in Pisces in the second house likely indicates a person whose best assets revolve around developing faith in themselves and learning to take risks and bet on themselves that they have what it takes. They may view financial resources as fluid, always coming and going, trusting the universe to provide for them when needed and at the same time being generous in how they spend those resources. They may also be at risk for being naive or unrealistic about money and budgeting, chronically overestimating how much they have or absent-mindedly spending.

Place Jupiter in Pisces but in the fifth house and this may be a person whose spiritual growth centers on allowing themselves to get lost in the moment and let their creativity and imagination have free rein. They may have a strong sense of intuition when they let themselves run with it.

Put Jupiter in the fifth house but in Gemini instead and then the creativity, play, and being in the moment of the fifth house activities take on the flavor and style of the quickness and cleverness of Gemini, and the joy that comes from following their curiosity around by the nose like a child.

Question Everything

You can ask these questions of Jupiter in your chart, and the sign and house in which this planet resides will reveal the answers:

- What experiences encourage you to feel limitless and free?
- What experiences do you seek out to reinforce a sense of joy and positivity?
- In what areas do you feel inclined to feel your way by optimism and hope rather than caution?
- Where and how in life are you vulnerable to overdoing it?
- In what areas might you be vulnerable to overconfidence or naive optimism?

SATURN

Saturn represents all the classic character-building experiences and traits: responsibility, hard work, self-discipline, and commitment. Saturn represents maturity and the processes by which we mature. The process of maturity is inherently built on working within limitations and learning to work through them, with them, or sometimes around them. Building inner strength and discipline cannot happen without obstacles to overcome. Limits may seem frustrating, but they provide us with something to push against, which forces us to grow in ways we might not have if everything came easily. When we lift weights at the gym to strengthen our muscles, it is the resistance of the weight that allows us to build that muscle at all. Saturn is about the recognition of (healthy) limits and working within them.

We don't always simply need to look on the bright side to appreciate limits. Saturn governs not only healthy limits, but helpful and even comforting ones as well. It may be easiest to think of limits as something inherently negative because it's a word that is most commonly understood as lack, as we focus on what the limit *prevents* us from. But limits can also define parameters and help us outline our goals and priorities. Limits can help us understand what is and what isn't and provide a sense of security as well as a structure to work within. When we're able to see what we can't do, it often helps us begin the work of doing what we *can.*

Saturn is certainly at work when we are taking on responsibilities, such as chores or homework in youth or projects and commitments in adulthood. With a steady (but not overbearing) weight on our shoulders, we can keep our feet on the ground and learn how to make things happen in a realistic world. Saturnian responsibility can be taken one step further, into the realm of accountability, where we are not just fulfilling our obligations but are actually taking ownership of our role in a situation, goal, or outcome. We may feel a sense of duty in the area Saturn governs in our chart, but we can choose to respond by ignoring it, grudgingly accepting it, or taking it on and making it our own. When we choose the latter, we are taking control—we accept obligations we feel naturally inclined toward. In this process, it becomes important to distinguish between socially or culturally imposed guilt and obligation versus our own real sense of internal duty, or else resentment, not accomplishment, will be our reward.

Saturn work is never easy. Unlike Jupiter, its bounty is not won by natural talent or optimistic risk-taking but by the things that we have to work for and make a steady, constant effort to attain. It is not about reaching beyond boundaries, but working within them, and the strength and benefits we can gain from doing so. Saturn's work can be challenging for us either because we have a setback or limitation that makes that work particularly challenging for us or simply because to acquire a skill requires practice over the long term. Where Saturn lies in your chart indicates where you have your work cut out for you as well as the nature of the gains you'll acquire in doing the work.

Saturn isn't without its rewards; in fact, it brings about rewards like no other planet can. The achievements that require sacrifices of time, commitment, and diligence, as well as any number of other sacrifices, are the things that are most prized above all else because they are so rare and precious. A happy thirty-year marriage, a doctorate degree, a grown son or daughter we are proud of, a mortgage paid off, a talent honed to perfection—these do not happen through hope alone. It is the *commitment* to a goal, as well as a commitment to the *continued effort* toward that goal, that brings about life's grand prizes. Saturn is the pride and sense of accomplishment you feel from something earned versus something simply given.

Saturn's placement in your chart represents where you may experience a sense of being blocked or limited, where you'll need to apply yourself steadily in order to see gains. Sometimes limitations can leave us feeling like there is no way to achieve something, but it's often this limitation that turns us back on ourselves, forcing us to summon the self-discipline and tenacity required for success.

Self-discipline, self-control, self-sufficiency, self-possession—many of the terms that describe Saturn begin with the word *self* because Saturn represents what we must often do alone because no one will or can do it for us. We may also *feel* alone in the area of our lives that Saturn governs for this reason. No one can give us self-discipline; we must govern ourselves and learn to do for ourselves. It's part of growing up, which is why Saturn is the planet of maturity.

When we are children, our parents enforce rules that we must follow. We follow those limitations because we must, but eventually we set our own as we mature. With maturity comes the ability to self-govern, to become our own grown-up, and inherent in that process is the recognition that no one sets external consequences for you for not doing the work and no one will do the work for you, so if you want it done, you'd better do it yourself.

When Saturn represents a weight we find too unbearable, we can become depressed and avoidant in that area of life. While sometimes there's no way around it but to find a way to summon the discipline and the patience to do the work, we may also need to ask for help in getting on our feet. Saturn work isn't about self-punishment or self-denial *for its own sake* but about self-empowerment through realistic and sustainable methods.

External authorities abound throughout our lives. When we are children it's our parents, teachers, and babysitters. When we are adults it's bosses, judges, and police officers. All of these roles are about setting and enforcing rules and limits. As we grow, these rules shape our behavior and provide a structure for us to follow to integrate ourselves more easily into society as we become an adult. At best, Saturnian authorities are mentors, showing us the way. As we reach and continue through adulthood, our task becomes to internalize the wisdom from these authorities and govern ourselves with internal guidelines of conduct and wisdom, not just the external rules that confine our behavior. We can then become the mentors and pass on our hard-won wisdom.

Of course, not all authorities are benevolent guides, nor do they always know what's right for us. Saturn is also about discerning the wisdom of a rule or law, sometimes embracing and following the rules and traditions we inherited and other times reworking the old structure and crafting a new guideline according to our own accumulated wisdom. We must often do that with our own rules and habits that we've internalized over our lifetime thus far, which may have once served us but are now unnecessarily limiting or even damaging us, preventing further growth. The nature of Saturn's position in our chart can also illustrate where we may experiences roadblocks to our own growth because we need to make changes to an outdated or crumbling system of rules or beliefs.

Saturn Misapplied

The misuse of Saturn's energy usually centers on something in our lives or ourselves becoming stuck, either because we have allowed ourselves to become rigid in a particular way or because avoiding Saturn's work has brought on a mountain of consequences that seem insurmountable. Saturn rules things that take time to build and will last over time, such as buildings, organizations, habits (healthy or otherwise), and even our own skeleton, the structure that holds up our body. Saturnian structures can support and bear a lot of weight, but if they don't retain a small amount of flexibility and aren't taken care of, they can become too rigid, trapping what they were meant to protect or support. A skeleton is flexible enough to accommodate growth and pressure and a tall building is strong enough to stand but flexible enough to sway slightly in a strong wind, bolstering its ability to endure.

Where Saturn lies in your natal chart can indicate the structures—metaphorical or literal, internal or external—that you must build and maintain over your life for success in that area of life, even when it takes more effort than it seems to for others. Lack of doing so can result in an immature response to that area of life and undesired consequences that perhaps could have been avoided. These consequences are not typically meant as punishment, but are just a result of natural law. For example, if you do not maintain a healthy diet, poor health and obesity will be the natural result. Regular maintenance on a relationship helps sustain it; the lack of doing so can lead to its demise.

Keywords Clarified

Just as the Moon has been linked symbolically as mother, Saturn has been called father,[9] and Saturn's placement in your natal chart has been said to have implications regarding your father and what your relationship with your father was like. The traditional, stereotypical view of father has been one of disciplinarian and teacher, as opposed to the stereotypical view of mother, which has been nurturer. As Saturn represents the idea of *authority* and the role it plays in our lives, the traditional idea of father makes a good fit, metaphorically. However, as a literal representation of your father's personality or his role in your life, it often falls short. Just as your mother has her own natal chart, so does your father, and his natal chart will reveal more about him than your own Saturn.

Saturn has been referred to as a karmic planet, although an entire natal chart could be considered karmic from certain perspectives. One reason why Saturn may seem karmic is that it is the planet of natural law and consequence. What we sow, we inevitably reap. But karma isn't just arbitrary crime and punishment; it is essentially habit. It is what builds up and stays after constant repetition. Actions or inactions create ripple effects in our lives and the lives we affect.

Saturn in Action

Saturn placed in Leo in the eleventh house can indicate a person who has challenges to overcome in freely expressing themselves confidently

---

9. Aside from Saturn, the Sun has also been identified with the father, reflecting the repeated dualistic symbolism in many cultures of father-mother, male-female, Sun-Moon.

for all to see. They may feel awkward, limited, or insecure when trying to fit in with social and peer groups, seeming more shy than they might naturally be in other settings. Participating or building a peer group in which they feel free to shine may take time and persistence as they develop and practice skills that help them do the work and gain the rewards of a supportive tribe. Doing these things that are difficult, awkward, or take perseverance may also eventually enable them to build a sense of natural authority, charisma, and confidence, such as a person who overcomes a fear of public presentation and grows to be comfortable enough in that spotlight over time with practice. Even still, they may always have to strive to continue to maintain that confidence.

Placing Saturn in Leo but in the third house would shift the activities that are needed in order to practice and gain a sense of confidence and self-expression from peer focus to the challenges of articulating one's thoughts and opinions (third house) or pushing through limitations (Saturn) in their thinking and communication style (third house), and developing mental and communication strengths in order to gain the confidence they long for.

Question Everything

You can ask these questions of Saturn's condition in your chart, and the answers will rise to the top:

- What kind of challenges might you face due to lack of skill, patience, commitment, or advantage?
- What kind of authority might you perceive in others that you ultimately need to claim for yourself?
- Where and in what ways will perseverance most likely pay off for you?
- What kind of behaviors or attitudes can you find yourself too entrenched in?

GENERATIONAL PLANETS

Traditionally, astrological practice included only the seven visible planets, from the Sun up to Saturn. Saturn represents limits, tradition, the law, and death. It was the last planet and it represented the endpoint. The discovery of Uranus and the outer planets took us beyond this rigid boundary. Uranus breaks the rules, going beyond the boundaries of law and convention. Neptune goes beyond the material realm, transcending the trappings of what is "real." Pluto goes beyond the realm of death itself, through metaphorical rebirth.

Uranus, Neptune, and Pluto are often referred to as the "outer planets," a term that is sometimes used in conjunction with the idea that their meanings are generational and not specific to an individual's experience of life. While it is true that the outer planets remain in a sign for a relatively long period of time (Uranus averages 7 years, Neptune averages 14 years, and Pluto averages 20 years[10]), their influence via sign and house placement is meaningful on an individual level *as well as* on a collective level. Just as we all are influenced by the zeitgeist of our time, we also hold a spark of it that we internalize and make our own, participating in and contributing to the cultural norms of the times in which we live. The vibe of the times not only influences us, but lives *through* us, simultaneously.

While the sign in which an outer planet resides in your chart is significant to your experience of that planetary energy, it is often the house placement of the planet that helps to reveal the individual expression of each of the outer planets in our personal lives.

URANUS

Uranus represents the need for individuation: to find and express what is truly the essence of you, independent of how you've been de-

---

10. These are averages. Pluto's orbit, in particular, is very elliptical, so, relatively speaking, it zips through the signs of Scorpio and Sagittarius and drags through the signs of Taurus and Gemini, ranging from 10–12 years up to 30 years spent in a sign.

fined according to your race, culture, sexual orientation, gender, family, country, or any other way that society's rules can apply.

Living in an organized society brings benefits that are too numerous to count. Benefits from scientific discoveries, technological inventions, and medical advances abound. Safety, for the most part, does lie in numbers, as well as adherence to the social contracts and laws (spoken and unspoken). However, any given culture we find ourselves a part of will have collective opinions about the way its individuals live their lives, and will subtly and sometimes not so subtly pressure the individuals that stand out to get with the program. This is not always as obvious as the bully picking on the weak or the popular kids excluding the standout. Sometimes the pressure comes from well-meaning people who want us to be safe or enjoy the benefits of fitting in. Also, pressure may disguise itself as well intentioned, but simply be a method to control someone or get them "figured out" in order to ease their own discomfort about the unpredictability of humans and life.

When faced with the pressure of the collective, it is all too easy to succumb and conform, whether we secretly rebel inside while giving the appearance of fitting in or whether we allow ourselves to be convinced by the stories others are telling us about ourselves. We simply don't have enough confidence or experience with ourselves and life when we are children, for example, to overcome the threat of punishment from authority for disobedience or to go it alone in a world where we are not enabled to care for ourselves like we are when we are grown.

Our trust in authority figures in our lives can be healthy, natural, and helpful, and yet at some point we must revisit some of the things we were taught and compare them to the signals we are receiving from our inner self and make some course corrections if need be. We do this by utilizing Uranus's urging to stand apart, not only in body and habit but also in perception and the way we think about what we've seen and what we've been taught. We must stand outside of the norms in order to view them as an outsider so we can enable ourselves to even begin to see that there's another way, another definition, another story. When we do this, we can see that some of these norms are not law, but are merely *consensus:* what everyone seems to be agreeing is good, right, or normal. In the case of individuation, majority doesn't rule.

Uranus often provides us with a clue about our path to individuation with the discomfort we feel about being encouraged to fall into line with a norm we simply don't identify with. When we're young, we may not know ourselves or society's norms well enough to recognize what this discomfort is about and be able to articulate it, sometimes prompting us to ignore these confusing feelings. In adolescence, we may make efforts to push the boundaries in honest but clumsy and sometimes misguided attempts to gain the freedom to express our own individuality.

As we get older, we may have a better ability to understand and articulate (even if only to ourselves) where this discomfort stems from. We may realize that we don't agree with the governing religious or political principles that our family or others in our society seem to, or perhaps there is something more obviously different about us, such as our appearance (by choice or not) that sets us apart; but it is this contrast that teaches us the most about what it is to be different and what that can mean for us, both positively and negatively. Positively, our awareness of our differences can prompt us to nurture a unique part of our personality that we can take pride in. Negatively, we may feel alienated or insecure about our differences, especially if we've received ridicule or judgment because of them. We can learn valuable lessons about ourselves from these experiences, but it's our own internal discomfort when we behave in a way that society approves of yet somehow feels alien to us, or our sense of disconnect when we see others participating in events or experiences that seem to make them happy but have the opposite effect on us, that can really point the way to our individuation path.

There may be miles between knowing the path and walking the path of individuation. If the path to individuation leads away from the easy norms, we must break away and make our own path. The area in your chart in which Uranus resides is where you will be prompted to do that—and not always just once, but repeatedly, whether it's through making a choice that you have to continue to defend time and again or whether your path is a series of choices that continue to take you further and further away from where you started.

Under Uranus's influence, we march to the beat of a different drummer, but, fortunately and unfortunately, sometimes only we can hear that beat. Uranus can represent unique gifts that we can develop and offer to the world; history is filled with people who stood out and, because they did, made a huge difference, even if that's not what they set out to do. Inventors, revolutionaries, and geniuses all personify the principle of Uranus. By thinking and acting outside of the accepted norms, we can be a part of changing these norms entirely. By the same token, Uranus is where we may be vulnerable to feeling like an outsider, whether it is ourselves or others who make us feel set apart or misunderstood. Since no one but us can hear that personal Uranus beat, we may look quite strange to others when we dance to it. Shallow popularity may be overrated, but the need to feel accepted and included is primal, and where Uranus lies in our chart tells us where we may be walking a fine line between the world and ourselves.

If we are able to disentangle ourselves from the things that compromise our true selves too much to walk our own path, we may still feel like an outsider. It is not easy to hold to your own, and even if others accept and even appreciate you for it, you may still feel misunderstood by a majority of people. When we walk our own path, we don't just walk it, we *forge* it. That is why where Uranus lies in our chart is where we have the opportunity to form or join our own "band of misfits"—allies who find themselves in the same boat and can understand the struggles we face as well as why we face them. We can also look to others who set out on their own path as our mentors. To be truly Uranian, however, may also require us to be willing to stand apart even from them at some point. We don't have to be lonely, but we do have to strike out on our own.

It's important to note that while Uranus often inspires revolutionary talk, not everyone is an extreme example of Uranian aberrance and anarchy. We're not all wildly bizarre or weapon-wielding rebels; in fact, most of us aren't, overall. But the Uranus call to individuation is still there for all of us, whether it whispers or shouts, whether it requires small or big sacrifices. Our personal experience may be small in the context of the grand history of revolutionaries, but the internal struggles and the rewards we experience are valid. While we don't all feel moved to storm the White House or stand on a picket line, we all have a little revolutionary in us. Where Uranus lies in our chart is where we are most likely to push back when we feel our rights or the rights of others are being tread on.

Why would anyone endure these pressures? Some of us don't, with good reason. Some of us decide the price of nonconformity is too great a risk, and indeed, there is no shame in this. We may lose support, opportunity, and acceptance to a threatening and frightening degree. Many who have embodied Uranus in the collective consciousness of society are those who have lost their jobs, families, and even their lives in response to being true to themselves at all costs. But for some, there comes a point when they can no longer pay the price they are paying to silence their true selves and live an inauthentic life. The cost to suppress and betray the self is too great.

Uranus is our "inner rebel," but rebelliousness is not the purpose of Uranus; it's only a mechanism for change when our desire to express our individuality is being suppressed, by ourselves or others. We see Uranus's rebelliousness on a grand scale any time a country erupts in civil war or large-scale protests are staged, but we can recognize it every day when we act against what someone else wishes for us because it conflicts with our true self. When a woman makes the voluntary choice not to marry or have children, when a person quits their six-figure salary in corporate America to open a yogurt stand on the beach, when a person admits to being an atheist in a god-oriented culture—these are everyday examples of people leaving the beaten path. That's Uranus in action.

Uranian behavior is often easier to see and understand when we can identify where someone is rebelling against cultural and societal norms, but to merely define Uranus as our inner rebel is misleading. All Uranus requires is that we are true to ourselves, and that process often has us examining the examples we've been presented with and the ways in which our desires may contrast with them, but they aren't always in contrast. If we have the courage to engage in this process and choose our authentic path *even if it happens to be supported by consensus*, we've embraced healthy Uranus.

Just as a child may react to her mother's rules by doing the exact opposite of her mother's wishes to assert her independence, Uranus can manifest as the proverbial rebel without a cause, being contrary for the sake of being contrary, not for any real purpose but simply to prove and assert one's right to be an individual. This is not inherently good or bad, but it can disguise the real issue at stake and, in some cases, even prevent someone from acting according to their true desires. If what we want just happens to fit in with what society wants for us but we don't want to feel like society is dictating who we can be, we might be in danger of opposing ourselves in an effort to oppose society. This is how Uranian rebellion can go awry. Uranus is not rebellion, it is independence. Rebellion may or may not be necessary. One doesn't set out to be a rebel. One sets out to be oneself.

Uranus often has us employing rebellion as a useful tool, but the purpose of individuation is not simply to be different than anyone around you. Uranus's method is to allow you to detach from the subtle pressures from the environment around you so you can get the necessary breathing room to hear yourself. Also, one moment of rebellion is not what Uranus aspires to—you must continue to evaluate your life, behaviors, and needs wherever Uranus influences your chart. The unfolding of one's individuality is a lifelong process, and Uranus, while not the only planet involved in this process, is often at the forefront, getting us to wake up where we've fallen asleep, to change our lives when we've changed on the inside and life has failed to catch up with us.

Sometimes in an effort to fit in and go with the program, we may suppress our desire to do things differently in accordance with what feels right for us, often out of fear. This may be an especially tempting strategy when the stakes are high, such as trying to avoid hurting a loved one or to avoid losing our jobs or, in extreme cases, our lives. It's often in these cases that our suppression can backfire. We may find ourselves expelling that suppressed energy in a "safer" part of our lives, such as fighting the dress code at work with disproportionate vehemence when really it may be a build-up of other areas of life that don't get to express freely and authentically. Breaking trivial or inconsequential rules such as some minor social protocol or a workplace dress code in order to make a statement about our right to freely express ourselves doesn't usually lead to what we truly want. In cases like these, the benefits of fitting in (or appearing to) may not outweigh the cost of hiding our true selves, and can cause waves elsewhere that result in nothing more than blowing off steam (and the consequences that may come with doing so). In general, the misuse of Uranus's energy usually centers on unfocused rebellion or exaggerated contrariness.

Keywords Clarified

Some of the keywords for Uranus are rebel or anarchist, which are apt terms but miss the purpose of Uranus by a hair. Uranus's purpose isn't rebellion, but freedom. Rebellion is sometimes a necessary method by which to bring those things about. Genius is also a keyword associated with Uranus, because genius is not just intelligence but also the ability to think differently about something and therefore understand something that no one else has yet understood. The genius, scientist, and the inventor are personifications of Uranus in that they are about experimenting to find new discoveries and thinking differently than anyone else has in order to come to new conclusions. They are certainly out-of-the-box thinkers. The outcast is yet another personification of Uranus, which isn't always a literal experience of being expelled from a family or from society but can represent the internalized feeling of not belonging. This is common with Uranus since a measure of belonging is often a quality of sameness or the ability to fit in, where Uranus is the proverbial square peg in the round hole.

All of these keywords and personifications can be traced back to the core idea of Uranus: the path of individuation. Simply assuming that Uranus's placement in a natal chart indicates where or how that person utilizes technology most, or is apt to invent something, takes these ideas and applies them too literally, often with incorrect results. Utilizing them as metaphors to understand how a person's natal Uranus placement enables them to "invent" their own rules will get you right to the heart of the meaning of Uranus in any natal chart.

Uranus in Action

If Uranus is placed in Libra in the ninth house, it might represent someone who has a different philosophy or worldview than most of the people in the culture the person grew up in or is surrounded by, such as someone with a different religious or political point of view compared to that of their family or the people in their neighborhood. They may differ primarily in their philosophy compared to others they are surrounded by when it comes to issues about partnership or perhaps education, especially as they grow into adulthood and have more freedom to explore their true beliefs, which may differ from what they were taught and were compelled to do as a child. They may even be an advocate for establishing or changing the established laws if they feel human rights are being violated in a way that treats others unfairly.

If Uranus is in Libra in the first house, this person might express Uranus energy in a more obvious way. It will likely be more apparent that this person stands out in a crowd due to something unique about their demeanor or appearance overall. With Uranus in Libra, they might use the contrast of interacting with others as a way to understand their own individuality, making them understand more clearly the key qualities that define them when they see the differing qualities in others.

Question Everything

To understand the Uranus principle in action in your natal chart, ask Uranian questions of the house and sign in which this planet resides.

- Where might you have a naturally different viewpoint or experience of life than the norm?
- In what area of life might you potentially feel alienated?
- Where in your life are you most unwilling to compromise?
- When you feel boxed in, how do you rebel?

NEPTUNE

Neptune represents our need to experience the mystical, the ethereal, and the spiritual. Everything Neptune governs represents a method toward transcendence. In the Neptunian realms of intuition, imagination, and inspiration, we seek to take ourselves beyond what we know into what we sense or what might be. As a connection to source, to the divine, to God, or whatever we call the big picture, we seek to transcend the physical into the metaphysical and spiritual. When we are drawn to ease another's suffering through compassion and empathy for a fellow creature, we transcend the boundaries of the self. Even the dream realm, another domain of Neptune, goes beyond the boundaries of consciousness.

Neptune symbolizes the part of us that recognizes it is part of a whole and therefore longs for unity with that whole, whether we call it the collective unconscious, humanity, the universe, source, or God. It is our yearning for the infinite, the divine, the perfect. We channel our yearning for the infinite through the house and sign in which Neptune lies in our chart. This area of our life may be where and how we seek fantastical experiences, where and how we want to transcend everyday life.

The Neptunian function aligns with an idea that is sometimes called the *subtle body*. Many terms attempting to define this idea exist in a variety of beliefs and literature as it's been co-opted and redefined over time, including the astral body, energy body, light body, or simply one's spirit or soul. The subtle body is thought to be associated with one's aura: an energy field surrounding the body, whose color can indicate one's overall emotional or physical health and personality. The location of Neptune can represent how we attune to or are made aware of our subtle body, where our sensitivity lies outside of the conscious realm.

While Neptune experiences allow us to experience a touch of magic, the ordinary has a way of creeping back in. Whether it's the growl of our stomach or the ringing of the alarm clock, the shift can be disheartening, a rude awakening from a lovely dream (sometimes literally). For some, this crash feels rougher, and they may attempt to avoid transcendent experiences altogether or just the opposite—attempt to never come back down to earth. The location of Neptune in our chart may be where we are vulnerable to escapist behaviors. While certain drugs are said to facilitate the process of expanding consciousness, many of them, including alcohol, are often used to escape from the pressures or sorrows of the everyday world, which is why Neptune is often prominent in the charts of those who struggle with drug and/or alcohol addiction. Of course, one need not use drugs or alcohol to escape. The same outlets that can facilitate our imagination can also be used as numbing agents. Too much food, television, or any other form of entertainment can also provide an effective hiding place to escape from reality, which is only really a bad thing when it becomes chronic.

Just a hop, skip, and jump from the desire for spiritual transcendence is emotional transcendence, or empathy. While Venus is the part of us that seeks personal love (Eros), Neptune is akin to a divine love (agape), through which operates a sense of connection and love for humanity or for the human element that unites us all. Neptune's location in our chart can illustrate where we may more easily tap into a sense of compassion or "oneness" with others.

The more united we are with others, the more selfless we are inclined to be, so Neptune's placement in your chart can also tell you where you may be vulnerable to being too yielding, even allowing yourself to be a victim to someone or something (whether or not it's intentional on their part). When our desire or ability to empathize with another overwhelms our need for self-interest, we can do great acts of service, giving wholeheartedly and lovingly. However, the difference between giving selflessly and losing the self lies in whether we allow ourselves to be depleted. Giving of ourselves generously through compassion and giving *up* ourselves entirely through martyrdom bring two entirely different effects. The former can be tiring yet fills you up, while the latter can leave you empty and resentful. Where Neptune resides in your chart is where you are learning to walk this fine line.

Understanding Neptune is like trying to understand consciousness itself, for that is also at the heart of Neptune symbolism. When we daydream or meditate, we are, in essence, trying to experience consciousness itself, independent of the body. Like Neo in the Matrix films, we are trying to free our mind.

This desire for transcendence leaves us with a difficult challenge: how to experience the unreal while living in reality. Any time we send our consciousness to frolic in a daydream, or get lost in an entirely different world through a book or film, we are embracing Neptune. It is not enough to conceive of an idea; it is the act of *getting lost* in something, where we feel it at a deeper level and allow it to overwhelm us, even if just for a time, that is Neptune's joy. During a Neptunian experience, we feel suspended as we surrender to the timelessness of the moment.

Because our potential for empathy and intuition is highest wherever Neptune touches our chart, the combination of the two can yield a kind of inner knowing—about ourselves, others, or our world. Heightened psychic sensitivity or intuitive awareness can be honed through the sign and house in which Neptune lies in your chart. However, it is important to remember that Neptune does not deal in facts or absolutes; it provides a channel to one's highest self, and the knowledge we draw down is impressionistic, subjective, and always changing with every moment that develops, like drinking from a constantly flowing river. Following Neptunian intuition is a bit like following a single flame in the dark—we often don't have the whole image and must surrender ourselves to following where it leads us. We can be vulnerable to projecting our own desires and assumptions onto what we see as a filter, trying to force a meaning that may not be inherent. Neptune lessons usually center on the collision of the impossible and possible, the ideal and the real, the imagined and the actual.

Because Neptune transcends the boundaries of the real, it is not limited by the laws of our natural and social world. Our imagination is a blank canvas and the sky is the limit. Because we are not solely spiritual creatures but also have a physical body and needs, we can straddle both the natural world and the spiritual world. The challenge of Neptune comes when we try to bring things from the Neptunian world into the physical world as is. Dreams often make no sense when we wake and attempt to explain them. Rich symbols full of meaning fall flat when applied literally.

The things we wish were real and imagine could be real have to surrender to the laws of reality and may actually collapse altogether underneath them. We may imagine an idea or a belief thoroughly and invest in it, but it can be dashed to pieces when it meets the test of reality unless a translation of sorts can be made. Whether we imagine the perfect lover, the tallest building, or the ideal government, all these perfect ideas must meet and compromise with the complications and capabilities of the humans in charge and the natural laws of the world.

Keywords Clarified

Neptune is frequently classified as the spiritual planet, which often brings with it connotations of God and religious devotion, but Neptune demands a broader definition of spirituality that includes everyone of every religion or even no religion. At its most basic, the word spiritual can be said simply to mean "of the spirit," as opposed to being earthly or physical. We all wonder, we all imagine, we all have hunches. Although unfortunately they are frequently pitted against each other, both science and religion seek to delve into these mysteries and use the tools of imagination as steppingstones to investigate the many wonders of human life.

Religion is a common vehicle for the Neptunian experience of transcendence, and for some people, some of the time, it does the trick. It provides a gateway to a sense of mystery, transcendence, and communion. Religion itself, however, whether it is as simple as the axiom "do unto others as you would have them do unto you" or whether it is a full tradition of philosophies, rules, and rituals, can only facilitate transcendence. It is the yearning and opening of our consciousness that turns something from a mundane experience into a spiritual one, which is what Neptune is most aligned with.

Neptune in Action

With Neptune placed in the eleventh house, the source for inspiration and the natural inclination toward empathy will likely come from participation with the public. The sense of community and unity with others will be broadly defined by those groups the person feels empathy with, out of a need to protect or defend those who need extra help, such as animals, underpaid teachers, single parents, or a multitude of other possibilities. The person may be drawn to causes to help those less fortunate and to behaviors that build a sense of oneness with others. If Neptune in this house is in the sign of Sagittarius, this might take on the Sagittarian flavor of a love of adventure and all things new and foreign, such as combining these urges to work in large peace organizations that work globally rather than locally, like the Peace Corps or Doctors Without Borders (if the rest of the person's chart is not geared more toward home matters or introversion). On the flip side, Neptunian empathy may lead to vulnerability to being swayed by others' opinions or easily manipulated by others' emotionally fueled agendas.

Placed instead in the first house, which hosts the Ascendant, Neptune might lend a compassionate and openhearted approach to life in general, as well as an attitude of wonder and openmindedness toward whatever or whoever crosses the person's path. Since the first house is also the house of self and Neptune tends to blur boundaries, it might be easy, for better or worse, for this person to take on the qualities and characteristics that others project onto them or that they perceive in others (a very useful placement for actors!). This can allow them the flexibility and ability to reflect the needs and moods of others around them but can also leave them vulnerable to losing themselves.

Question Everything

You can ask these questions of Neptune's condition in your chart to get the answers to rise to the top:

- What lifestyles, philosophies, people, or experiences do you find especially inspiring?
- What experiences or activities give you a sense of touching the divine, whatever that represents to you?
- What do you daydream or fantasize about?
- Where and in what ways do you need to let go and allow intuition to guide you?

PLUTO

Sometimes we grow in our lives in a way that is contained, steady, and measured, such as when we develop new skills and practice them, Saturnian-style. There is some growth that takes place when we are simply willing to leap into the new, as Jupiter encourages us to do. Then there's Pluto, where the growth process tends to be messier. When we grow into a new pair of shoes, we may discard or recycle the old pair, but it's a forward transition. We leave something behind and step into something new that feels better. Growth via Pluto's method often begins with a dismantling. The caterpillar cannot become the butterfly without a surrender to what seems to be potentially annihilating. Death, then re-birth, is Pluto's way.

Pluto is often discussed with abstract, breathy statements about transformation and everything being for the best. The truth is that while there *are* many good things that come with Plutonian territory, none are easy or quick. Courage is required in all Plutonian matters, whether we are facing the beauty or the beast inside of ourselves or inherent in life itself. While Pluto can illustrate where we contain a deep well of survival strength inside of ourselves, we often only call on it in times of dire need or fear, so the good is often couched in the bad. Sayings like "It's always darkest before the dawn" or "You don't know how strong you are until being strong is your only choice" are proof of that awareness.

Untested, we may not know the depths of our strength. If we have not yet been through a tour of our own personal underworld, we won't have the experiential knowledge that comes with surviving hell, including both the vulnerability and the sense of raw strength that are the potential rewards of such a journey.

Pluto, much like Saturn, is often looked on with initial dread by astrologers. We know we have to talk about the hard, scary stuff now. While it's almost always representative of an intense part of us and is often a doorway to our own personal underworld, Pluto isn't always in hellhound mode. True, it may never represent bunnies and puppies but it's often from Pluto that we access our sense of meaning in life. Pluto penetrates to the core of something, and you can't fool it—all you can do is attempt to avoid what it shows you, and never for long.

Pluto can point us toward a deep sense of purposefulness. Pluto's location in your chart can reveal the issues that strike a deep chord in you, even if you are repelled by what they represent just as much as you are drawn to them. People with Pluto prominently placed in their chart, such as close to their Sun, Moon, Ascendant, or Midheaven, of-ten have a striking sense of purpose, a deep-rooted knowledge that they are meant to do something important. This is not to be confused with worldly importance or fame, of course, but a sense of conviction fueled by passion and meaning. They may not have it any more figured out than the rest of us, but they are pushed to go to their edges in the process. They may engage with situations that are intense in their very nature, such as those that involve life-or-death choices or require support or rescue in dire or frightening circumstances.

Not everyone who serves on the front lines of life has a strong Pluto, but Pluto's location in your chart can show you where you have the greatest capacity for growth through courage. This kind of courage leads to empowerment. When we are living healthy Pluto, we can tap into a sense of true empowerment. Pluto power doesn't come from a sense of grandiosity, but from humility and endurance when we go beyond what we thought we were capable of.

Uranus may want to push the boundaries of authority and establishment, but Pluto wants to push the boundaries of life itself, and past any line that may be well intended but keeps us from our personal truth.

Psychologist Carl Jung coined the term *the shadow* to symbolize the darkness surrounding the things about ourselves that we cannot consciously acknowledge. It's a fine thing to strive to be our best selves, but when we deny part of ourselves in that effort, we can become fragmented and lost to ourselves. Jung said he'd "rather be whole than good," maybe because to be *only* good is to deny growth. The things we fear or despise about ourselves, others, or the world often hold the biggest clues toward growth and empowerment and reveal something we may not have wanted to admit about ourselves.

Pluto's location in your chart can illustrate where it's sometimes most needful but also most dangerous to lie to yourself, because the things we don't acknowledge about ourselves, our lives, or the people in it don't go away, but simply hide where they can still go on affecting us in ways we may not prefer, uninhibited, unseen, and uncontrolled.

We're all aware we're going to die, but while death may creep into our consciousness from time to time, we aren't always thinking about it or haunted by it. Pluto wants to show us the truth about ourselves and about life, and the fact that we're all going to die is one of the biggies. While this awareness is a double-edged sword and risks overwhelming us with fear or depression, the conscious awareness of death can also push us into life, to fill us with a desire to live to our edges because, as you know, you've only got one life to live. "No, *really*," Pluto might add.

Living with awareness of our own fragility and being conscious that life could end at any minute can be overwhelming, but it also has a way of getting us to cut through the noise of everyday living and focus on the things that really matter. Nobody's perfect, but this awareness can help push us into living life fully engaged. Pluto's location in your chart can reveal the kinds of experiences that can shake you up and jog your memory about what's really important. Whether we enjoy that wakeup call or not is another story!

Pluto and Fear

At the core of every manifestation of Pluto's dark side is fear. We all have some kind of trigger or tender spot that holds the key to the nature of our deepest fear. Plutonian fears are not mere phobias or anxieties, but deep, primal wounds or aches in the psyche that remain vulnerable throughout our lives. The nature of your fear and how it shows up in your life is revealed by Pluto's placement in your own natal chart.

Where Pluto lies in your chart represents the manner and area of life in which you are called to go to your edges by pushing through fears. You cannot muscle your way through Pluto experiences, however, by simply telling yourself to toughen up. There is something about Pluto work that undoes us, stripping us down to the vulnerable child within, in order to empower us in a real sense, not just puff us up.

Pluto fears, at their root, are never very complex and are not even that unique. A handful of fears is enough to plague the human race: death, loss, abandonment, and annihilation are among the topics on that short list. The stories and events that shaped the particular wounds surrounding the fear may be unnumbered, but when they are boiled down to their essence, they all involve something that we feel helpless about or afraid of.

Pluto fears can be so intense, overwhelming, or complex that they can be difficult to pinpoint directly; sometimes Pluto is easier to see by looking at the evidence of it in one's life. Pluto fears can reveal themselves in our lives through a variety of behaviors, but it's common to see one or more of the following clues, especially in patterns of behaviors and repeated situations.

Defense Mechanisms

Pluto can be difficult to spot because our ego is invested in keeping us sane and strong, and looking fears in the face often makes us feel, well, weak and crazy. Often we can only see Pluto by looking for evidence of it. Routinely employed defense mechanisms are often the best place to start looking. A psychological defense mechanism is a strategy of thoughts and behaviors that we may employ to cope with things that cause us anxiety or emotional pain. Unconsciously attracting the wrong type of partners may be a way to avoid the anxiety of losing someone you love. Sabotaging yourself when you get close to success may be a way to avoid the anxiety of failing at something you really wanted.

We don't have to stare into the abyss every moment of every day; we'd all go mad. There are reasons for defense mechanisms that are helpful and valuable. They can enable us to keep waking up in the morning or survive a difficult aspect of childhood. The difference lies in how permanent those defense mechanisms become. Transforming Pluto pain into power often requires dismantling some of the defenses that no longer serve us.

Specific defense mechanisms that we have unconsciously created around a certain issue will usually repeat in situational patterns in our lives. Additionally, situations may also repeat themselves in our lives even when we *seemingly* have nothing to do with their creation. Sometimes the types of people who represent our Pluto to us can repeatedly enter our lives, such as always finding yourself with an abusive boss or a deadbeat partner. Sometimes we don't see or cannot understand a truth about ourselves, but we may see its shadow or re-flection on the faces of the people we keep meeting.

No planet, not even Pluto, has a monopoly on defense mecha-nisms, but it is often the things we are most afraid of that defense mechanisms stem from.

Woundedness

Often, a defense mechanism is created in response to a traumatic event or situation that wounded us. While we can be wounded as adults, the vulnerability of childhood is a common birthing ground for defense mechanisms that we may carry into adulthood. Tragedies suffered in childhood, some too unthinkable to mention, can have lasting effects. Some people may spend a lifetime working through a trauma that oc-curred when they were too young and vulnerable to process it at the time.

Sometimes we have a story to explain our wounds, but not in ev-ery, or even most, cases. Pluto can't always be traced back to some tragedy we experienced in childhood. Some of us didn't have a house burn down or suffer child abuse, thank goodness! The Pluto wound, therefore, isn't always a wound from overwhelming, traumatic dam-age as much as an area of one's life where a *vulnerability to wounded-ness* lies. Even if we do have a story, it may sometimes seem grossly anticlimactic because the first time this tender spot is triggered, it can overwhelm us, marking itself in our memory even if the event itself isn't inherently traumatic. One woman who identified her most pri-mal fear as abandonment tells the story of her wound occurring when her father stepped over her on his way out the door while she was playing as a very young child. This moment, which seems unimport-ant and probably even occurred more than once, became the *symbol* of her wound. It was not the act itself, but the way it triggered this vulnerability to blossom into her awareness. In some cases, it's not what *really* happened that wounds us as much as it's the way it im-printed itself on us at the time and the story we told (and continue to tell) ourselves about it as it lives in our memory. Not everything is universally wounding. Different things will affect two people in different ways depending not necessarily on the intensity or nature of the event but on how it's received and the nature of the personality experiencing it.

An additional way the evidence of a Pluto wound can show up in our lives is not only through avoidant behaviors, where we try to avoid a repeat of the event or situation that wounded us, but through the opposite approach, where we anxiously seek to fill a need that we don't realize is insatiable, at least in the way that we are trying to fill it. When Pluto wounds form around something that we felt we lacked or didn't get enough of at an early age, we may seek out people or experiences that seem to hold the key to satiating that need, stopping the ache of yearning. This is not simple desire or longing for a true love or a fulfilling career; there is a desperation behind it that is fueled by the fear and the pain of whatever is lacking.

Not every slight or hurt we experience in childhood or beyond relates to Pluto. It's the ones that stick with us, affect our subsequent behaviors, and even shape our lives through recurrent themes that are more likely to be connected to Pluto.

Unhealthy Attachments

Pluto can also reveal itself by way of someone or something that we are deeply attached to. Healthy attachments, such as the bonding of an infant securely to its mother or the love found in satisfying adult relationships, are not the territory here, but rather the kind of attachment that comes with an unhealthy level of intensity or fear laced through it, where it becomes obsessive, manic, and desperate. The things or people we frantically cling to can often reveal what we are most afraid of. The thing we may be attached to can act as a buffer between us and the nakedness of our fear. It is not always a person—it can also be a place, an object, or an idea. But the object of our attachment, in these cases, is often a representation of the source of the fear itself, an embodiment of it.

If we are deeply afraid of being abandoned, for example, we may find ourselves in a romantic relationship where we are excessively jealous or we allow ourselves to be abused or taken for granted, or any number of other coping behaviors that are meant to prevent the loss of our partner *at all costs*. At the heart of the matter is the issue that really needs to be dealt with: not the problem with the partner but the pattern of behavior that fuels that unhealthy partnership (and probably others before). The source of obsession can be masked by the form it has taken, and if one form is lost, another takes its place, as a stand-in for us to play out the defense mechanisms that mask our fears.

Power in Powerlessness

Perhaps it may not seem all that dangerous to be attached to something. If it makes us feel better, what could be the harm? In addition to taking the great risk of placing the burden of maintaining our peace of mind onto one sole thing, we have also given our power to it. That object, idea, or person now holds a power over us whether they want it or not, and the further trouble is, in our effort to avoid the thing we are most afraid of, we may create it. Someone whose fears center around death or illness may literally worry themselves sick. Someone who is afraid of being alone may drive a partner away by emotionally suffocating the person.

Why would we give our power away, even unconsciously, and then lament and long to take it back? Is it an attempt to avoid taking responsibility for that power? There is a certain safety in projecting our fears onto something or someone else, the same safety that is subtly and insidiously inherent in a perpetual victim attitude: we have something to blame and can be satisfied, if not happy, with that explanation when the inevitable happens and we are hurt. It helps to have a god, a spouse, a boss, or a bank to rail against. But if we never uncover the real issue, we cannot transform our relationship to it, and we will keep meeting that god, that spouse, that boss, or that bank over and over again.

Living Healthy Pluto

Naming the fear is key to a healthy engagement with Pluto. As mentioned, Pluto fears are often hard to identify at their basest level, often because doing so is so uncomfortable that not only do we not want to, but sometimes we can't. Much of the time, even saying the fear out loud can sound ridiculous, as if it is too simple a thing to cause such trouble. Sometimes that happens because we are avoiding the emotional reality of it and are intellectualizing it (another defense mechanism). Even when we do connect deeply to the fear as we name it, the words may sound innocuous as a concept but the feelings behind it will be very real and cripplingly intense. Bringing the fear out into the light allows us to take stock of it, make a strategy around it, and see that in some ways it has less power over us in the light of consciousness.

Face the fear, or rather face the situations that spark the issue you're afraid of. Willingly entering a situation where you know you are safe enough but that sends your anxiety off the charts can provide the opportunity for you to empower yourself. You may not feel powerful in the moment, but if you remind yourself that you are doing this willingly and can change your mind at any time, it can help you summon courage.

Anxiety and fear are two different things. Fear is what you experience when in an actual dangerous situation. Anxiety is what you experience when *contemplating the possibility* of being in a dangerous situation. Anxiety is a state of the *anticipation* of danger. Transforming Plutonian anxiety is often not about experiencing the tragedy and devastation you're afraid of but about battling the anxiety of having to do so and not letting it control your life. Opening the door for a child who is afraid there is a monster in the closet is a way to extinguish the anxiety. Avoiding the closet, leaving the lights on, or sleeping in another room (defense mechanisms) are ways to attempt to avoid focusing on the fear, but they actually help to feed it, perpetuating a sense that one cannot handle what's behind that door. Granted, the door may have to be opened every night and courage summoned again and again, but surrendering to the fear and going *through* it is sometimes the only thing that does not leave us powerless. A child does not have to be eaten by the monster to address the fear. The fear *is* the monster.

Healing Pluto

Healing is a powerful and affirming word. Healing means we can feel better, be free of something, and be whole again. However, healing doesn't happen with Pluto issues the way we might think of a wound scabbing over and growing into new, whole skin again. The things we are afraid of or that have hurt us in extreme ways can always be triggered. The source of our fear doesn't stop existing, and when life situations trigger a Pluto fear, we are afraid again. Even if we succeed temporarily at insulating ourselves from our fear, Pluto can be a bottomless pit. We can never get enough love, security, or fill-in-the-blank to be satisfied, to quiet the desperate inner voice, if we focus only on making the pain go away or quelling the longing.

Healing Pluto issues happens not by trying to eradicate the fear and its source in us but by learning to understand our fears, identify the triggers, and act consciously when they come up to manage them, using the magnitude of that powerful energy and *transforming our response to it*. In this way we can stop perpetuating destructive patterns and defense mechanisms that don't serve us, freeing the energy that is caught up in hiding from our fears. Our fears can stand in the way of accessing some parts of our truest, deepest selves and the things in life that can hold the most meaning for us if we're willing to seek them out. As Joseph Campbell said, "Where you stumble, there lies your treasure. The very cave you are afraid to enter turns out to be the source of what you are looking for."

Facing our fears, participating in formal and informal therapy, confronting our past's hold on our future—all of these things can bring Plutonian transformation as we learn the truth about and release old pain. We can't always stop the fear from being triggered, but we can learn how to manage it when it arises.

Keywords Clarified

Transformation is the favorite keyword when it comes to Pluto, but what does it mean to transform? Transformation is not a makeover, where we decorate the outside of something or give it a polish; it is a total redo from the inside, which means an undoing must take place first. Where Pluto resides in our natal chart represents where we have the most capability for radical transformation, if we are willing to undo ourselves and strip ourselves clean of our false securities and unfulfilled hungers. We will also find ourselves facing deep fears about what we might lose and what's waiting on the other side of that loss in the process. The urge toward transformation can be either triggered by external circumstances that force change or initiated from recognizing an inner state of readiness. When it comes to facing our fears and the uncertainty of change, it may even take both an inner and an outer shift to push us to transform.

Transforming the fear isn't just learning to hide from it better or building better insulation against it. It's facing it and being changed by it, embracing the alchemical process of taking the "poison" and transmuting it into something beneficial and entirely different. When something dies, it makes room for the new to be born, and the energy release in the death can actually facilitate the birthing of the new. Whether the lead-up takes months, years, or decades, when we finally accept and lean in to this metaphorical death, the transformation can finally come to completion, sometimes instantaneously.

Pluto in Action

Pluto in the seventh house in a natal chart represents deep lessons around partnership. Partnerships can teach anyone some significant lessons, but when Pluto is in this house, those lessons are particularly intense. Pluto in the seventh house can show up as any number of issues around trust and commitment to another, such as a fear of trusting others enough to let them in close and be very involved in your life, a fear of dependency (on either your part or your partner's), or a good old-fashioned fear of commitment (although this can come from several potential sources).

With Pluto in the seventh house, fears or wounds around commitment can come in many forms. This can show up as a chronic avoidance of any kind of closeness even when there is a yearning for it. It can show up as serial monogamy with partners who are incapable of committing or are inappropriate for us, possibly as a way to avoid triggering our *own* fear of having to be vulnerable with a truly appropriate and committed partner. When we truly open ourselves up to another, trusting them deeply and irrevocably entwining our lives, we may feel that we would be utterly annihilated if we were to lose them, either to betrayal, apathy, or death. That subconscious but powerful fear of loss can lead us to invent defense mechanisms that keep what we want out of reach, providing us with poor substitutes instead.

If Pluto is in Leo in the seventh house, the fears and issues might be flavored with notes of an insatiable need to be appreciated, seen, and adored enough to trust a partner's love and let it in. In Virgo, it might manifest as unworthiness or criticism as the tools to keep another from getting in too deeply. If Pluto is in Virgo but in the eleventh house, the wounds involving criticism or feelings of unworthiness might translate to insecurity with peers or people in general, feeling alone or like we don't measure up. We might be wounded more deeply by the social challenges that most of us typically experience in youth.

Question Everything

You can ask these questions of Pluto's condition in your chart to begin to uncover the meaning of this complex symbol:

- What is the nature of the wound(s) you may have experienced in early life?
- What experiences or beliefs might you be vulnerable to attaching yourself to in order to avoid a repeat of wounding or fear?

- What kinds of experiences frighten you so much that you might avoid them through the use of defense mechanisms?
- What might be the nature of destructive patterns in your life?
- Where do you need to surrender deeply to inherent external powerlessness in order to regain a sense of true power and courage?

CHAPTER 6
THE MOON'S NODES

ASTRONOMY OF THE NODES

Recall that the apparent path the Sun takes around the earth is called the ecliptic, and the band of the zodiac lies along this circle. This circle does not center on the middle of the earth at the equator, but lies at an angle around the earth. The apparent path the Moon makes around the earth is also at an angle, but is not at the same angle as the ecliptic. The angle of the Sun's path and that of the Moon's path differ by about 5°, not quite aligning.

Every month the Moon crosses the path of the ecliptic two times, once as it follows its own orbit north of the ecliptic and once as it follows its path south of the ecliptic. When the Moon meets up with the ecliptic as it continues its orbit around the earth, that meeting point is called a *node*, or more specifically the *South Node* or the *North Node*, depending on the direction the Moon is heading when it crosses the ecliptic. Essentially, when the Sun and Moon cross paths, there's a node.

Every planet has nodes, because every planet crosses the ecliptic. However, the Moon's nodes have been discussed most prominently in popular astrological literature, possibly because the Moon is the earth's only satellite and takes on great significance because of that. (The Moon is second only to the Sun in its impact on earthly life.)[11]

THE SOUTH NODE

The South Node represents our comfort zone, the habitual ways of thinking and behaving that feel easiest for us. It's a comfort zone because we feel comfortable when we know what to expect from life, others, or ourselves when we think and behave in certain ways that we are used to. We feel comfortable when we know what we're doing.

The South Node can be seen as a set of attitudes and behaviors that we know and do well, comparable to the idea of natural talent. In fact, it's common to find people utilizing the natural talents of their South Node in their professions, because it comes easily to them, such as a Gemini South Node being a writer or teacher or a Libra South Node specializing in marriage counseling.

You can often see the South Node present in a couple of specific ways. The South Node can sometimes illustrate circumstances or attitudes with which a person grew up as a young child—the kind of environmental imprint that permeated their childhood, either in its entirety or brief but impactful childhood experiences. For example, you may see someone with Neptune conjunct the South Node who grew up with an absent or alcoholic parent, or someone with the South Node in Aquarius who had some physical, cultural, or circumstantial difference that set them apart from others from the start, like a physical handicap from birth or being the only kid in a vastly different religion from the rest of the neighborhood. This is by no means *always* the case; however, it is very common. In these cases, the childhood foundation doesn't replace the idea that the South Node represents the person's own internalized habits and perspectives, but the child-

---

11. If the topic of planetary nodes piques your interest, investigate the work of astrologer Mark Jones, whose work can be found in the resources section in the back of this book. This angle relationships between the Sun, Moon, and Earth can also be used to understand eclipses.

hood circumstances can often play a role, big or small, in the forming of the habitual responses of the South Node.

The South Node of the Moon also represents the foundation and compulsions of the past. The past can be defined as simply as your childhood or as far-reaching as your past lives, depending on your belief system. Our past informs how we act in the present and will act in the future, whether we are repeating it or learning from it. Our past experiences shape our current perspective.

When viewing the South Node in this way, we can recognize the strength of a lifetime of habit or a certain foundational orientation on which we build our entire lives going forward. The Moon represents our emotional bodies and our unconscious selves, in part. Therefore, the nodes of the Moon play out on this instinctual level. The emotional "memory" of the South Node is not about explicit memories from childhood or past lives; it is the mood, the instinctual, implicit memory of the past.

While the South Node and what it represents can be comfortable and valuable to us, it also represents behaviors and attitudes that come so easily that they can impede growth, just as anything we do habitually out of security rather than intention can lead to stagnation. Restlessness on a deep soul level can manifest when we perpetually relive South Node material. The attitudes of the South Node may also represent a blind spot because we are too good at seeing ourselves, others, and life from this perspective, which may discourage us from trying on new perspectives. As humans, we see what we expect to see and often try to quickly fit it into our existing paradigm instead of sitting temporarily with confusion or allowing what we see to threaten or redefine that paradigm.

THE NORTH NODE

If the South Node is much that's familiar and easy, the North Node is much that's foreign and challenging. The sign and house in which the North Node lies in the natal chart are clues to the kinds of circumstances and behaviors (house) that may help expand a person's world, and the characteristics (sign) that can be developed to counteract or balance some of the excesses or pitfalls that the South Node represents.

When we encounter what our North Node represents in our lives, we are in unfamiliar territory and may not always recognize it or even welcome it. Some astrologers look at the North Node as the ultimate in karmic importance, as if it's the soul's purpose, but truly, the entire chart as a whole represents the way forward. The North Node can simply be looked at as a kind of energy that can help bring balance and promote growth for someone. When we open ourselves up to the kind of attitudes and experiences of the North Node, we are able to encounter the *new*, which can prompt us toward growth if we so choose and, at the very least, give us a glimpse of another approach to life that's vastly different from what we're accustomed to.

Because the North and South Nodes lie at either end of an axis, it's helpful to think of them as extreme ends of a spectrum. Go too far toward the South Node and you will be stuck. Go too far toward the North Node and you will be overwhelmed.

THE NODES IN ACTION

A Scorpio South Node person will automatically have a Taurus North Node, as Taurus and Scorpio are opposing signs. Someone with this node set may have a tendency to gravitate toward emotional intensity, either in their circumstances or personality. They may have a natural instinct for sniffing out what's hidden in any situation, whether it's a person or a situation that seems to be about more than meets the eye. They may enjoy work that involves solving mysteries or research because of their hunger to get to the bottom of things. Because Scorpio looks beneath the surface, Scorpio South Node people are unlikely to be satisfied until they've uncovered a secret, and will often approach life suspiciously, as if they are waiting for the punch line or the other shoe to drop.

Since the South Node can illustrate not only characteristics and habits that we embody but also the "stew" we were born into and grew up in, a Scorpio South Node, in some cases, may indicate a childhood that was emotionally charged somehow, perhaps with an intense or moody parent, or a painful or difficult component in the family/home environment, or something else along similar lines.

Embracing a Taurus North Node, then, would mean learning to stabilize one's life and self, discovering ways to bring peace and equilibrium into one's life when needed. The house would further illustrate the methods in which the person could do so, whether a physical outlet such as yoga or gardening or a mental or spiritual outlet like meditation, or any other countless possibilities in between. Developing an appreciation for and trust in the simple and straightforward in life can help them see that not everything need be complex and dramatic. While the Scorpio South Node person might be used to dramatic, sudden change (by choice or not), the Taurus North Node encourages them to develop the ability to see things grow and change little by little, over time.

Although a traumatic background is not necessarily a given with a Scorpio South Node, there may be a history of soul trauma, either in the early or past life, however you choose to frame it. In traumatic circumstances, there can be a sense of disembodiment, a feeling of withdrawal or disconnection from the wounding situation. A Taurus North Node, in this case, could be about developing a trust of the physical, learning to embody their physical being and be comfortable inside their skin.

In the case of the reverse situation, a natal chart with a Scorpio *North* Node and a Taurus *South* Node, we would look to the potential pitfalls and excesses of Taurus for clues as to the path of growth. If Scorpio is often in various states of upheaval, either circumstantially or emotionally, Taurus, its counterpart, is often in such a state of equilibrium that it can slide into stagnation. A Taurus South Node person may be so disinclined toward change that they try to avoid it at all costs, staying in jobs, situations, and relationships or out of momentum along the path of least resistance. They may deny or suppress strong emotions in themselves or avoid volatile situations, yet there is a *need* for upheaval, drama, and complexity in their life that can break them out of their sleepy state, should it overtake them, and into a life that is more *alive*, even if less predictable. It doesn't mean they need to turn themselves into a drama queen or king, but to learn to navigate and sometimes embrace the drama of life and let it deepen them, rather than avoid it.

None of these possibilities are certain, nor are they immoral or inherently bad. They are simply potential examples of how the energies can be used in healthy or unhealthy ways.[12]

---

12. There are two methods commonly used to calculate the position of the nodes: the true node, which accounts for a slight wobble as the earth spins on its axis, and the mean node, which averages the wobble out in its calculations. Despite the inference one could make from their names, there is no good or bad rule when it comes to which calculation an astrologer prefers to use, and the two nodes are typically no more than a degree or so apart. Ultimately, the most important thing to remember is that the true and mean nodes are not two separate things; they are only two different ways to calculate the same thing. All charts in this book use the true node.

CHAPTER 7

THE SIGNS

THE ROLE THE SIGNS PLAY

While the planets represent basic human needs, the signs in which the planets fall in your natal chart reveal the specifics of how those needs are best met and the way in which those needs express themselves. The signs are the adjectives, the flavor, the *style* and characteristics that bring the agendas of the planets to life. We all share a basic human need for communication and learning (Mercury), but what topics do you like to learn about most? What are the methods by which you most easily learn something new? What do you like to talk about and what is the manner in which you share your thoughts? It is the sign that reveals the answer to these questions and contributes to shaping our personalities—not just one human in a sea of humans, but a unique individual with particular preferences and characteristics.

Because the signs are the most popularized and well-known component of the language of astrology, they are the most subject to shallow understanding and stereotyping, which has sometimes resulted in a watered-down version of each sign that limits our understanding of these powerful archetypes. When you read a description of your sign in most popular astrology books, newspapers, or magazines, what you are reading is the author's interpretation (or repetition) of a list of behaviors and personality traits that your sign is likely to manifest.

For example, it's been frequently observed that Virgos behave in fastidious ways or an Aries behaves impulsively, so naturally it's assumed that all Virgos *are* fastidious and to be an Aries *is* to be impulsive. These behaviors are then seen as the law of each sign. But these behaviors and observations are merely some *manifestations* of each sign, not its core truths. There can be dozens of behaviors and personality traits that come from each sign, and they are as varied and complex as the people exhibiting them.

Manifestations of each sign can vary depending on the person wearing them and the other components in their natal chart, but it's also a common mistake to assume that the behavior we're attributing to a certain sign *is at the heart of the sign's meaning*. The truths that are most important and central to each sign don't vary as much at their core, but only in the way they express themselves when worn on one person or the next. They are central ideas that have a multitude of expressions. A sign has a small handful of core truths, or *roots*, from which all of these changeable behavioral manifestations, or *branches*, stem.

Beginner astrology students are often taught to memorize a list of these manifestations, or keywords, about each sign, which is usually a lengthy list and in the end does very little to promote deep understanding of the core truths of each sign. This leaves astrology students frustrated by the inability to make a chart come alive, but the fault lies in the method, not in the student. If we understand the core truths about each sign, memorization of keywords becomes less important.

INTRODUCING ARCHETYPES

An archetype is a concept that is universal, seen in every culture and every time period, an idea or symbol that is almost primal and inherent to the collective consciousness. It can be an idea, a type of person, or a story or myth we've heard retold throughout history. For example, one of the most common archetypes is "mother." We all have had a mother, who gave birth to us, and that individual person has individual personality traits that express who she is. But the *archetype* of mother embodies not the individual personality traits of your mother, but the universal concept of mother: one who gives birth, nurtures, protects. While we may not all literally be mothers, we all have the mother archetype within us, whether we are male or female, young or old, whether we give birth to literal or metaphorical children. Any time we create or nurture something, we are drawing on the mother archetype within, and we can all tap into a primal, pre-verbal knowing about what we call *mother*.

The signs can be thought of in this way, as a collection of archetypes that embody the traits and experiences contained within each sign. Just as we can think of many ways someone might behave when they embody the mother archetype, we can think of many ways that a sign might behave when we understand that sign's core principles. Each sign will likely contain more than one archetype. For example, Aries might represent the daredevil archetype but also the leader archetype. Scorpio might represent the detective and/or the shaman. We don't have to know that Scorpio is "intense, dramatic, secretive, and loyal" and memorize these adjectives (and more) to understand Scorpio. Both the detective and the shaman, though very different archetypes, represent the Scorpionic desire to dig deep, whether it be in getting to the truth at the bottom of a mystery or getting beneath the surface of life into the underworld. These archetypes help us relate to and understand what's at the heart of each astrological sign or symbol, and derive from that understanding a sense of how Scorpio might behave, the experiences it might seek out, and the trials it may experience. If we understand that one of the core truths of Scorpio lies in the need to experience life in the deepest way possible, we can understand that a Scorpio might be prone to going to extremes, for example. Many keywords and behaviors commonly assigned to Scorpio embody this one core truth, and if we understand it, we can make our own keyword list at any moment, one that always fluidly draws on the root of the sign, rather than memorize a collection of flat and seemingly disconnected personality traits.

One of the reasons it's so fun and interesting to study astrology is that we can see ourselves and those we know reflected in what we study almost right away, especially in the signs, since they are most people's first encounter with astrology. It's not only fun but also very helpful to try to connect what you study with the people you know, in order to see astrology come to life. In describing the behavior and needs of the signs, it's instinctual to personify each of them. However, it's very important to remember that *you* are not an "[insert sign here]." To say "your Sun sign is Aries" is not synonymous with saying "you *are* Aries." You are a whole and complex person, and the signs in which the planets in your chart reside are representative of the archetypes at work within you and working through you, mingling with the other influences on your personality and creating a unique blend that no astrology profile can sum up alone. You are more than the sum of your parts.

The meanings of the twelve individual signs discussed in this chapter encompass not only positive expressions but also potential hang-ups. No astrology symbol represents something that is all bad or all good. You will gain deeper empathy and further insight into a natal chart if you can remember that there is an underlying connection of need beneath the positive and negative ends of any sign's spectrum of expression.

In many cases, the negative expression of a sign's characteristics can show up because of a misuse of or misunderstanding about the nature of the need that is trying to be fulfilled. For example, Virgo longs for perfection via constant improvement and self-control, but if perspective isn't maintained, this sign can get carried away with the method, exerting control over everything and everybody, perhaps because something yet unidentified or beyond its control feels chaotic.

In other cases, the negative expression of a sign can be the result of being too good at something or having too much of something, such as Libra's natural skill at seeing both sides of an issue resulting in having difficulty actually picking a side when necessity dictates. Likewise, the positive expressions aren't always just sitting on the surface, waiting to be expressed; they often must be cultivated and directed to get the best out of them.

ARIES

As the first sign, Aries embodies the primal nature of life itself, the perpetual birth of the cosmic soul. Life, in order to begin and continue to survive, must be aggressive, dominant, and passionate. It must also be able and willing to defend itself, acting instinctually and sometimes immediately to do so. Symbolically, Aries is represented by the ram, illustrated by a ram's willingness to run headfirst at life to establish dominance and display strength. Like the ram, Aries must charge in headfirst, uncrippled by reluctance, doubt, or fear.

The primary need of Aries is to exist. There are so many things in life that make it difficult to exist or threaten continued existence, and they must be pushed through, overcome, and fought against to continue to exist and thrive. Whether Aries' physical existence is challenged by direct illness or physical attack, or its identity challenged by subtle constructs of society that quell its spirit with admonishments to "'wait your turn" or "play nice," Aries does not like to be constrained, marginalized, or defeated. It doesn't want to survive merely by continuing to breathe in and out until life ends. Many behaviors exhibited by Aries are done simply to say "I am here."

Natural selection is a theory that was developed by Charles Darwin in an attempt to describe the mechanism by which evolution occurs. The expression "survival of the fittest" is often attributed to Darwin as well, but it was coined by a man named Herbert Spencer when drawing parallels between the natural selection theory and his own observations about surviving and thriving in society. In common use, the phrase has come to indicate the belief or philosophy that those who are the most "fit" are most likely to survive and thrive, measured by those traits that equip one best to handle life's challenges.

Inherent in this idea is competition. In a world with vast but finite resources, determination of who is the most fit is often dependent on who has access to the most resources. Aries has an inherent impulse to go after what it wants according to this instinct not out of a selfish desire to take from others but to ensure its own survival. In a modern world that is more removed from the everyday realities of battling for one's food and usually fighting savage beasts only in the metaphorical sense, this can seem overdramatized. Yet the instinct still beats in the heart of the Aries archetype. Aries tends toward competitiveness because it is born to conquer and survive, therefore competing where necessary, pitting itself against another or even itself. Aries can become excited and more motivated when it has something or someone to beat, seeing it as a chance to test and prove itself.

Certainly Aries' competitive spirit, like anything else, can be overdone. Aries is prone to seeing or making conflict where there need be none, or putting more importance on winning than other goals that may be equally important. Aries is designed to run ahead toward its own desires, even if it accidentally runs over someone in the process. Sometimes Aries may delight when that happens because it means it has won or triumphed, or it may not even be aware that has happened, being as focused as it was on the finish line. However, sometimes Aries needs to be reminded that when *everything* is a competition, there can be only a winner and a loser, and there are situations that call for more inclusive solutions.

Although all humans may have a deep and primal survival instinct, in some ways the sign of Aries is an embodiment of it. Life doesn't ask whether it's okay with anyone else that it's here; it just is. As we've seen, sometimes it has to eliminate its competition in an effort to survive, but most often Aries just wants to be free to do its thing, and it will become impatient when people or circumstances thwart its will. This includes circumstances where it is more socially acceptable to stand back, be agreeable, smile even when it's insincere, or lie to avoid hurt feelings. Aries' method is directness; with Aries, what you see is what you get. Aries prefers to act in a straightforward and unapologetic manner, calling it like they see it and not beating around the bush. This sign admires and prefers to act with passion and boldness over reserve and restraint.

While Aries isn't typically thought of as the sign of invention (out-of-the-box-thinker Aquarius or curious and intellectual Gemini may come first to mind), Aries' desire to discover (and conquer!) new territory tends to make this sign quite innovative. Innovators René Descartes and Leonardo da Vinci were Aries-born. Along with the desire to innovate can come an entrepreneurial spirit—the drive to put one's ideas into action, such as famous Ariens financier J. P. Morgan and Google co-founder Larry Page. At age fourteen, Aries Laura Dekker became the youngest person to sail solo around the world. In the 2013 film *Maidentrip*, Laura told a journalist that she didn't care about being in history books, and while she thought it would be a "rush" to set a world record, she narrowed it down to the most important point: "I asked myself, 'Can you do this?' And I answered, 'I'm going to try.' So I'm curious if I can and if I make it I'll know I can; I've crossed a boundary. That is my only goal."

Strategy and commitment, of course, go hand in hand with innovation to make one a true entrepreneur rather than just someone with a good idea, and the archetype of Aries alone does not necessarily include those traits, which are more reflective of a desire to see goals through rather than the bursting spirit of the new. Aries loves a new beginning and sees it as an expression of the creation impulse: life. However, Aries may not always have the desire or fortitude to follow an idea or plan through beyond the initial establishment. Once it becomes an institution, Aries has already moved on to conquer new territory and discover new horizons, because its heart lies in the drive to bring the new and overcome obstacles in the process.

Initiative and an ability to tolerate risk are inherent for innovators; they have to be able to be the brave one, carving a path through uncharted territory for the rest to follow. Anyone embodying Aries energy must discover this reserve of courage within if they are to respond to this need. Aries symbolizes not only the explorer but also the warrior, the one who is willing to face fear and danger. While others may admire this sign's bravery and willingness to leap into action, this ability manifests in Aries not out of a desire to impress but an instinctual ability to act and react quickly. Modern-day warriors such as firefighters don't do what they do *in the moment that they do it* because they are trying to be a hero; they do it because immediate action must be taken and they don't ignore their instinctual response to *just do it*. That's why it's been said that there's a fine line between bravery and stupidity. Courage isn't about strategy and it's not simply the absence of fear; it's action, sometimes impulsive and reckless, and it's usually the success or failure of the action that is the basis for it being judged as stupid or brave.

It's not just unthinking impulsiveness that drives Aries to take risks, however. The classic image of the Aries daredevil stems from this desire to court life, and for Aries, life is courted and experienced most boldly when found on the edge of death. Those with Aries featured strongly in their natal chart will often find some outlet for living on that edge, whether it's in the way they act, dress, talk, or pursue their interests.

Aries isn't always the warrior or the brute, but it doesn't exactly embrace its tender side overtly or easily. It can love fiercely and come to the defense of its loved ones ferociously, but for all its directness and risk-taking, Aries may not always have an easy time expressing softer feelings. Showing weakness or tenderness, even for good reason, can be difficult, for it leaves this sign feeling exposed and vulnerable, a kind of risk that can leave one feeling weaker, not stronger (at least not apparently). Aries may show its affection through loyalty or through playful teasing, but a "true warrior" doesn't cry, let down its guard, or come undone, this sign may subconsciously tell itself.

Keywords Revisited

Pop astrology sometimes makes Aries sound like it's always spoiling for a fight, but it really comes down to a matter of what it chooses to do with its energy. Aries is made to move, push, and explore. If its energy remains unfocused or restrained for too long, Aries gets restless, and conflict can result from a buildup of that energy, which also serves as a useful release, like before and after a storm. Aries is easily frustrated when it's restrained, whether the restraint stems from external situations or is self-imposed, as freedom is a key component to maintaining its health and sanity. Not every Aries will be combative, however; this sign may get a false reputation for being combative simply because it is not as likely as some other signs to shy away from conflict or demur. Also, Aries doesn't only seek conflict when it's bored or restless. There are other ways to release energy, such as physical outlets like exercise or sports.

Aries is sometimes called the most selfish sign, but perhaps self-oriented may be a more accurate description. Aries is often called the sign of the self, perhaps because everything in our lives begins with, stems from, and returns to "me." We are the center of our own lives, acting from our own will and trying to fill our own needs, and Aries instinctually understands that best.

Aries *can* be selfish at times, not wanting to share or consider others in its decisions, but so can anyone else. Aries is often just the most unapologetic and obvious about it. Because it is fueled by its own passion and will for what it wants, Aries may seem more selfish than some other signs, but in a society sometimes taught to sacrifice individual needs for perceived polite but occasionally misguided reasons, Aries can keep things balanced simply by following its instinct to take care of itself.

Mars Rules

Each sign corresponds to a certain planet, a concept that is referred to as *rulership*.[13] Mars naturally rules the sign of Aries, because they both are inherently about our will: the directness of self-reinforcing Aries makes for a convenient expression of our desire nature expressed through Mars.

Aries in Action

Mercury in the sign of Aries will communicate best and most authentically when it can be direct. It wants to get to the point and does so

---

13. You'll learn more about rulership in section three.

rapidly, so a person with Mercury in Aries may talk fast. They may also be fast learners, but will appreciate leaping right in and learning by doing rather than reading all the instructions or doing tedious research. They may enjoy a good debate, not merely as an intellectual exercise but for the competition. They may not easily back down from an idea and can tend to be combative in defending their ideas, which can turn a conversation into an argument, even unintentionally. They will tend to shoot from the hip when communicating and can be prone to speaking without thinking, especially when they are passionate about a topic. They have a penchant for strong, one-sided opinions, which may not always be as a result of a well-thought-out argument as much as impulsive tendencies.

In the tenth house, Mercury in Aries may be well known for this kind of communication style. They may find themselves in leadership positions (officially or unofficially) that center around their ability to aggressively pursue and gather information and/or present it in a passionate or forthright way. They may be well suited for situations in which a strong voice is needed.

With Jupiter in Aries, a person will experience a natural sense of "luck" as well as increased faith in life and themselves when they take risks, without hesitation. Although impulsiveness can often lead to a misstep for many, a Jupiter-in-Aries person may often experience just the opposite, where acting impulsively toward something they want to attempt may actually increase their chances of success as they learn to trust their instincts. It can also increase their innate ability to summon courage when they need it. Their confidence rises when they tackle the unknown and are willing to simply try, without a carefully controlled plan. With this placement in the tenth house, they may be known for their ability to inspire others with their courage and willingness to act. They may find themselves in leadership positions that center on encouraging others to find their strengths or release their fears. They may excel at motivating others to do their best, especially in a coaching capacity.

TAURUS

The Aries archetype roars the cosmic spirit into existence through courage, fervor, and force. After the primal scream of Aries' AM comes the Taurus BE. Taurus is symbolized by the bull, which tends to conjure cartoon images of a great beast charging down a little man holding a red cloth, but most of the time the raging bull is simply a cow, content to graze where it stands.

Taurus does not seek to push itself into blazing existence, but to plainly be—peaceful, calm, at ease with itself and the world. To some, this may look like confidence, to others laziness, and to yet others resolution; but whatever it's judged to be, Taurus's natural state and core need is centeredness, through stability and peacefulness.

In the new age, words like peacefulness and centeredness lead us to imagine the guru meditating on the mountaintop. Peacefulness is not necessarily piousness or transcendent spirituality; for Taurus, peace is often sought through indulgence rather than transcendence. The activities that bring one down to earth in an immediate way are the pathways that Taurus prefers to walk, whether through experiences that refresh and enliven the senses or a familiar routine that calmly reassures the soul that life will continue.

The Taurus archetype symbolizes the need for continuity, which builds on itself and allows the setting down of roots. It feels good to Taurus to be able to trust that it can depend on circumstances and people in its life to remain consistent. Therefore, Taurus likes to have a sense of control over its environment, not necessarily to direct it or be in charge but to feel confident that it knows what's coming up next and knows how to handle itself when it does. Taurus itself tends to possess the traits of patience, endurance, and a single-mindedness that allows it to continue moving along its chosen path. This sign is not in a hurry to get to the end of that path but enjoys seeing it stretch out before it, taking comfort in its predictability. Taurus may stay with the same job or partner or in the same home for decades because stable external circumstances make it easier for its inner state to reflect the same stability.

Through this doorway of steadfastness and dependability can also enter the flip side: inflexibility and stubbornness. The tenaciousness of Taurus can allow it to accomplish long-term goals that others haven't the dedication for, but it may not always be out of intentional perseverance as much as coasting off of momentum once it's established. If Taurus find itself in a situation or relationship, for example, that has long since passed its expiration date, its desire to stick with the known can allow a bad situation to continue much too long or even become worse, bringing stability but no peace. The house in which Taurus planets lie will provide further insight into the situations or beliefs that they are prone to clinging to most stubbornly.

Naturally, the desire for stability tends to make Taurus risk-averse overall, digging in its heels instinctively when change threatens to topple over a well-ordered life. This sign is reluctant to stray from the proven, tried-and-true methods and plans to which it has grown accustomed. Every human alive can be said to be resistant to change under the right circumstances, and often the key factor is whether or not the change was their choice. But Taurus needs to plant its feet and feel the ground solid underneath, so change has to take place in a rhythm that feels natural, to allow for slow adaptation rather than be thrust into an entirely unknown scenario all at once, even if it's Taurus's idea. Taurus may need to get used to an idea before it's willing to move its feet; pushing this sign only creates an equal resistance in it. If Taurus succumbs entirely to its initial resistance, stagnation, not contentment, will be the result.

Taurus has an innate understanding of the benefits of slowing down and taking its time to enjoy something. It tends to want to avoid complications and therefore has an innate ability to get to the heart of a matter, reducing ideas, tasks, or problems down until the solution is plain, which it will state matter-of-factly. This sign takes things at face value and can usually be understood in the same way.

Taurus can exude a quiet calmness that puts others around it at ease and often comes across as sincere and grounded. It has no patience for pretense or drama; healthy Taurus is comfortable in its own skin and unconsciously gives others permission to relax and be at ease within themselves. Taurus is often called easygoing and can tend to be quite amiable, but that stems from the desire to keep things easy and steer clear of over-complication whenever convenient, and not from bending over backwards to meet another's needs, which is a much more complex endeavor. This sign is typically unflappable, although when pushed past its limits it will draw a firm line that it may never cross. When it "sees red," the cow becomes the bull, snorting and stamping its feet!

Comfort can lead to contentment, so Taurus is known for enjoying its creature comforts. Taurus is called a sensual sign because it is prone to seek out things that please the senses, from aromatherapy to comfort food. It is the most animalistic of signs in this way, not because it is violent or primal but because it tends to be in tune with its senses. A luxurious but comfortable environment can work wonders on its mood and sense of well-being.

Many Tauruses are nature lovers, enjoying working directly with the earth through gardening or the peaceful stillness of bird watching. However, while the classic image of the mountain man is one of many apt symbols for Taurus, it doesn't mean birds alight on their shoulder when out for a walk or that they love to go camping every weekend (a rock in one's back while sleeping certainly isn't comfortable!). But the Taurean ideal of comfort can be applied metaphorically, not just physically, and being out in nature can appeal to the back-to-basics vibe of Taurus, so it's common to find that a connection with nature in some form is deeply moving for Taurus.

Keywords Revisited

The most popular keyword for Taurus is stubborn, which we've already outlined, but a another common one is materialistic. This may stem from the Taurean love of nice things, or, more specifically, *things that make it feel nice.* The pursuit of comfort is very motivating to Taurus, and since it so naturally navigates the world through the five senses, it may frequently seek out comfort from luxury items. However, comfort can come from intangibles as well and may be a more fulfilling choice for some with strong Taurus energy, depending on where and how it expresses within the context of the rest of a person's chart. Decadent food and soft blankets can potentially fulfill that desire, just as a camping retreat can bring comfort to the soul or a massage can calm the mind and heart. Taurus does not have a monopoly on retail therapy (although it may sometimes certainly lead the charge!).

Taurus is certainly capable of realizing that too much stuff can bring a level of burden and complexity that is the antithesis of the comfort, peace, and simplicity it is seeking. Taurus is not fulfilled by the shallow pursuit of wealth but by the confidence that continuity brings. If Taurus does become materialistic to an unhealthy degree, this can often stem from a desire to bolster itself against the tide of change and uncertainty that life naturally brings. Taurus may unconsciously feel that if it has enough money in savings or food in the pantry (or whatever it has deemed as its safeguard), it can stave off any disaster. But recognizing when enough is enough is the key. It's human nature to want to avoid change in some way or to some degree because it can feel like our survival is threatened, but because stability is high on this sign's list of priorities, it's more common to see it with Taurus.

Venus Rules

Taurus shares its ruler, Venus, with Libra. Venus acts easily through the Taurean desire for simple pleasures and things that soothe, and Taurus's love of the sensual is a natural outlet for Venus's appetite to experience things of beauty.

Taurus in Action

Someone with a Taurus Moon will feel most nurtured by a sense of constancy, especially taking comfort in their routine such as that morning stop at their one and only favorite coffee shop. Since the Moon has a correlation with our domestic needs, a nurturing home will need to feel comfortable and relaxed above all, a place where they can put their feet up with no fussiness. Their moods tend to be stable but can take a dive if they have a chaotic start to the day or an emotional conflict, and it may take a while for them to be able to turn their mood around. A Taurus Moon will certainly have emotions and will even be deeply affected by them, but they may be reluctant to admit it to others or even themselves when they are affected strongly by something.

In the sixth house, the Taurus routine becomes an even greater necessity for a Moon-in-Taurus person, both at work and in their daily lives. They will enjoy work that has a steady pace and a steady paycheck, with clear expectations regarding their tasks. A high-stress job will take its toll quickly, as will an environment with a high turnover. They may also enjoy work that has a material component to it, where they are working with raw materials or with their hands in such a way that they can see and feel what they produce right up front.

GEMINI

From the steadfast and solidly planted feet of Taurus to a mind constantly in motion, Gemini rouses the cosmic soul from its sleep with questions to answer and ideas to pursue.

The twins symbolize Gemini for two reasons (appropriately). First, Gemini's hunger to learn so fast and experience so much makes it seem like Gemini lives two lives instead of just one; and second, the twins reflect Gemini's ability to see so many perspectives that it's almost always of two (or more) minds. There is a singularity of experience and purpose in Aries and Taurus that is now expanded in the dual nature of Gemini.

Gemini needs to *know*, and many of this sign's skills and inclinations serve as a tool kit for that mission. Gemini loves to learn, loves to understand what it is learning, and loves to communicate it in some form, but Gemini isn't necessarily out to memorize the dictionary or get a doctorate degree on every imaginable topic. It's the process of thinking up a great question and then getting that delicious "hit" of discovering the answer that is like a drug to Gemini. If you've ever reached for an answer to a question like "What was the name of that actress who played in the movie about the guy with the hair in that one town?" and fallen over in ecstasy when you were somehow able to determine the answer (thanks, Internet), then you've shared Gemini's joy.

Gemini is not typically attached to *what* the answer is or whether it is proven right; it tends to be openminded enough that the discovery process is rewarding in itself. It might as well have been a Gemini who said "I think, therefore I am." Thinking is (almost) enough for this sign to live on, but what or who is doing the thinking? That's how Descartes [14] felt he was able to conclusively prove (or at least was not able to *disprove*) his existence—there had to be an "I" to do the thinking. But thought itself can run an entire gamut between question and conclusion, and the archetype of Gemini is not simply to find answers but also to learn how to keep one's eyes open—to *see* and witness and observe with as little bias as possible.

They say perspective is everything, and nobody knows that better than Gemini. As with a mirror ball, Geminis know the truth has many facets, so much so that they can't help but be aware that truth is relative and lies in the eye, or mind, of the beholder. While that allows them to contemplate multiple perspectives, furthering their education and enabling them to learn more with every turn, it's also what makes this sign so good at "spin": swaying opinion (theirs or someone else's) in one direction or the other according to how they decide to combine and present the facts, as well as what they strategically leave out.

While Gemini may be good at spin-doctoring, it's not always done with malicious intent, or even any intent, for that matter, but is simply a result of this sign's ability to come to different conclusions based on different perspectives. Gemini is a great debater, but when it comes

---

14. The French philosopher Descartes (an Aries with Mars in Gemini) is known for having said "I think (Gemini), therefore I am (Aries)" in an attempt to prove his own existence.

to the ever-present internal debate going on in the mind of the twins, they can sometimes paint themselves into a corner, asking themselves so many questions and coming up with so many different answers to the same question that they wind up with fewer conclusions and more confusion than they started with. The twins can also be too good at rationalization, backing up whatever they wanted to do or believe anyway with a few pieces of data to justify the conclusion.

The Geminian mind is curious, responsive, and versatile, able to leap from topic to topic in a single bound. Gemini is quick with an answer, or at least an opinion or follow-up question. This curiosity and versatility serves this sign well; when focused, Gemini's mental stamina is exceptional, but when unfocused, its curiosity can encourage a short attention span, fragmented thinking, and mental burnout. Its attention can so easily be shifted and split that it can be difficult to focus in one direction sometimes, especially when Gemini is physically or mentally exhausted.

Gemini represents versatility not only in mind but in body as well. Geminis may exhibit this with quick reflexes and good dexterity or simply in consistently being on the go. They are quite restless and always in search of stimulation, so much so that they can burn out physically as well as mentally if they don't slow down when their body warns them to. They are pulled in so many directions by so many interests or social engagements that they are simply prone to overdoing it when it comes to the sheer number of daily activities. They excel at juggling many things at once, however, because they are good at quickly focusing and responding in the moment. They don't think about the "ball" that is in the air but about the ball about to fall into their lap, catching it at the right moment and sending it up again quickly before the next ball demands their attention.

Above all else, Gemini is known most for its love of communication, a keyword that's usually at the top of the list of Gemini's qualities. Communication is a two-lane highway, with input going in one direction in the form of reading, listening, and observing and output going in the other direction in the form of speaking, singing, writing, hand signals, or any other way Gemini can think of to tell its story or share what it knows. The energy that builds up from these stimulating exchanges is not draining but enlivening to Gemini.

Keywords Revisited

Gemini does like to share information, but that doesn't mean it runs at the mouth all the time. Excessive talkativeness, often assigned to Gemini's list of faults, may not be the chosen method of sharing information, as there are other ways to do so. The overall personality may dictate whether it's more important to share information than to gather it, as well as what information it likes to share and at what length. It's not uncommon to ask a question of a Gemini and get a windfall of answers, only some of which are related to your question!

Second on the list of overused keywords for Gemini might be fickle. Because Gemini is motivated by curiosity, it is in constant search of stimulation. Stagnancy in any form is anathema to Gemini. Gemini is life's little scientist, playfully experimenting by asking questions and pressing buttons (sometimes mischievously!), so the actions it takes aren't always indicative of a desire to commit to something (whether it's an idea, person, or situation), but rather a curiosity about it. If curiosity was and continues to be the only motivation in any given experience, Gemini will move on once that purpose is fulfilled.

Mercury Rules

Mercury holds dual rulership of the signs Gemini and Virgo, because they each represent an easy path for Mercury's natural function. Mercury's love of exchanging information suits the flexible, communicative sign of Gemini quite well.

Gemini in Action

Someone with Saturn in Gemini may seek out the kind of information that defines clear boundaries and provides facts and practical know-how. While Gemini needs to know, the Saturnian urge tends to limit how far they'll pursue something and in what way they will seek answers to their questions in order to get to the point. If they can rise to the Saturnian pressure to utilize self-discipline, they may enjoy the benefits of becoming a master of a certain topic or field of study, which can provide a great deal of pride and self-confidence. They are likely to feel more comfortable with rigorous or scientific areas of study where the questions tend to have reliable and proven answers rather than flaky speculation.

Placed in the ninth house, Saturn in Gemini may prefer a formal route of study such as an academic degree, which can put them through their paces and enable them to feel they have a stamp of approval from authorities whose expertise invokes respect. Depending on other placements in their chart, they may have to work hard at maintaining flexibility in their ideas and their perspectives; they may sometimes become fixated on method rather than purpose. They are vulnerable to getting caught up in proving their intelligence or trying to assert their authority through what they know.

CANCER

In the energy of the first three signs there exists a quality of "now-ness," with the impulsiveness of Aries, the in-the-moment beingness of Taurus, and the surge of pleasure at the moment of clarity for Gemini. As we reach Cancer, the cosmic soul dives into the ocean of feeling that permeates the total being.

The crab, carrying its home on its back, explores the world from within its safe haven. Never approaching it directly, but always from the side, the crab is wary; it knows that under its hard shell it's completely vulnerable.

Although the symbol of the crab may make Cancer seem closed and hard, nothing could be further from the truth. Cancer feels deeply, and thrives when it is able to show the depth of its feelings, especially to those it trusts and cares about. What is most important to Cancer is to be able to do that safely; it senses the dangers of walking around with its naked heart exposed. Were this world the mythic Garden of Eden, there would be no need for a shell. Hurts and slights over the years can harden its shell with bitterness if Cancer lets it, but to express from the heart, the heart must remain soft. Like the crab, Cancer must periodically soften its own shell and break from it, a difficult but necessary process for emotional growth.

Inside Cancer's shell, everything is amplified, and the inner waves of the emotional tide can get high. The depth of its feelings is not easy to manage but is an important Cancer commodity: the emotional current that may be ignored, stifled, or discounted by some signs is the very means by which Cancer explores and knows its own heart deeply. To learn how to ride the waves and allow the current to flow while not being drowned is Cancer's challenge. To accept and honor its own feelings is important; if Cancer fights this, it diminishes its very nature, but it loses perspective if it permits its emotions to have free rein indiscriminately.

This amplification exaggerates Cancer's inner sense of vulnerability; it is so tuned in to its inner emotional states that it assumes everyone else can sense this as well, seeing its tender spots. Although Cancer can be prone to hiding any hurt or discontent deliberately (either out of self-protective privacy or to avoid being overwhelmed by emotion), it may also genuinely not realize that what is so obvious to it about how and why it feels what it feels is not always so obvious to others. If this sign is feeling hurt, it is feeling vulnerable, so revealing that it is hurt often just makes it feel even more vulnerable.

Cancers takes everything personally, for better or worse. They are the least inclined toward superficial pursuits or status and they prioritize matters of the heart. When you are gifted with the trust and love of a Cancer, their affection for you will know no bounds. They don't easily let go of those they love and are very loyal and devoted, with a tendency to take others under their wing. When hurt, they tend more toward retreat, sulking, or giving the silent treatment until they are ready to open up again. This behavior may sometimes be a form of punishment for the one who hurt them, but many times it can also be an instinctual method to calm the emotional waters enough to be able to make sense of their feelings enough to talk about them. They may tend to hold grudges longer than some signs, especially because their tenderness makes wounds seem to cut especially deep, even when harm was not intended or even known. Patience and thoughtfulness go a long way to coax Cancer back out of the shell. Their sensitivity and complexity can sometimes make for a delicate temperament that, to more aloof or unflappable signs, seems too easy to offend.

Cancer is one of three water signs,[15] along with Scorpio and Pisces. While Pisces may be the great ocean and Scorpio the deep well, Cancer is the safe harbor. Not only the emotions of the present but also the emotions of the past fill these waters. Some signs are perpetually looking forward and some are content to live moment to moment, but heart-centered and security-loving Cancer usually has strong emotional ties to the past and doesn't like to let anything slip from their crab claws, forgotten. Although this quality can make it challenging for Cancer to let go of past wishes, hurts, or regrets, it can also foster a love of things like family traditions with a nostalgic heart. Additionally, the continuity of the past can be not only heartwarming but also reassuring, as Cancer craves security.

Perhaps it is their awareness of their own vulnerability that makes Cancers so easily attuned to the vulnerability in others, especially those that are obviously vulnerable, such as children, animals, or simply someone in pain who needs care and shelter. It's also part of the reason that they sometimes focus on others rather than themselves; it's much easier for them to take gentle care of another's soft spot than to trust someone with their own.

Cancer has an innate desire to heal and nurture, whether it's plants, animals, people or anything else. They instinctively protect what's in their care, or even what's simply within arm's length! Walk into the home of someone with a strong Cancer influence and you'll undoubtedly be offered food and drink, metaphorically if not literally. Healthy

---

15. You'll learn about the sign elements in section three.

Cancers seem to intuitively know where it hurts and what will make it better.

Cancer tends to express itself in subtle or indirect ways. Just as a crab walks sideways, so Cancer tends to approach situations in a careful, roundabout way. Their empathy is strong and close to the surface, like Pisces, so they must approach life's intense situations with care. It is not difficult to get to know a Cancer, but to know them well and intimately takes time. The Cancer shell can sometimes protect them too well, making it difficult for others to know what their needs are or whether something is weighing heavy on their heart. When they are feeling most tender, they may actually put on their toughest face. In general, Cancers are more comfortable giving than receiving, and it's this characteristic that can lead to an imbalance in their lives: neglect.

This one-sided dynamic can foster unhealthy dependence in others, setting up expectations that Cancer is an unending font of nurture. If Cancers do not reveal themselves, then they cannot receive, and a cycle of dependence can unfold; the more others take, the more depleted Cancers are, and the more depleted Cancers are, the harder it is for them to summon the courage ask for what they need before it becomes dire. In order to allow themselves to be loved and get their needs met, they have to be open enough to communicate their needs and allow themselves to receive from another. Whether it's a reluctance to leave themselves open enough to be hurt, a fear that they may be rejected when someone truly sees their insides, or getting caught up in the role of "mom," they can feel isolated, unseen, and uncared for, which can build up into depression and loneliness, even if they are surrounded by lots of "dependents."

An imbalance of dependence can go both ways. While Cancers tend to care for and nourish others, they may also simultaneously get too caught up in what they hope to receive from others. This is not to say that they don't deserve the love and care that they themselves can offer, but that expectations and longings unsaid can eat away at them. We all long to have our needs anticipated and met like only Mom can from time to time, and Cancers are no different. However, their level of attentiveness and the efforts they sometimes go to in order to show care and appreciation for others while sacrificing their own needs (when taken to an unhealthy degree) can go unmatched. In extreme or chronic situations, Cancers can build up resentment in their lives and relationships when their needs go unmet, either because their needs remain unspoken or because they keep wishing or expecting others will meet the needs that they may need to find a way to meet themselves. Emotional game-playing and forcing others to jump through hoops, although sometimes unintentional, can result.

Cancer shares Taurus's need for security. Knowing they can count on something or someone allows them to open up and relax more, letting down their guard. Although it's emotional security they are looking for, much of it is fostered by physical manifestations of security, especially financial security but also a safe haven. Whether that haven is their own home or as small a thing as their own cozy bed, a sense of security sustains and recharges this sign. It is not unusual for Cancers to be homebodies or lean toward introversion, although the rest of the chart will greatly affect whether these traits are present. Emotionally speaking, Cancers need a lot of reassurance and support from family and friends. Because they are deeply centered by security, they can be highly sensitive to change and become fretful or generally anxious when change threatens that security.

Keywords Revisited

Much of the literature on Cancer in astrology focuses on this sign's desire to nurture but often presents it in a very narrow context, reductively making Cancers seem baby-hungry. Not all Cancers long to be parents, nor has something gone amiss if they don't. There is a very real part of this sign that wants to nourish and heal, foster and protect, but that doesn't always translate into babies, family, and homemaking.

The Moon Rules

The Moon naturally rules the sign of Cancer. Just as Cancer has a nurturing and caring style, the Moon is the tender part of us that wants to give and receive care in a way that encourages a feeling of safety and the ability to trust to allow emotional openness and vulnerability.

Cancer in Action

Someone with Venus in Cancer will likely prefer relationships with people who are kind, gentle, and sensitive but also protective and loyal. Brash or strong-willed people may seem rude or thoughtless, triggering the Venus-in-Cancer person to remain on their guard even if they otherwise like the person. They will most easily demonstrate their feelings for another by taking care of them in little ways that show their attentiveness and will respond well to friends or partners when they demonstrate their own thoughtfulness in regard to Cancer's needs and wants. Venus in Cancer may not easily reveal their feelings, so loving patience from a partner will be the best way to allow Cancer to open up to them. They don't respond well to being pried open. They may be prone to jealousy or possessiveness if they are feeling insecure about themselves or their partner.

With Venus in Cancer in the eleventh house, the previous paragraph will still apply, but additionally, their loving and nurturing tendencies will extend out to the world. Charity work of some kind may not be out of the question, although there are many possible outlets for them to show their support and love for their fellow humans. No matter their chosen method of expression, whether it's social work, running a bed and breakfast, volunteering, playing the neighborhood mom, or one of a thousand other ways, the urge to protect and support others will shine through.

LEO

From the protective cocoon of emotional security, the cosmic soul must break out of the shell and show itself through expressing what is genuine and precious to it and about it. Leo is the birth of self that has incubated in the Cancerian womb. It is no longer enough to be, feel, or think; now to be alive is to demonstrate it openly and uninhibitedly.

Multiple mythological references depict the lion as a majestic creature, the "king of the jungle." Whether through the power of their roar or the grandeur of their mane, lions possess a powerful presence that, like Leo, cannot be ignored. Yet what is a lion without its pack—it's pride? What is a Leo without its court—its audience? The lion's roar must be heard.

To be heard, seen, and appreciated, Leo must *engage* with life, stepping out into the sunshine and extending itself out into the world in some way. Although many of this sign may be outgoing to some degree, the Leo energy is not about simple extraversion (the high need for frequent stimulus, most of it social); it is about the meeting of Self and the experience of Life in a way that inspires one to create and express, to play and revel. One of Leo's mottos might be "Eat, drink, and be merry," but not out of ignorance, negligence, or carelessness. Life is not to be wasted, but savored.

Essential to keeping Leo's fire stoked is a strong sense of pride. Leo's display may lean more toward the playful or toward the serious and dignified, depending on the rest of the natal chart, but even if they seem to be playing the fool, they will not be the butt of anyone's joke. Leos don't just want to be on stage, they want to be at their best and brightest when in the spotlight. Like a cat, they always want to appear to land on their feet. Leo is not so much the class clown but has the self-possession and poise embodied by royalty.

Leo is one of a few signs that is noted for its leadership qualities. Although the royal Leo doesn't shy away from getting a little commanding with its subjects now and then, it is usually the way that Leo naturally draws others in, rather than an inclination to boss others around or lay down rules and regulations, that makes it leadership material. It may not necessarily lead through careful planning, but it can easily inspire with its enthusiasm and vision.

Leo has an appreciation for luxury and opulence. Leo can be quite hedonistic and enjoys its indulgences, not out of gluttony or greed but out of a desire to enjoy life to the fullest; self-denial would diminish Leo. This sign may occasionally overindulge in its particular vice, but not necessarily due to addiction or helplessness; Leo typically has too much pride to allow things to go that far if it can help it. Leo is also inclined toward generosity and despises pettiness in itself or others; like royalty opening their court, there is enough for all to enjoy and Leo relishes in sharing its pleasures with others.

At the center of Leo beats a dramatic heart. It has an appreciation for the epic journey of the hero, the well-timed grand entrance, or the romantic line that causes others to swoon. The dignity and grandeur of the iconic moment appeal greatly to Leo, and this appreciation of the theatrical is often considered melodramatic by signs that have no appetite for it. Leo prefers to do things with a sense of flair, showmanship, and elegance, which will usually show up in its personal style, speech, or interests (depending on the house through which Leo expresses itself in the natal chart). However, Leo never wants to appear to be trying too hard to impress lest the grandness of the effect be spoiled.

Leo is not constantly the gregarious, loud-mouthed caricature that it's often expected to be, but Leo's charm and charisma are legendary for a reason. All of these qualities tend to be magnified when in the presence of others, fueled by the receptivity of those around it in a symbiotic flow.

Although pure Leo often enjoys social interaction, Leo's magnetism can isolate it in an unusual way. When Leo is *on*, its natural charisma draws others in, like moths to a flame. It feels *good* to be around someone who is confident and inclusive and to enjoy whatever the performer offers. This star quality can sometimes eclipse Leo itself, because the light this sign shines can be so bright that it can blind others to the depth of who Leo is. The "audience" may fixate only on what they want to see, the one-dimensional aspect of what Leo presents onstage and not the whole self, just as fans often confuse actors' intent and personality with the roles they play. This can create deep loneliness in Leo that is difficult to express and nearly invisible to others.

The pressure to perform, literally or symbolically, is something Leo is sensitive to. Sometimes Leo feels like it has to *put on* a show, potentially masking its own heartfelt authenticity in the process of projecting a more impressive, entertaining, or charismatic version of itself. In truth, Leo has quite a bit of charisma, but it is better fueled by simple confidence rather than the applause of the audience alone. That doesn't mean appreciation from others is unneeded; appreciation has a way of lighting Leo up, but this fuel cannot burn without Leo's own inner spark.

If Leo gets caught up in the show, others can usually sense this sign's lack of sincerity and may respond negatively, assuming Leo is simply showing off, desperate for attention and approval. It's usually insecurity, not arrogance, that fuels this stereotypical Leo behavior, and it can create a vicious cycle. The more Leo senses it is being shunned, the more it may try to gain back its self-possession and pride by putting on an arrogant face or feigning bravado, which in turn can lead those around this sign to be more put off in backlash. Leo is at its best and is most fulfilled when it's inviting others to play at its party in the spirit of openness and joy, not collecting groupies or striving for enough acceptance or validation to drown out the insecurity that we all feel from time to time. In this generosity of spirit, Leo doesn't have anything to prove, and its natural light shines through.

Leo, like every other sign, has a private side and certainly doesn't always prefer to be in the spotlight, especially when in need of replenishment and inspiration. Follow them offstage when they are ready to be alone in their dressing room and you will be escorted out with grace and swiftness. Although the word *diva* is often used to describe someone who is spoiled and self-centered, Leo embodies the true regality, presence, and star quality of a diva, but a diva needs time to prepare. They don't tend to shift quickly from one thing to the next and will typically only do so when they are good and ready. You can't rush greatness!

Leo is often called the sign of self-expression, which is creativity in action. Creativity in this sense is not about art or artistic talent as much as it is the desire to share oneself in some demonstrative way. Whether it's a poem, a joke, a work of art, a performance, or something they've been moved by, there is a longing to share it and an equal trepidation about doing so in case it is not received well or, even worse, ignored. There is a risk in sharing part of yourself, not just through direct means, such as revealing a personal flaw or secret wish, but by what you offer from your heart, what you think is good, noble, lovely, worthy and having it seen, appreciated, and validated.

In the larger sense and in whatever form their self-expression takes, Leo wants to make a mark on the world, to engage with the classic hero's journey. Rather than the concern for legacy and tradition that Capricorn embodies, Leo is more concerned about greatness during life, not afterward. Healthy Leo isn't about striving for fame or taking the spotlight, but about the desire to inspire others. To them, a hero is someone who is thought well of because of their great deeds, not their self-promotion skills.

Keywords Revisited

Hopefully you're convinced by now that Leos are not all spotlight-craving extroverts. Typically Leo has enough grace and dignity to avoid engaging in obvious attention-getting behaviors, but that doesn't mean there isn't a level of egocentricity present. They don't tend toward accommodating behaviors like Libra, nor does an excess of humility benefit them like it does Virgo; although the absence of humility can have them forget that they may be the main character in their own story but theirs is not the only story that matters.

The Sun Rules

The Sun naturally rules the sign of Leo, because the Sun is the symbol for our most central self and finds it can easily take center stage in the story of one's life with the expressive and joyful sign of Leo. It seems contradictory that the lion sleeps during the day and is active at night, after the Sun has set. It's a good thing a healthy Leo supplies more than enough of their own light!

Leo in Action

A natal chart with Venus placed in Leo will likely have a great deal of warmth, charm, and magnetism with their friends and lovers. Although Leo enjoys being adored and appreciated, they also excel at returning this in kind when inspired by their love, especially with Venus in this demonstrative and affectionate sign. They find the glow of new love highly inspiring and love to offer (and receive) grand romantic gestures. More hurtful than unkindness is inattentiveness or indifference, especially for Venus in Leo. They don't do well being taken for granted, so when love starts to get too comfortable and familiar, they'll need a partner who can continue to put them high on their list of life's priorities, taking the time to give them the proper attention. They'll sometimes need gentle reminders not to take all their friends or romantic partners for granted as well, or making assumptions about what is and isn't okay with their partner. Leo needs a partner with a great deal of passion, who is willing to make love and/or war with ferocity (depending on the tone of the rest of the chart). Being treated with dignity is also of utmost importance; ridicule, even couched in playful humor, is a quick turn-off.

With Venus in Leo placed in the second house, some of Leo's love of extravagance may shine through in the types of things they spend their money on, especially objects of beauty for their home, wardrobe, or collections. They may especially enjoy giving and receiving gifts. Outside of the arena of love, they may have an interest in art or fashion, and if the rest of their chart reinforces it, Venus in Leo in the second house may excel at making money in artistic or creative fields.

VIRGO

From the broad expression and joyful celebration of self in Leo, the cosmic soul comes down to Earth, entering the humility and precise focus of Virgo. The symbol for Virgo, although outdated and misguided in this modern age, is the virgin, originally applied as a symbol of purity. The theme of purity runs throughout the Virgoan territory, with topics of perfectionism, efficiency, and the classic focus on health. "Clean and simple" is Virgo's motto. Virgo's symbol is often depicted holding a sheaf of wheat, which could be a nod to the bounty of harvest time in the Northern Hemisphere when the Sun is traveling through Virgo, but could also reference Virgo's tireless, hardworking nature, as there's a lot to be done at harvest time.

At its core, Virgo needs to grow, to refine and improve itself endlessly. It is built to work and strive. Equally important is the *feeling* that one is growing; Virgo thrills at the sense of progress and is spurred on further when it can see it's nearing its current goal. Virgo's natural inclination toward continual analysis and assessment enables it to constantly track its progress as well as note what is left to be done, whether it's a personal or professional goal or an ever-present list of tasks to complete. Although Virgo is almost constantly goal-oriented, it is not the attainment of a goal that is Virgo's joy, but the *process*. Virgo *is* process, which is why Virgo can't sit still for long even after attaining a goal; its restless nature won't let it rest!

Virgo is at once both an idealistic and realistic sign. Virgos have all the tools of practicality, reasonableness, and levelheadedness at their disposal, but they are never satisfied with the status quo and always have their sights set on the ideal. Virgos think realistically and analytically, so they are unlikely to *consciously* think that they can reach the level of perfection that represents their ideal, but unconsciously they may still continue to strive for it. This tension is at the heart of Virgo's makeup. To be perfect is not Virgo's true goal; however, sometimes Virgo gets so wrapped up in what they are trying to achieve that they can lose sight of when enough is good enough and find themselves disappointed even with their best efforts.

The trick Virgo is prone to playing on itself is to constantly raise the bar. Once it achieves or gets near to achieving something, it automatically resets its expectations to continue to be in striving mode. It's this instinct that can bring out the best in Virgo, to push just a little harder or a little longer and get just a little more done before the end, but it's also what can leave Virgo feeling constantly inferior, always falling short of its goal.

Due to the combination of a realistic ability to self-assess and the ideal of perfection, Virgos have an inherent sense of humility because they always see just how much they have yet to grow. Their humility is an important tool; without it they would be unable to self-assess properly, unwilling as they'd be to see any flaws that might threaten their self-worth. You can certainly have too much of a good thing in this case, and Virgo is vulnerable to overdosing on humility to the point where it can become self-loathing or encroach too much on their sense of worth. This and a potential perfectionist complex can haunt Virgo to the point where they feel that they themselves or anything they do are never enough.

Virgo must therefore be careful not to confuse their steady, underlying sense of worth with their sense of progress, which always fluctuates. It can be difficult for Virgo to do this because they have such a strong need to feel useful and to fulfill a sense of purpose. It's not enough for Virgo to exist; they must be *contributing* in some way with their existence. The planets and house involving Virgo in a natal chart will give specifics as to the ways and means through which Virgo most wants to make this contribution.

While Virgo doesn't mind contributing in a generic sense, it's a sign of exactitude and can experience greater joy and consequently a stronger sense of value when they have a specific skill or set of skills to offer. Building and refining a variety of skills fulfills their need for growth, and offering this set of skills to others fulfills their need to contribute. To fill a specific need with a specific matching skill thrills Virgo with its targeted precision.

Also in line with their love of precision is their proclivity for efficiency. Whether in energy or resources, Virgos have an aversion to waste or excess and tend toward conservation and direction of efforts or resources as well as moderation in general.

While Virgo's humility may have them shunning the spotlight, their ability to think practically and see what needs to be done makes them excellent at giving direction. Virgos don't have to lead and in fact may be reluctant to do so, but they do need to be *in control*—of themselves as well as events and situations in which they are invested in a good outcome.

Virgo may exercise this control in the present, keeping things running smoothly like a well-oiled machine, but they often apply this to the future through damage control. Because Virgo is so process-oriented, its consciousness is well grounded in cause and effect, and it often projects its awareness into the future to see whether a process may be vulnerable to being interrupted or thwarted. A Virgo was probably the first to say "an ounce of prevention is worth a pound of cure," and anticipating problems that may develop is what helps Virgo stay in control of things so well. However, at some point the future becomes less predictable as Virgo casts their gaze further ahead to the point where their effectiveness is limited and anxiety looms.

Whoever first said "if you want something done right, you've got to do it yourself" was probably a Virgo as well. This sign's desire to control makes it difficult for them to let go and trust others to get things done, especially because they tend to have a precise way they think it *should* be done. This can lead to the classic criticalness that Virgo is notorious for. Virgo sees the process and detail of what and how something needs to be done. Because they approach every situation in problem-solving mode, their critical eye is an excellent tool for all kinds of detailed work.

This same matter-of-fact problem-solving approach can be misconstrued and unwelcome if Virgo applies it to people rather than problems, whether they are overstepping the bounds of what they can and should control or less than tactfully delivering unsolicited advice. They don't intend to be harsh or belittling; they just want to help fix whatever is broken and can get caught up in the fixing rather than recognizing that the delicate balance of interpersonal relationships is nuanced and not mechanical. This doesn't mean that Virgo is never judgmental of others, and it certainly isn't the only sign with that tendency, but if they are behaving in a bossy or controlling manner, it isn't always intended as insult, but instinct.

On the other end of this control spectrum lies Virgo's frenemy, anxiety. The more Virgos feel in control of themselves or their surroundings, the less anxiety they feel. This tendency can be Virgo's friend, as focused anxiety can motivate them to take care of whatever they are anxious about and/or do whatever it is that's waiting to be done, increasing their sense of productivity and self-satisfaction. However, anxiety and its relationship to control represent a double-edged sword for Virgo. If Virgo attempts to control the uncontrollable or the unknown, such as other people's behavior or the outcome of uncertain future events, they'll be fighting a battle that can't be won, backfiring to *increase* not only their anxiety level but also potentially their sense of personal failure. They may react by trying to increase their level of control by either clamping down harder or putting themselves in charge of even more tasks, which will continue to send them on a downward spiral.

Even healthy Virgo is rarely in a relaxed state but is often in some state of alert. Tasks left to be done, both now and in preparation for the future, bombard its mental borders. Virgo must be vigilant to prevent their analytic mind from running amok with anxiety at all the potential problems on the horizon. This continual state of nervous energy running through Virgo can be emotionally and physically wearing, even at low levels, which can leave Virgo vulnerable to mild to moderate health issues or sensitivities that are anxiety-related and exacerbated by stress.

Keywords Revisited

Virgo is often depicted as a neat freak, with images of someone as a tidy, fastidious type with hair slicked back in an impossibly tight bun, walking into their pristine living space with pursed lips, testing for dust with white gloves and washing their hands over and over (because they're all germaphobes too, don't you know). In reality, most Virgos do not come close to these stereotypes. These clichés seem to stem from Virgo's need to create and maintain order. How Virgos choose to impose this order can be anything; the chart will hold clues as to where this urge to organize may be expressed, but it doesn't always take *physical* form.

Virgo is also often accused of not being able to see the forest for the trees, implying that it tends to focus too much on small things of no consequence and miss the big picture. Virgo's efficiency coupled with its powers of analysis make it very good at spotting tiny flaws and pinpointing details that need to be tweaked in order to make everything run more smoothly, and if anyone knows the devil is in the details, it's Virgo. Virgo doesn't ever lose sight of a goal, but if it replaces the end goal with the intense focus of getting the immediate goal taken care of, it can lose its way temporarily, expending more energy than is warranted overall.

Mercury Rules

Mercury has a dual rulership with the signs Gemini and Virgo, because they each represent an easy path for Mercury's natural function. Virgo's love of analyzing data and putting it to practical use allows Mercury not only to gather information efficiently but to understand and apply it as well.

Virgo in Action

When Virgo is the sign on the Ascendant, this person will approach the world with a matter-of-fact attitude, wanting always to get right down to business in whatever they're doing. They may even tend to walk fast in order to get right to their destination, or communicate sometimes abruptly as they want to get right to the point. They simply don't want to waste time on superfluous nonsense!

A Mars in Virgo person will tend to be careful and thoughtful with the way they spend their energy, whatever their task is, but especially in the physical world. Not everyone with Mars in Virgo will be a health or exercise nut, but they will tend to have a heightened awareness and interest in maintaining their health, whether it's a focus on good health practices, avoiding unhealthy ones, or sometimes giving in to their vulnerability to engage in hypochondria. Mars represents passion as well as energy, and a Mars in Virgo person will pride themselves on maintaining control and being self-motivated, able to direct their energy efficiently. However, while their self-control makes them less prone to outbursts or losing their temper, they may tend toward frequent impatience and may become extra critical (of themselves and/or others) or complain excessively when they are tense. They may be prone to holding their tension in and have difficulty releasing or expressing feelings such as anger or passion out of a fear of losing control. Releasing their tension physically through exercise can be beneficial to their mental, emotional, and physical health.

LIBRA

If Leo's expressiveness lies at one end of the spectrum and Virgo's humility and attention to detail lie at the other, then the cosmic soul is ready for "just right" through Libra's search for equilibrium. Libra is represented by the symbol of the scales, weighing the difference between people, ideas, or even objects or images as it strives to maintain balance within and without.

Libra's core need is harmony through balance. Most of its behaviors stem from this need, which can take a number of forms, from harmony and beauty, to justice in law and order, to agreement between people (or at least understanding and tolerance). Libra is always aware when one side of anything is out of balance with its counterpart—the greater the imbalance, the greater the internal stress for Libra.

As the scales, Libra is always in a mode of comparison between one "weight" and another. Libra is exceptionally sensitive to things that are out of balance, so it is always in a subtle but constant state of assessment and adjustment. This makes Libra very good at *managing* the tension of opposites through counterbalance, but also hyper sensitive to it.

Like Lady Justice holding the scales while blindfolded, Libra is classically fair-minded and impartial, willing to put personal opinions and feelings aside to weigh the facts and perspectives involved in any particular issue or conflict. While they may have a personal opinion or preference, Libra seeks to give both sides of an issue equal consideration and can hold two opposing ideas with mental dexterity. This does not preclude Libra from *unconsciously* favoring one viewpoint or the other, but it tends to strive for impartiality and objectivity.

Because it can see dual perspectives, this sign tends toward moderation in its ideas and reactions, somewhere between extreme viewpoints that may lie at either end of an issue's spectrum. They tend to react with an equal force when presented with one-sided or grossly subjective declarative statements, arguing the other viewpoint in an effort to set things back to a balanced position.

While the Libra archetype encompasses this balancing of ideas, the specific location of Libra in a natal chart, as well as potentially competing factors such as the placement of thought-processing and opinion-forming Mercury, will determine where and how Libra's need for balance through fair-mindedness manifests.

Because Libra is very skilled at harmonizing opposing ideas, it will typically be able to identify with each point of view in some way and can naturally arrive at a point where each is equal in importance and value. The scales balance, but, like a deadlocked jury, a stalemate may be the result, which can paralyze Libra if a decision needs to be made or action taken. Libra's indecision is often affected by stress or pressure not just from juggling multiple perspectives but also from managing their desire to please, or at least not frustrate, the people who may be affected by their decision. Always finding themselves in the middle, they aim to please, but they sometimes find it difficult, if not impossible, to please everyone.

Libra's ability to maintain balance and harmony often shines through in relationships. This does not necessarily mean that Libra is more skilled at relationships than other signs, but that it is the sign most sensitive to and focused on "the space between you and me," an underlying awareness that shapes its behavior. Libra instinctively knows how to make others comfortable in social settings. This extends not only to common, obvious things, such as a friendly demeanor, polite conversation, and a knowledge of basic social graces, but also to things like anticipating others' needs or listening actively and asking questions to let someone know that they are heard and appreciated. With Libra, chivalry is not dead; they know that the simple things can have a profound effect, greasing the wheels of sometimes otherwise clumsy or awkward social interactions.

Although Libra easily makes friendly overtures, they don't necessarily mean to become everyone's best friend, nor do they always enjoy the small talk they excel at. They are vulnerable to standing too long after the meeting or in line at the store, smiling and nodding in an effort to be polite while a stranger goes on about traffic or the weather for much too long. So they often find themselves walking a fine line between authentic politeness and insincerity. Libra may be accused of being fake more often than some signs because of this; their authenticity comes through most often when they are with someone they trust, because they are able to relax and feel less pressured to be the ever-smiling host/ess. This is one reason why Libras are at their best in one-on-one interactions rather than large groups. While they can excel in both situations, they are naturally built to focus on one person, giving them their undivided time and attention.

Potential side effects from Libra's desire for harmony between people can crop up. There is a line between striving to make others feel comfortable and understood and sacrificing one's own opinions, needs, and authenticity in order to do so. Libras must always remember to advocate for themselves as well as others, or their desire for true balance cannot be achieved. With their sincere desire to be accommodating, they can become too good at it, making themselves a secondary character in their own life instead of the hero or heroine of their story. This can backfire on Libra because the more they sacrifice their own needs and desires and the more amiable they try to be in the name of relationship harmony and support, the more they undercut the relationship rather than support it. This sign can disappear, leaving nothing left for their partner to connect to. They must remind themselves that their true goal is the *unity* of opposites, not the melding of opposites.

Libra is always trying to build a bridge between people, even when that doesn't involve them directly, so they excel in situations that require mediation or peacekeeping to help others come together. However, while Libra can be very good at managing tension between people, that doesn't mean it is a comfortable process, especially when they are personally involved. Confrontation is very uncomfortable for Libra, and in an effort to manage or diffuse tension in their personal relationships, they sometimes default to avoiding it altogether, whether it's just avoiding the subject of the conflict or going so far as to avoid the person or people involved altogether. Unfortunately, while this may or may not remove the trigger, the tension is still there, unresolved. Avoiding conflict can be a useful technique to keep the peace, but in some cases, friendships and opportunities can be lost needlessly when the tension of things unsaid or potential conflict outweighs the joy in a friendship or the potential in an opportunity. In order to fully achieve the harmony that Libra craves, the tension must be dissipated through conflict management, not avoided.

If this sign cannot escape the situation or people involved, they may protect themselves by pretending that everything is all right when it isn't, at least not for them. Many people may do this from time to time if it's not the moment or place to discuss a matter or it's not worth the risk, but Libra can be vulnerable to allowing this to become a habitual technique. This can also lead to passive-aggressive behaviors if they cannot find a way to diffuse their own tension about the matter themselves.

The Libran scale weighs all things. Sometimes Libras put *themselves* on the scale and need another person to stand on the other side. They often seek validation from others in a variety of ways, to help them manage the tension of the scales. They may ask another's opinion on a matter in order to finalize a decision they're pressed to make or seek support from a friend when they are in conflict with someone and need validation to help them find peace after or during conflict.

This need doesn't necessarily spring from a low sense of self-worth; it simply helps them in their assessment and adjustment process. Libra is in a constant mode of comparison and often employs others' opinions and support as resources in that process.

While this sign's involvement in handling interpersonal issues often takes center stage in their behaviors, a not insignificant part of Libra's desire for balance is reflected in their orientation toward beauty as a means of experiencing harmony. Whatever the preferred medium, art and beauty create an inner peacefulness for Libra that provides relief from tension and a soul recharge that they don't have to strive for but can simply bask in and enjoy. Depending on any mitigating factors in a natal chart, someone with a strong Libra influence will be highly affected by the look and feel of their environment, their mood and sense of well-being bolstered by peaceful and beautiful surroundings—it can make or break an experience for them.

Keywords Revisited

Libra is most commonly known as the relationship sign. While this is not inaccurate, it tends to make every Libra sound like a love-obsessed teenager. A romantic partnership is just one among many examples of relationship, a word that here refers to the idea of two or more things being connected as well as the awareness of the quality of the space between them.

Peacekeeper is also a word often used for Libra, but it tends to mask just how surprisingly argumentative Libra can be. Libra has the skill for argument yet has a distaste for conflict. While Libra longs for balance, and to be in conflict is to be out of balance (if only for the duration of the conflict), Libra has a hard time abiding one-sidedness, unfairness, and injustice. Depending on what combinations shape the rest of the natal chart, this sign may simply bite their tongue in silent disagreement or may engage in discussion to correct the imbalance; it will depend on whether or not they decide to sacrifice their need for social peace or their need for balanced thinking. Libra is therefore the best devil's advocate of all the signs, being the sign of the diplomat, the judge, and the lawyer.

Venus Rules

Venus has a dual rulership through the signs Taurus and Libra. Libra reflects Venus's desire for relating because of its ability to note and adjust to the needs of others as well as reaching out to others for companionship and validation. Libra also shares Venus's interest in aesthetics and seeks harmony through beauty.

Libra in Action

With Mars in Libra, the person's need to exercise their will and go after their desires may be tempered by consideration of the needs of those around them and how their actions may impact them. For someone with Mars in Libra, it may not just be about what they want but also what their spouse, child, coworker, or friend wants as well, especially if the action may hinder another person in some way. With Mars in Libra in the fourth house, their motivation for harmony will be concentrated in their home space, focusing on how to maintain harmony between family members or even just housemates in order to feel at peace in their home. They may even have a penchant for interior design or at least be sensitive to their environment and how it contributes to a balanced inner state (or doesn't!). They will be very sensitive to conflict (Mars) in the home, especially in the pre-conflict state because they will feel and be affected by the tension building long before it has broken.

Mercury in Libra will emphasize the balanced approach in the style of thinking, with a tendency toward a flexible point of view and an aptitude for objective thinking. A person with Mercury in Libra may especially enjoy getting feedback from others in their decision-making process and benefit from bouncing ideas off of other people to concretize their decisions. Mercury in Libra in the fourth house will continue to emphasize a peaceful and balanced home environment but will shift the focus to Mercurial needs, such as frequent communication or status updates between family members or house-mates for a sense of ongoing collaboration.

SCORPIO

The cosmic soul descends from the heavenly grace of Libra to the severity of the underworld in Scorpio, a sign of intensity and extremes, uninterested in anything that hides the naked truth. While Libra appreciates and deftly navigates a carefully structured social world, Scorpio knows that just under the fragile façade of polite society lies the *real* world, untamed, raw, and sometimes frightening.

Scorpio has accumulated a small number of symbols to represent it over time, such as the eagle because of its piercing vision, and the Scorpion because of its sting, but it's the phoenix that seems to encompass the spirit of Scorpio best. The phoenix is a mythical bird, born from flame and also consumed by it at death, to rise again from the ashes. In most references, the phoenix is not immortal; the same bird does not rise from its own ashes to live again, but a new phoenix is born from the ashes of its predecessor. It is a symbol of renewal: born again but never the same.

Like Virgo, Scorpio is often caught between the proverbial rock and a hard place. While Virgo exists between the desire for perfection and the constant awareness of its distance from it, Scorpio longs to be consumed by life's intensity but also fights against being annihilated by it. Scorpios inherently have all the tools that drive them toward the depths and edges of life, but that doesn't mean they aren't scared by what they see; it simply means they cannot avoid it as easily as other signs may be able to. They *see* even when they wish they didn't, and to try and pretend they don't can make things worse.

At their most authentic and courageous, Scorpios live at the breaking point of life's learning curve, living at the edge of their strength and learning to handle the intensity that is part of their makeup. They hunger for the real, the raw, the unvarnished truth. Scorpio has a sensitive radar when it comes to digging up what is hidden. This sign seeks out that which lies beneath the surface, what is *un*obvious.

Scorpio loves to uncover secrets, break through taboos, and rip off the Band-Aids. Although Gemini is often considered the sign that wants to *know*, it's Scorpio that really excels at research because of its tenacity and obsessive nature. But Scorpios also come up against the hazards of seeing too much: imagining things that aren't there. Their natural suspicion makes them good at digging up truths, but when the secret they expect isn't there, they can become fixated and destructive.

Although this sign knows what's culturally expected, Scorpio often has little patience for social niceties and friendly small talk because it seems to be a charade, a pretense that reveals nothing of the truth that one can read between the lines of the social script. Ask a Scorpio how they are and rather than getting the expected "fine, thanks," they might be tempted to really tell you! Scorpio places more value and trust in the dark because it's less likely to be a comforting lie or a false smile. This sign tends not to take anything at face value, in fact, and can often take this to extremes, misjudging niceness for falseness.

Unhealthy Scorpio can let this suspicious nature go too far, destroying trust in an effort not to be taken for a fool. In many cases, this may be an overreaction to all the times others denied the truths they were afraid to admit yet Scorpio knew was there. Scorpios are not immune to hiding the truth from themselves, but they try never to do so willingly and detest it when others do, often considering it weakness. Unhealthy Scorpio may feel compelled to force others to see what they perceive as the cold, hard truth, often hurting and alienating others in the process. They don't always believe that one can be compassionate and truthful at the same time, and have an even tougher time understanding that though *they* would rather be hurt by the truth than comforted by a lie, others find that beating someone over the head with truth can be unnecessarily cruel—not to mention that Scorpio's "truth" is often not as black and white as they would like to think it is, and that they are as vulnerable to a subjective point of view as anyone else.

Nevertheless, Scorpios still have a knack for seeing and distilling penetrating psychological truths, and, just as they seek out catalysts for growth, they love to assist others in their own breakthroughs. They can stand with someone who is facing their own demons and offer them strength and loyalty, if not traditional comfort, even when others might shy away.

Although it can be unkind, they come by this compulsion to press the truth onto others honestly. Because Scorpios are more attuned to seeing where the monsters are than most other signs, they often feel they are facing those monsters alone. When others deny what Scorpio sees, it can feel like they themselves are being denied or invalidated. What they often long for from others is someone who has the strength to meet Scorpio head-on, not wilt at their intensity, deny what they see, or lie to spare their feelings. They appreciate others with whom they don't have to pull any punches and those who will be brutally honest with them even when anger or pain results.

Though they may strive for it, Scorpios are not always as honest with others as they want others to be with them. They do not like to feel vulnerable or weak and prefer to collect others' secrets rather than reveal their own. They are not always above using those secrets along with their own observations to subtly manipulate the behavior of others if it suits them. They get a thrill at being the only one in the know, the power behind the throne or the one who knows all the dirty secrets, because it makes them feel powerful and in control. When there is a secret to be had, they have an overwhelming desire to know it, sometimes disrespecting the boundaries or privacy of others in their quest to know what is hidden. Not every Scorpio will always succumb to these urges, but unless strong mitigating factors in the rest of the chart suggest otherwise, they will feel them, as it's inherent in the Scorpionic nature. Healthy Scorpio is an excellent keeper of secrets, and their ability to handle intense and taboo truths often has them hearing others' private confessions.

Scorpio cannot abide helplessness or powerlessness. They would rather face the monster in the closet than risk the possibility of the monster disempowering them. For Scorpio, there is a safety in the unsafe, a freedom in knowing that what doesn't kill you makes you stronger. Unlike Capricorn, for example, who contemplates worst-case scenarios out of self-defensive pessimism or damage-control instincts, Scorpio does it to alleviate the power that their fears have over them. Even if their fears come true, they are no longer a prisoner to anxiety or caught up in trying to prevent it.

Transformation implies change, and the willingness to change implies flexibility. However, Scorpio's tenacious, compulsive, driven nature makes them incongruously inflexible. The inner phoenix transforms after emotional turbulence boils over or pressure from outside circumstances forces the issue to the surface. They resist being overwhelmed by it until they cannot, but then they often choose to lean in to the change, leaping into the abyss. Once they reach that point of longing for destruction and renewal, as the molting phoenix losing its last feather, they succumb gladly, stripped and renewed ever stronger.

While its opposite sign, Taurus, seeks to endure through preservation, Scorpio seeks endurance through transformation. If one form ends, it can continue on in another, and to do so is inevitable from Scorpio's perspective. Scorpio, like Aries, is built to be tested and thrives on it. It is not uncommon to see those with a strong Scorpio influence in their chart to find outlets, even professions, that seem to be on the front lines of life, where crisis and chaos seem to reign. Whether it's the police or paramedics, crisis counselors or rehab, Scorpio is built to handle it. That does not mean that Scorpio is invulnerable—they have their breaking point just like everyone else. But they are uniquely equipped to process the difficult, the taboo, and the frightening because to them, that is where real life happens.

Scorpio is intimately associated with death and the dying process, always seeing themselves somewhere along it, metaphorically, at least. Scorpio can be afraid of death but also longs to succumb to it (not necessarily literally), as it is the ultimate mystery; there's always an edge to fall off or go beyond. This sign is ever aware that any moment could be their last, or the loss of their loved ones could be around the corner, and even though this knowledge is painful and frightening, they cannot look away from it. Their desire and ability to look into the dark is also what is always threatening to overcome them; they are always a little (or a lot) haunted. Scorpios rarely experience lightness of heart, and their inner emotional life is often quite turbulent. They are prone to moodiness and a morose frame of mind as a result.

Keywords Revisited

There are many stereotypes about Scorpio that can be traced back to the same source, such as possessiveness, jealousy, obsession, and the emphasis of its sexual nature. All these traditional keywords are examples of everyday feelings taken to their edges. Scorpio's method of engaging with life is to wholly consume and be consumed by it and therefore take situations, beliefs, actions to their extremes. This sign is also so driven toward this immersion that the emotional hunger to merge with their object of desire, whether it's a person or an experience, can consume them. For Scorpio, the only way out is through, or as Carl Jung said in *Memories, Dreams, Reflections*, "A man who has not passed through the inferno of his passions has never overcome them." To merge with something and therefore to wholly possess it and be forever transformed by it is Scorpio's way.

Pluto Rules

Pluto is the ruler of Scorpio because Scorpio's desire for intense experiences easily facilitates Pluto's desire to transform through death and rebirth. Before Pluto was discovered and "adopted" by this sign, Scorpio was also ruled by Mars, via the passionate and powerful nature of Scorpio and Mars's exercise of power and desire through will.

Scorpio in Action

Mercury placed in Scorpio indicates a propensity for getting to the bottom of something through investigation, research, and asking the hard questions. This person tends to be suspicious of easy, light-hearted answers and rarely takes any explanation at face value. They may not always reveal what they are thinking freely, preferring to make their judgments and assessments in secret while at the same time questioning others intensely about their own opinions. When they do reveal their opinions or thoughts, they may tend to express themselves abruptly or shockingly—telling it like it is even if it pushes the boundaries of safe and pleasant social rules for conversation.

One of their intellectual interests may be solving mysteries—they may enjoy true crime stories or study topics like forensics, for example. With Mercury in Scorpio in the twelfth house, these interests may lean more toward the hidden world of dreams or the study of symbolism, which still feeds the desire to penetrate mysteries and uncover truth but encompasses the twelfth house arena: the area of life in which we deal with the spiritual realm or the realm that is removed from everyday life. They may be interested in "out there" topics, such as conspiracy theories and UFOs, life after death, chaos theory, and quantum physics—all subjects that are inherently mysterious and out of the ordinary.

SAGITTARIUS

Leaving the velvet darkness of the caves of Scorpio, the cosmic soul craves the wide-open field of Sagittarius, with its expansive outlook and soaring positivity. It is not the deep, frightening truths that are sought now, but universal truths that lift and free the spirit.

Sagittarius is symbolized by the archer, who looks not at himself but toward the heavens for the bull's eye. Like the archer, Sagittarius is always looking upward and outward, scanning for its target and aiming for the center. Sagittarius is often depicted as a centaur with a bow in both hands. Half-human and half-horse, Sagittarius participates in two worlds; the powerful legs of the horse want to run unbridled across the broad expanse of life's terrain, and the head and heart of the human combine intellect and experience into wisdom and meaning.

Sagittarius is a sign of faith, a word reserved not solely for religion. Faith in oneself manifests as confidence, and faith in life as optimism. Faith in one's personal truth can come as a result of meaningful first-hand experiences.

Sagittarius almost always maintains a positive outlook in general, leaning toward optimism even when something seems like a long shot. In general, they are never down for long and bounce back quickly from setbacks. Whether they believe everything happens for a reason or not, they have a natural ability to turn any event toward a meaningful, positive end and use it to their advantage. Even if it's not true that everything happens for a reason, Sagittarius will find one!

Their positive outlook is not a strategy, but an instinctual response to life and something they rely on to keep tackling life's challenges. Their fuel is a constant sense of hope for the future and excitement about what life might bring tomorrow.

Like Scorpios, Sagittarians tend to throw themselves fully into whatever they are engaged in, not out of obsession but natural zeal. Like Gemini, they cannot tolerate boredom, but instead of information-gathering, they are adventure-seeking. While Gemini asks "why?" Sagittarius says "why not?" This sign is likely to try anything once, and the unfamiliarity of a new experience thrills rather than deters them.

Because of this enthusiasm for new experiences, Sagittarius racks up extraordinary adventures and will certainly have many stories to tell as they get older, including situations where they were in over their head and either didn't know it or didn't let it stop them (at least not entirely). Sagittarians tend to have such a positive outlook that, coupled with their spontaneity, they can too often embark on something without thinking it through.

It's this very combination that trips Sagittarius up, causing them to have to scramble at the last minute to get things done that they didn't plan for or foresee, or abandoning ideas halfway through when the practical reality catches up with their hopeful ideal. Yet it is also what often allows Sagittarius to succeed, at least in some measure. The Sagittarius inclination to see the positive outcomes of possibilities in life often makes them more likely to act, because they feel optimistic that they will have a good outcome. Not only will they tend to view a partial success, even via an unexpected outcome, as good enough because they make the best of any situation, but their enthusiasm and hopefulness will spur them on to see a situation through where others might consider it a lost cause and declare it a failure. In this way, Sagittarians often do succeed in the "impossible," because of their faith. Therefore, when they naïvely say "it'll all work out," they are often right, much to the surprise of their doubters!

Sagittarians have an innate confidence in themselves that draws others to them. Insecurity is inherent in the human condition, so they experience it like any other person, but they don't tend to turn the spotlight on themselves to examine their flaws, or waste time imagining that others are doing so. They naturally focus on the external experience of living, and they're so busy getting on with that that they have no time or patience for navel-gazing.

Like the release of the archer's arrow, Sagittarians are known for their direct and straightforward approach to life. Their openness makes it unnatural for them to hide anything or beat around the bush. While Sagittarians may not be any more or less deceitful than the average person, they tend to inspire trust from others because of their forthright and sincere style. This directness is not always out of a desire to be truthful as much as it is just easier for them to open their mouth and express whatever they are thinking without hesitation, which sometimes leaves too much room for the occasional foot in the mouth, as they are not known for their tact (that requires too much tedious mental game-playing for their taste). They can laugh at themselves more easily than anyone else, however, so they recover well from these mishaps.

Sagittarius is always on the move. They are restless, with the heart of the wanderer. Sometimes they seek knowledge and wisdom, sometimes they seek adventure, and they almost always seek fun. They are looking for the spark of life, the experience that provides a sense of meaning as they navigate the world.

It is not necessarily facts they are seeking, or the academic answers to life's big questions. Though they are philosophers at heart, they may not necessarily seek spiritual meaning through a search for the divine, though many do find spiritual outlets rewarding. It is the *feeling* of meaning that they are pursuing, the spark that tells them that here is something real; here is a truth. It is the feeling of rightness and profundity when their passion is ignited, when their arrow finds the target even if they don't fully understand what they've caught, that guides and motivates them.

It is not about a sacred search for the meaning of life but the joy that comes from experiencing something that fuels their enthusiasm. Sagittarians are no more or less likely to be religious as the next person, but their primary church is the church of life, not necessarily an attachment to doctrine. They seek out a unifying guiding principle rather than a smorgasbord of disparate ideas, and are drawn to systems of belief, thought, and practice that seem to tie their life experiences together in a meaningful way. When this sign stumbles on a belief, activity, or way of life that sparks their entire being, they tend to leap in with body and soul, holding nothing back. This allows them to fully surrender to an experience but also makes them vulnerable to clinging to the method and details of an experience as the Truth, rather than focusing on what that experience taught and provided them. Like the proverbial finger pointing at the Moon, they are always seeking the Moon but can get distracted by the finger if they don't keep their archer's aim true.

Their natural inclination to seek out universal truths, coupled with their ability to tie ideas together easily and their inherent confidence in themselves, make Sagittarians vulnerable to jumping to conclusions more easily than some. Because they are profoundly moved by experiences that drive their passions, they trust their personal experience, sometimes above all else, and may use that feeling of rightness to make assumptions that fit in with what they already believe.

When taken to an extreme, this sign's enthusiasm coupled with this tendency toward certainty can become so fervent that Sagittarians may succumb to self-righteousness—not out of snobbery or judgment of others, but because they feel so strongly and are so emotionally committed to the personal truth they've experienced that they are certain their way is the right way and cannot fathom otherwise. Their zeal for something flows outward from them easily, and in their passion they can become missionaries for their cause, whatever it may be. Their immersion in their own experience can make it difficult for them to accept that another's experience may be different and yet just as valid, and they may even feel threatened when others don't share their experience or come to the same conclusions, as if it invalidates their own experience.

Keywords Revisited

Sagittarius has been called the friendliest sign, and it's true that their effervescent and easygoing demeanor attracts others. Sagittarians typically give off an open vibe, both in mind and heart, so others are not intimidated to approach them. However, they may be friendly, but they also treasure their freedom. Relationships with people who start to make intense demands on their time or attention can feel confining or suffocating if it's more than they bargained for. Sagittarians are just as capable of maintaining close relationships as the next sign, but they need a lot of room to run free, so friends and partners that understand that or have similar needs can work out just fine.

Another keyword that has shown up for Sagittarius is happy-go-lucky. No one is happy all the time, and that includes Sagittarius, but this sign does tend toward an optimistic viewpoint and doesn't sweat the small stuff. Keeping their spirits up is a great way that Sagittarians handle life's downs, but they walk a fine line between remaining hopeful while acknowledging a challenge and propelling themselves through life with manic positivity while denying any negative feelings.

Jupiter Rules

Jupiter naturally rules Sagittarius, because Jupiter's desire to expand and focus on the possibilities expresses easily through Sagittarius's adventurous and optimistic style. They both like saying yes!

Sagittarius in Action

With Uranus in Sagittarius, the individual as well as the collective group that shares this placement carry with them a strong urge toward freedom. The path toward authentic self-expression lies along the lines of seeking out truths, big answers to the big questions. They'll likely wander far from home in search of themselves and their personal truth, whether literally leaving the land of their birth or figuratively seeking philosophies and traditions vastly different from those with which they were raised.

With Uranus in Sagittarius in the fourth house, these urges will play out against the backdrop of home and family (the terrain of the fourth house). This will bring out an added dimension of possibilities, such as the experience of being the black sheep of the family, set apart from their family in some significant way, or, by the same token, their entire family being set apart from their community in some way. A sense of belonging or home, based on their authentic self rather than simply their blood relations, may be important to them.

With Uranus in Sagittarius in the seventh house, the need for freedom will persist against the backdrop of one-to-one relationships. The need for the space to explore themselves and the world will involve finding the right partners, especially those friends and lovers who can be a buddy in adventure or at least not hold them back. Equally important will be learning the right way to compromise in relationships, which in some cases will include choosing independence over codependence.

CAPRICORN

In Capricorn, the unbridled enthusiasm of the centaur is reined in. Given boundaries and direction, the fuel of ambition and purpose is ignited. While Sagittarius explored the wide expansiveness of the earth, Capricorn takes the cosmic soul up to the mountain peaks that reach into the heavens.

Capricorn's desire to reach great heights is reflected in the symbol of the tenacious mountain goat. Just as the mountain goat reaches heights most other animals cannot through carefulness and perseverance, so Capricorn is specially suited to climb its own personal mountain, whatever that may be.

Capricorn is not *just* practical, efficient, and ambitious. It is not an automaton, inputting data and analyzing the best possible way to the goal like a robot. It is a sign that embodies the wisdom of the elder. Like Scorpio and Sagittarius, Capricorn also has more than one symbol. Through the symbol of the goat-fish (a mountain goat with the tail of a fish), Capricorn draws intuition and wisdom from the depths of the ocean in which its fish tail swims, but with its head and body above water, it navigates the world with clearheaded reason and foresight. Because it reaches such great heights, it is able to see the terrain before it, preparing itself and others for what lies ahead.

At the heart of what fuels Capricorn is respect—from others, but especially self-respect that is won through integrity and hard work. Like Sisyphus rolling the rock up the hill or Atlas with the world on his shoulders, this sign's sense of commitment and duty is fundamental to their makeup. Capricorns are always aware of what *should* be done and what a respectable person *should* do, and often take it upon themselves to do it, even when they don't want to. When they commit to doing something, they don't do it lightly. Although Capricorns are not saints, they have high expectations of themselves and their need for self-respect compels them to live with integrity. Because respect is so critical for them, they want to be held in high regard by others. Sometimes, however, if their desire to appear respectable supersedes their desire to *be* respectable, they can lose track of why they're doing things in the first place, gaining the respect of others but losing respect for themselves.

Capricorns are highly self-reliant and take pride in their ability to manage their own responsibilities. As such, they are good at pitching in where needed, getting things done quietly and efficiently and directing others to do the same when chaos descends and needs to be managed. They often find themselves picking up the slack.

Yet Capricorns often have a harder time being on the receiving end of help. They don't necessarily have to do everything themselves and will delegate when the expectations of each person's responsibilities are clear, but to accept help with something they feel is their responsibility can make them feel as though they are shirking their duty, inspiring feelings of humiliation rather than gratitude. This isn't true in every case, but it takes a special situation for a Capricorn to accept help; the more like charity or pity it seems, the harder it is for them to accept it. This doesn't mean that they don't sometimes need help, but on the rare occasions when they are in over their head, they may still be reluctant to ask for assistance, to their detriment.

Not out of optimism but pragmatism, Capricorns are least likely to cry over spilled milk. When an obstacle appears, they tend to skip over the urge to whine or rage and go straight to asking themselves "what can I do from here?" Like Virgo, they don't want to waste any time, but unlike Virgo, they don't tend to worry themselves sick by avoiding what might happen or over-controlling what could happen. They are always focused on the endpoint, on solving the problem and getting the results they want. They make a plan, and if things don't go according to plan, they may feel as much frustration and disappointment as the next person, but they tend to get on with plan B expediently.

This matter-of-fact attitude comes from their stoic nature. They know that trials come and go, yet they can keep climbing that mountain. Like Taurus, Capricorn tends to be patient and steadfast, not out of laziness or stubbornness but out of the realization that if people don't get what they want, it's often because they give up or allow themselves to get distracted. Capricorn's self-discipline and ability to endure is legendary. "Good things come to those that wait" might be their motto, though they might replace waiting with hard work. They don't sit around and wait for things to come to them but know that steady effort eventually pays off. They are able to endure temporary hardship for the long-term reward over the short-term thrill, and they typically avoid taking big risks because they prefer guaranteed results rather than the promise of a potential payoff that may never manifest. Because they are so focused on the big picture, they have an exceptional knack for strategy and the ability to prioritize anything into the most efficient order.

Capricorns consider themselves realists but are often called pessimists—a title they may only sometimes deserve. They do not like to be caught by surprise or feel like a fool when their hopes or expectations are not met. While they may avoid rigid expectations out of realism, they may sometimes go so far out of their way to avoid getting their hopes up that they seem to expect the worst of every situation. This can be a defense mechanism to protect them from disappointment or embarrassment.

Capricorn has been characterized as the "manager," both for their serious and business-like attitude and their propensity for making order out of chaos. Structure is just as important to Capricorn as it is to Virgo, although it's not about defining boundaries as much as it is the need to have an infrastructure that can support and enable future work. Capricorns understand the efficiency and contribution that organized efforts and rules can make and prefer to follow the rules to keep order. While some signs may favor freedom and anarchy over conformity, Capricorns understand the function and benefit of rules and order and are willing to conform to expectations not to sacrifice their identity but to maintain that order.

In order to have the will, stamina, and patience to achieve long-term goals and focus on the big picture, Capricorns have a demeanor that projects a serious nature but sometimes seems cold or indifferent. Their natural reserve can make it difficult for others to get to know them intimately, and they may sometimes seem imposing to others. They project a sense of authority that may have others looking to them to take the lead in certain situations, but socially can make them seem stiff or withdrawn, especially if the rest of their chart amplifies this impression.

Capricorns are known for enjoying solitude, but it's not typically out of unfriendliness. There is a steady internal push to be on the path toward whatever it is they've put on their plate to achieve, and when they are alone, they are free to move unhindered along that path. Solitude makes it easier for them to maintain focus on the end goal, whatever it may be, without guilt or obligation.

Keywords Revisited

Capricorn is often said to be cold, but this sign is just as capable of feeling love and compassion as the next person. However, Capricorns understand the importance of sometimes putting aside an emotion that might be fleeting for the larger goal and not letting themselves get sidetracked by temporary fluctuations. However, they can sometimes be a little too good at that, putting aside even the strong, repeating, or long-lasting emotional cues that may be trying to sidetrack them for good reason. They may not easily let go of a goal even when it becomes apparent that continuing toward it may come at too great an emotional cost to themselves and/or others.

Another common sentiment is that Capricorn is ambitious, but it's often expressed only in a certain context, as if every Capricorn should be a CEO or some other sort of master of the universe. In the best sense, the ambitious nature of this sign coupled with their patience can produce a wise and accomplished person, but only if the aim remains high and true. Being goal-oriented can mean that you don't stop until you are granted your PhD or you clear level 91 on a video game. Again, Capricorns are suited to climb whatever mountain they deem worthy or, failing that, whatever mountain lies in their path. Connected to this is the oft-used phrase "the ends justify the means," because Capricorn tends to focus on the end result, not what was sacrificed to get there.

Saturn Rules

Saturn naturally shares an affinity with Capricorn, because Saturn's need to promote discipline through restraint aligns easily with Capricorn's tendency to patiently see its plans through with steady and dedicated effort.

Capricorn in Action

A Capricorn Ascendant will likely present a face to the world that appears very formal or serious. Sometimes this can make them seem cold or intimidating to others, although that's rarely, if ever, their intention; they are simply self-contained, so they don't let a lot of their inner personality show through on the surface. Their overall approach to the world tends to be focused on the pragmatic: what needs to be done, in what order, and how, so that get-right-down-to-business attitude shows up in their overall demeanor.

Presenting a dignified face to the world is important to those with Capricorn rising. They avoid situations in which they are likely to feel out of control or foolish—what feels fun to other signs often feels over the top or unnecessarily excessive to them. They don't tend to be big partygoers. Social functions with a specific purpose, however, are easier for those with a Capricorn Ascendant to navigate, as it's clear why they are there and what their role, if any, is to be.

AQUARIUS

After the rule-following and (self-)imposed restriction of Capricorn, the cosmic soul longs for authenticity above admiration, individuality above conventionality, and freedom above security.

Those who know of the elemental correlations with the twelve signs often mistake Aquarius for a water sign. It is woven not only into the name itself (*aqua*) but also into the Aquarian symbol: the water bearer. But Aquarius is not weighed down by the depths of the emotional ocean; it pours the waters of life itself out from the vessel that shapes and contains it, freeing it.

At its core, Aquarius seeks freedom—not the wildness of being carefree or freewheeling, but independence of mind, heart, and spirit.

Like Scorpio, Aquarius seeks truth, but instead of digging into the dark to uncover secrets, they seek the light: the brightness of clear-thinking and objectivity, as free as possible from bias and prejudice. The other air signs (Gemini and Libra) prefer this in general, but while Gemini likes to twist and play with ideas through wordplay and experimentation and Libra aims to be fair-minded and see another's point of view, Aquarius strives to be free from emotional agendas, theirs and others', to think for themselves. Their notorious detachment extends

from this preference and permeates their personality. They are independent thinkers and don't appreciate manipulative attempts to sway their
opinion. They thrive in the attempt to pursue clarity of vision, preferring rational thinking over emotional partiality.

This doesn't mean that Aquarians are immune to subjectivity or
emotionally based opinions—they are human and can cling just as
stubbornly to their ideas as the next person. In order to remain true
to themselves, they must have the resilience of will and intellect to
hold fast against persuasion or cajoling, going against the grain if
happenstance requires them to (they are more willing to stand with
a minority or be at odds with the norm than some). When they get
caught up in the rightness of their personal opinions, subconsciously
resisting the opinions of others solely in an effort not to be swayed,
their stubbornness works against their ability to see clearly. Ego and
misguided rigidity can make it difficult for them to learn from others.
Thus, Aquarius running at less than optimal can seem to be a know-
it-all, not progressive-thinking but closed-minded.

Aquarius tends to seem somewhat emotionally detached as well, a
trait that is sometimes misconstrued as unkind indifference. They are
usually quite sociable and friendly yet can seem unexpectedly distant
or elusive when someone tries to elicit an emotional response or in-
vestment from them. Of course Aquarians enjoy friendship and love,
but emotional displays and the sometimes dramatic intensity that
accompanies close relationships can overwhelm or even repel them.
They may sometimes seem lacking in empathy to other signs who
have more emotionally conventional expectations of them.

Aquarians are not blindly loyal and are true to themselves above
all. Healthy Aquarius is typically honest and forthright about their
needs in this regard, but when underdeveloped, their need to be true
to themselves set against the pressure of expectation and conformity
can leave them divided and dishonest. This can spawn a sense of
alienation and loneliness if they feel they are not free to be who they
are to avoid disappointing others. It may always seem as though part

of them is observing life from the impassive position of an outsider, set apart, sometimes by choice.

Weird, unique, different—one or more of these words is often found in popular astrology literature on Aquarius, which makes it sound like they have the monopoly on uniqueness. No one does, of course, but their lessons and experiences often center on the contrast between who they are and who they are taught to be, so where they differ from others may stand out, especially to themselves. Beyond juvenile contrariness or rebellion (to which none of us are immune) or knee-jerk reactions to opinionated statements, the point of Aquarius is not to be weird or different but to be authentic.

To Aquarius, a free spirit may not simply be someone who does what they please but also someone who is free to live according to their own truth, and they place human rights and what is good for all, not just a select few, high on their list of important matters. Aquarius is often called a humanitarian, a word that often has people thinking of a pious soul who hugs puppies and is selfless without fail. A person who is also an Aquarius certainly could have these traits, but humanitarianism strictly in the Aquarian style is motivated more by the conviction that everyone is entitled to basic human and civil rights and is not fueled by empathy alone. Freedom denied or suppressed is what is most likely to engage Aquarian indignation and action more than a simple tug of the heartstrings.

Keywords Revisited

In addition to keywords we've clarified in the previous paragraphs, Aquarius is also sometimes associated with groups, due to its perceived relationship with the eleventh house since Aquarius is the eleventh sign. This can be confusing because Aquarians are also called individualistic, perceived to be a bit of a lone wolf and not wanting to run with the crowd, so how can they be drawn to groups or community at the same time? The distinction lies in the motivation: Aquarian energy does not urge a person to become *absorbed* in groupthink or lose their individuality to the will of the collective; however, Aquarius is highly attuned to the sense of "brotherhood" that all humanity participates in, and has a penchant for understanding what is needed for the good of all, not just the one, and how taking care of the collective can prove beneficial for each individual as well, even if Aquarius may sometimes be idealistic or impractical when it comes to putting ideas into action. Although this sign is thought to be a free spirit as just redefined, they will align themselves with grassroots and progressive organizations because they don't just want to be free to be uncommitted, they want to commit to freedom.

Uranus Rules

Uranus naturally rules the sign of Aquarius, because the Uranian agenda is to individuate, and Aquarius, with its detached, objective style, makes it easy for Uranus to stand apart from influences that would try to sway it from the path that leads to the expression of objective truth.

Before Uranus was discovered and adopted for Aquarius, Saturn ruled this sign, aligning its own government of realism and objectivity with the dispassionate nature of Aquarius.

Aquarius in Action

With the Moon's domain encompassing our emotional selves and Aquarius being a sign known for its detachment, this may first seem to be a confusing combination. However, everyone experiences emotions, and Moon in Aquarius is no exception. Like those with a Gemini or Libra Moon, an Aquarius Moon person tends to become most aware of their feelings via their thought processes, as though they are thinking their feelings. They are not drawn easily into anything that seeks to manipulate them through an emotional appeal, whether it's through media or advertising, a guilt trip from a family member, or peer pressure, and they tend to reject the coercion from others to feel the "normal" way that others do about certain topics or situations.

With the Moon in Aquarius in the seventh house, the person will encounter relationship themes in life centering on independence and individuality versus compromise and homogeny. Arguably, the de-pendence/independence axis lies at the foundation of relationship, and the question of balance between the two is always present, but for this person it will often take center stage, lying at the heart of any relationship conflicts and partner choices they make. Because emo-tional authenticity is of high importance to this person, relationships for them are more successful when they have a partner who is not threatened by their need to be true to themselves first, and when they are involved in unions where their independence can be maintained and respected. They may prefer relationship "rules" that tend toward the unconventional.

PISCES

The well-hardened "I" of Aquarius becomes water-soluble in Pisces. The boundaries of the self melt away, freeing the cosmic soul from the isolation of individuality and detachment and absorbing it into the greater all.

Pisces is represented by two fish swimming around each other, sometimes depicted in a yin/yang fashion, sometimes swimming away from each other yet tied at the tails. Although this may seem to repre-sent swimming in circles of confusion or self-contradiction, it can be said that as one fish swims toward heaven, the other swims along the earthly plane, not representing internal conflict but expressing the es-sence of Pisces: one who walks or swims between the worlds.

Within Pisces always remains a simultaneous desire to leave the world and engage with it. The tiresome, petty concerns and sometimes crushing reality of life's difficulties and sorrows can be emotionally over-whelming, and they long to manifest the divine on Earth in any form through sharing and/or seeking joy, wonder, imagination, lightness, and peace. Like salmon returning to the mouth of the river to spawn in a never-ending cycle of immortality, Pisces the fish always senses and longs for the source, whatever name or definition they give it.

Just like the Geminian twins, the scales of Libra, and the half-man, half-horse of Sagittarius, the two fishes of Pisces reflect another duality: the dual awareness of what something appears to be as perceived by the five senses and what can only be perceived intuitively. Pisces' intuition comes from their heightened empathy and a tendency to value what their emotional body is telling them. They are not second-guessing or suspicious but are simply governed by what they sense, not always what they see.

Pisces' awareness is big and diffuse. They are almost more broad than deep, their attention drawn not typically toward an egocentric focus but into imagination and beyond. They seem to live moment to moment and, at the same time, have their inner eye fixed on eternity. They tend to be the least worldly minded of all the signs. While the opposite sign, Virgo, focuses on the minute details and can lose track of the big picture, Pisces may often ignore the little details because it has an inherent sense that sweating the small stuff is pointless in the grand scheme of things. This part of their nature is the source of their innocent yet profound wisdom, but it also makes them arrive late for meetings, miss payments, or forget any number of mundane day-to-day tasks that require constant attention. They may often daydream and lose track of time, especially as children. This is not to say that Pisces are necessarily irresponsible, but only that they sometimes have to exert more diligence than some signs to deal with the minutiae of everyday life.

Experiences that ground this sign in the mundane world but still allow them to carry the magical world with them can be beneficial in helping them walk these two paths simultaneously. If they attend too long to the world of fantasy and spirit, they may have a difficult time dealing with the demands of life, sometimes turning to escapist activities in order to keep the realities of the world out. If they attend too long to the mundane world, without the benefit of creative inspiration or spiritual rest, they can burn out quickly, vulnerable as they are to depression, illness, and lethargy. Meditation, yoga, and other peaceful ways to holistically fulfill both spiritual and physical needs can be healing and grounding.

The other two water signs,[16] Cancer and Scorpio, have protective shells that help contain their depths, but the soft, iridescent skin of the fish cannot offer the same. Pisces' vulnerability and receptivity are heightened by the ocean's current around them, and they will typically wear their joy and sorrow on the surface as they are experienced. They respond easily to the emotions of others, which is why they are known as the most empathetic sign, and their compassion and intuition derive from their natural emotional attunement and gentle nature.

This sensitivity makes it necessary for Pisces to be more alert to their environment, as they are more easily affected by it, usually emotionally but sometimes also physically and psychically. We all need to escape from time to time, but strategic and periodic retreat is essential for Pisces. They need the downtime to heal, recharge, and collect themselves. Though not always the case, their sensitivity can also show up physically, from something as simple as a need for extra sleep to a higher vulnerability to stress-related illness. Simple solitude and a peaceful environment are quite effective at recharging them.

Though Pisces needs to escape at times (and so do we all, to a certain extent), escapism can be a slippery slope. Escapism that is not about refreshment but about numbing the self can be a bottomless pit—a never-ending need. Pisces is especially vulnerable to drug or alcohol addiction, but too much of anything—television, food, sleep, entertainment—can provide a way to avoid life's responsibilities and necessities.

Like Sagittarius, one of Pisces' favorite fuels is faith. "If you can dream it, you can do it" might be a fitting motto for them. Although they are not immune to disappointment, they tend to prefer to trust that things will work out or are all for the greater good, whether it's out of optimism or belief in a higher power or anything in between. Although this may seem naive and can certainly end up backfiring in disappointment, belief is a strong motivator for Pisces. They are built

---

16. Signs are grouped into four elements—fire, earth, air, and water—as outlined in section three.

to respond to inspiration as well as offer others inspiration. When you are in the presence of a strong Pisces, they'll get you believing too.

Because this sign is least likely to limit their imagination, they also tend to have a creative mind, which runs off their second favorite fuel: inspiration. To be inspired, or "in spirit," is enlivening. They may have a love of art, music, fantasy fiction and film, games, role-playing, costume parties—anything that takes them into a world that can only be imagined. Although some signs may feel that these kinds of activities take one away from the real self, for Pisces it's a way of inviting their real self to shine through.

Sometimes what Pisces *wishes* or *wants* to believe is true overcomes their ability to face the truth about what *is*, yet forcing them to cast off their illusions without care does them a disservice. What can empower fierce signs such as Scorpio or Aries can fray and crush Pisces to the point of ineffectiveness; it is simply not their way. The window dressing that covers the stark view allows a little gauze between them and the harsh world to help them gently see and accept what is there. Pisces may seem naive, but it's not always naiveté or denial; when it comes down to it, it's a kind of semi-conscious strategy: looking for the good and believing in what is possible makes it easier for them to wake up and do it all over again tomorrow.

These fish folk excel at going with the flow due to their flexible and openhearted nature. Stagnant water just will not do; although they don't tend to be full of angst, they are still restless and enjoy the current of the new, which inspires and refreshes them. On the flip side, they may go with the flow too well and can benefit from helpful and supportive boundaries so they don't find themselves drifting in every (or the wrong) direction. While they may be able to imagine an idea, they may not always have the stamina and resolve of some other signs to follow through, and their peaceful nature may have them floating down only the easiest rivers, even if they don't intend it. They don't do well in overly strict, harsh, or tense situations, such as high-pressure offices with frequent deadlines or tests, as the tension in such environments tends to short-circuit them. As their moods shift, so does their perspective; this is another facet of their mutable nature that tends to make them easy to get along with but can sometimes make them seem unreliable or flaky.

Like Libra, Pisces is a natural peacekeeper; but while Libra may work to build bridges between viewpoints, Pisces is more willing to surrender to keep the peace, as it is typically a pacifist at heart and wants to avoid unnecessary strife and conflict. Their kindhearted nature makes it especially hurtful for them to hurt or defend themselves against another unless absolutely necessary. Although the rest of the chart will have its say, those with a strong Piscean influence in their chart are vulnerable to sacrificing themselves or their own needs for others or for whatever they think is the greater good. In part, this is because they are outstandingly unselfish, but they can also lean toward the idealistic and naive and are inclined to see only the best in people. They are also more willing to forgive, as it's difficult for them to maintain the kind of stubbornness that holding a grudge requires. Under the right circumstances, their giving nature can be a godsend to those they help, but their desire to save people from themselves can have a detrimental effect not only on them but also on the person they are trying to save. Their urge toward forgiveness and compassion can have them giving others too many second chances, enabling someone to take them for granted or abuse them.

When this goes too far, the tension between getting their needs met but avoiding hurting or giving up on others leads to inner conflict or passive-aggressive behaviors as they wrestle with themselves. Although this aspect of their yielding temperament can be perceived as weakness by some, and is a behavior that *can* certainly stem from a lack of courage, it is not always out of weakness, but out of a different kind of strength: the ability to let things go.

Keywords Revisited

Sensitive is a common Pisces keyword that is not inappropriate but has a double-layered meaning. Sensitivity is often understood to mean that Pisces can get their feelings hurt easily or tend to take everything too personally. Indeed, these characteristics may both be true of Pisces, and those with a strong Piscean influence in their chart may have been told this in one way or another throughout their lives in an inherently (even if unintentionally) shaming way. Sensitivity has another meaning, however, and turning a negative into a positive is not only helpful, but clarifying, in this case. Sensitivity can also mean to be highly sensitized or attuned to something. Turn your speakers up as high as they can go while you're bouncing around cleaning the house and it may be loud, but put that same level of volume directly in your ear and you will be overwhelmed, your hearing potentially damaged. Pisces is already highly attuned to subtle signals that often emanate on emotional wavelengths, so they simply reach the threshold of overwhelm more quickly than others.

Neptune Rules

Neptune expresses itself comfortably in its ruling sign of Pisces, because Neptune's desire to transcend fits right in with the Piscean qualities of openness, imagination, and compassion.

Before Neptune was discovered and adopted by Pisces, Jupiter also ruled this sign, because Pisces reflected Jupiter's attitude toward limitlessness as a dissolver of boundaries, and the Piscean urge toward empathy and compassion was a nice complement to the typically generous nature of Jupiter.

Pisces in Action

A person with a Pisces Ascendant will tend to approach the world with an openhearted and openminded attitude. The "front door" to them may sometimes seem to be a screen door, metaphorically speaking, with a constant exchange of energy in and out of them as they interact with the world, taking it in and sending themselves out. They navigate the world intuitively, feeling their way, and may be exceptionally sensitive to their surroundings, for better or worse. While we all may see ourselves differently than the world sees us, a Pisces rising person may sometimes experience a sense of mild shock when they see themselves in photos or in the mirror, because they often focus on what they (and others) *feel* like rather than strictly on appearance. The condition of the Ascendant and first house also contribute to one's overall physical constitution, so a Pisces Ascendant may be especially sensitive to their environment physically as well.

CHAPTER 8
THE HOUSES

THE ROLE THE HOUSES PLAY

The houses symbolize the activities of life in its various arenas. You are probably already familiar with this sort of broad categorization if you have ever referred to events happening in your work life as opposed to your home life, or your family life versus your social life. Each house corresponds with a categorization of different types of activities and behaviors that human life is made up of. Anything you *do* can be categorized in a particular house in the natal chart. Visiting your therapist? That's the territory of the eighth house. Talking on the phone? You're in the third house now. Spending time at home? That's the shelter of the fourth house.

Planets in a natal chart will always fall within the boundaries of a particular house. When you attempt to fulfill the needs of one of the planets in your natal chart (representing a particular need within yourself), you will do it in the style of the sign that planet is acting through, and also most often in the area of life, the house, in which that planet resides in your natal chart, utilizing the behaviors and activities that are symbolized by that house.

If you have the planet Uranus, symbolizing individuality and uniqueness, in the sign of Gemini, a sign that loves ideas, information, and communication, and it resides in your sixth house of work, one simple synthesis of these symbols could reveal your love of bringing and finding unique and original ideas to the workplace, and working in a profession and/or environment that allows you the freedom of brainstorming and experimentation to get the job done.

Having a planet placed in a certain house doesn't mean you will only utilize that planet's energy in that particular house. If Mercury is placed in your ninth house of philosophy and education, for example, you certainly won't stop thinking when you close your textbook or stop communicating if it's not about Socrates. Instead, planets in houses will tend to show the circumstances in which that planet comes alive most easily, indicating in this instance that there is a particular enlivening of Mercurial function when thinking or in conversation about philosophical matters, in a broad sense, highlighting favorite topics to learn, think about, and discuss.

EMPTY HOUSES

You may have realized that there are more houses than there are planets, and since it's common to find planets grouped together, you will have empty houses in your natal chart (houses with no planets in them). This is a standard occurrence in natal charts, and it does not mean that you don't participate in any of the activities that the empty house encompasses. Empty houses simply mean that those activities are not a hotbed of continual activity for the kinds of lessons and experiences that are of key importance in the development of your life. You *will* experience developments and changes, highs and lows, in all areas of life throughout your lifetime, but some areas of your life may be more developmentally intensive and some activities in your life may hold more interest for you. The houses that govern those areas and activities are typically where you find planets.

Even if you do not have a planet in a particular house, that house cusp falls within the boundaries of a sign, and that sign's style shines through that house's activities in your life. If you have Virgo on the cusp of your second house, you are more likely to approach money matters with care, planning, and frugality, unless other factors in your chart compete with that. Also, the planet that naturally "rules" the sign on a house cusp can also, by extension, have something to say about the activities in that house. Using the ruling planet in this way will be discussed further in section three.

The houses are an attempt to define all the potential activities and behaviors of our lives in twelve categories. That's obviously a big challenge and leaves each house covering a lot of ground in an individual life. Everything from visiting your neighbor, to going to work, to running errands, to contemplating the meaning of life, to clipping your toenails can be found within a particular house's territory. Therefore, when trying to understand the meaning of a house, it's helpful to think of the one or two major themes that the house speaks to, just as with the signs. When you understand the underlying house theme(s), you can use that to trace any behavior, action, and situation to its governing house, and identify a myriad of different activities all bearing the same theme but expressed in a variety of ways.

It's often challenging for astrology students to differentiate the influence of the signs from that of the houses in a meaningful way. A helpful axiom to keep you thinking clearly about their distinction comes from Steven Forrest: We *are* our signs and we *do* our houses.

HOUSE SYSTEMS

Astrology is almost as old as dirt. As it has evolved, many variations and offshoots have occurred over the centuries. One such variation arose in the arena of house division. The calculations that determine where one house begins and another house ends vary among different house systems that have been created over the centuries. Variance between most house systems only affects the inner houses, with the first house, fourth house, seventh house, and tenth house (also called the *angles*) remaining the same with each house system, although some house systems show greater variance than others. Currently, the Placidus house system is most popular, with Porphyry, Koch, Whole Sign, and Equal House also widely used.

Just as no one can definitively declare any religion the one true way, likewise each astrologer has their own reasoning behind their use of a certain house system, and while it can seem confusing at first to know which is best for you, it is up to you to decide. It is the author's opinion that the universe will speak to you in whatever language you ask it to.[17]

ANGLES

The beginning cusps of four houses (the first, fourth, seventh, and tenth) mark the angles of an astrology chart.[18] Astronomically, the four angles are determined by the great circles as they intersect with each other, as discussed in section one. Symbolically, the angles represent the cycle of the Sun as we experience its light on Earth. The cusp of the first house, also called the Ascendant, represents the moment of dawn, the birth of the light for the new day. Rising into the sky, the Sun reaches the Midheaven, the cusp of the tenth house, when the Sun is high in the sky, brightly illuminating everything and minimizing the shadows. Descending toward the horizon, it reaches the cusp of the seventh house, the Descendant, and sinking below the horizon it reaches its lowest point at the fourth house cusp, or Nadir, the quiet privacy of midnight and the womb from which it will soon rise again.

The meanings of the angles are not much different from those of the houses they border, but the angles are thought of as distinct points in natal astrology and can receive aspects from planets. For the most

---

17. The charts in this book are calculated according to the Porphyry house system, but experimentation with other house systems is always encouraged and could even be considered a rite of passage for a budding astrologer. One way to begin to test these systems is to create your own natal chart using each of them. Although not an objective method for testing, it will help you become familiar with the variances between each house system and begin to decide which house system you prefer to use.

18. This is true in most house systems. In some house systems, the angles "float" within their respective houses. This may not seem significant, but it is important to note the actual degree of the angle to correctly identify planets in aspect to it. Most of the time, and in the charts in this book, the angles and cusps of their respective houses are one and the same.

part, an angle has the same meaning and influence as the house it borders, yet the closer a planet is to an angle, the more prominent or obvious the planet's influence tends to be in the area of life it represents.

FIRST HOUSE: HOUSE OF SELF

The Ascendant marks the beginning cusp of the first house. The Ascendant represents the first characteristics about us that people observe on first encounter, sometimes even before they've spoken to us. It is our contact point with the world and vice versa. If you were a building, then the Ascendant would be your front door. The front door serves to channel traffic in and out of the building, letting people in and out as well as sometimes keeping people safe inside and locking out those who don't belong. The Ascendant metaphorically serves this purpose. It is not only how you step out into the world, but also how you take it in.

The Ascendant plays an important part in first impressions. How we come across to others is only part of the role the Ascendant plays, but it is an important one. Understanding the simple idea of whether you come across as curious and talkative, regal and charismatic, or friendly and accommodating can help you begin to understand your rising sign and the role it plays in your chart. How others respond to your style of approach, how you seem to be, can be quite significant. Your own natural style is not better or worse than any other style, but a healthy Ascendant will serve as this natural and seamless connection to the world, whereas an unhealthy Ascendant often feels awkward, a clunky interface that makes everyone feel uncomfortable, such as when you're trying to pretend to be someone you're not or fit in somewhere you don't and aren't sure whether you're doing it convincingly. Whether or not someone likes you or considers you to have made a good impression on them is *not* a function of your natural style of interaction, unencumbered by self-consciousness or strategy.

Equally important is the Ascendant's role in your style of approach to the world around you, not just its reaction to you. What is your attitude toward the world and life in general—not your thoughts, feelings, or moral judgments about it, but your instinctual bearing toward it? Do you leap into life without looking, enthusiastically and naively saying yes to every situation, or are you more laid-back or careful in your attitude? Someone with Virgo rising may approach life with the overall attitude of trying to understand, categorize, and even control how life comes at them, while a Pisces Ascendant may be more inclined to take things as they come, seeing and approaching the world as a fluid, changing experience from moment to moment, and so on. Likewise, each sign will respond comfortably or uncomfortably to different situations. Capricorn or Virgo rising may feel more comfortable in situations where the activities are more formal or structured and the expectations are clear, whereas Sagittarius or Pisces rising may feel awkward or stifled by the level of expectations placed on the way they should act or do things the "right" way.

The sign of your Ascendant and any planetary aspects to it can indicate what kinds of situations you will seek out or avoid in everyday life according to your comfort level. As we go about our daily lives, we may interact with any number of strangers. When we ask strangers for the time of day, smile at them or avoid eye contact as we pass, maneuver around them in the grocery store, or walk next to them (but not too closely) when crossing the street, we are using our Ascendant. Our complex, multi-layered self needs a streamlined *interface* with the world, a way to interact with everyday life outside of our own skin that feels natural to us but still keeps us protected and "put together" as we carry ourselves along the flow of everyday interactions with the world around us.

In her book *The Ascendant*, author and astrologer Jodie Forrest said the Ascendant adapts to the outside world in a particular way partly "because of the nature of the inner world" and partly to "protect or to express the rest of the chart." The Ascendant is a channel for that inner world to express itself in an authentic way while still being able to interact with the environment's demands. By the same token, it can also serve as protection for that inner world, for the rest of the chart, to keep the world from trampling unheeded through our vulnerable insides. This is why the Ascendant is not just a mask, but an *interface.*

Just as we grow and change, so do our methods of utilizing our Ascendant. Jodie Forrest also calls the Ascendant a "*learned response to our interactions with our environment.*" Over time, we learn what works best and what doesn't to interact seamlessly with our environment. While the core *style* of our Ascendant remains constant, the methods we employ within that style continue to evolve within the comfort zone of our rising sign. We become more socialized as we interact with the world and other people, learning what is acceptable and not acceptable within our culture, and in doing so, we refine our Ascendant within the bounds of its sign. We still utilize our natural style, but we tweak it here and there to interact easily with what the world expects and how our culture and environment respond to us, including such things as the expected niceties being exchanged, the level of personal space expected, and how conscious we are of our effect on others in the first place. In this way, the construct of the Ascendant is a developmental process, both conscious and unconscious.

Beyond the Ascendant

Including but also beyond the focal point of the Ascendant is the realm of the first house, the house of self. This house covers all the activities we undertake where we act in our own best interest with our own desires in mind, not with the purpose of inconveniencing or ignoring others but to fulfill our own individual needs that exist entirely separate from what others may think or need from us. When we are at work, we may be obligated to consider the needs and comforts of our coworkers, and our behaviors are mitigated by that knowledge. Here in the first house, we are focused solely on the activities that serve the "I."

The kinds of activities that are inherent to the first house are difficult to specify because they are so ingrained in our everyday behavior, as opposed to other houses where the divisions of certain types of activities are clear, such as work tasks versus hobbies or socially motivated behaviors versus personal behaviors. Sometimes we can see them in contrast to the things we *aren't* doing for others.

Much of what we do in life may not be in deference to other people and yet may still not be of a first house nature. Even when motivated by our own interests, this house is not just about what we want (second house) or what we like to do (fifth house) but, more simply, what we *are*. Activities here are of an *immediate* nature, such as taking care of our personal or physical needs, or things of an instinctual nature, such as our mannerisms; they are behaviors that are an extension of who we are rather than strategic or conscious acts. The sign and planets here clarify the style in which we carry out these instinctive behaviors.

First House Emphasis

A person with one or more planets in the first house will tend to identify strongly with the needs that those planets represent, sometimes seeming to be a personification of that planet itself. This is especially true the closer the planet lies to the Ascendant; the person may seem to "lead" with that planetary tone. Someone with Mars in the first house may have an underlying forcefulness or heat that seems to radiate from them, even if Mars is in a gentler or non-aggressive sign. Someone with Saturn in first house might naturally radiate an aura of authority or reserve, even if it is in a typically lighthearted sign. Likewise, these planets may color the way we see the world, in addition to the filter of the sign overlaid.

A significant number of planets in the first house may indicate a person dealing with matters of putting themselves first, acting from confidence, and embracing their full *presence* in the world. They may do this well, too well, or need some practice, depending on the planets and sign here as well as the rest of the balance in the chart. Overdone, the person may dominate the immediate environment around them, with a potential to seem self-absorbed, either out of unawareness or self-promotion. This can be present no matter what the sign, although the more fiery or passionate signs, such as Aries, Leo, or Sagittarius, may do this with a boisterous and big personality, whereas signs like Capricorn or Scorpio may give off a commanding and self-possessed vibe. Underutilized, a first house person may too easily blend into their environment or shrink into the background, taking up no space at all in their own life.

Ultimately, the fulfillment of first house planets lies in practicing the right amount of *initiative* in meeting the needs of planets here, in the style of the sign in which they fall. Planets here need the backing and application of one's *will* to direct and act on their energy, as opposed to simply reacting to the world passively or waiting for something to happen.

Keywords Revisited

Some have called the Ascendant a mask that you present to the world, but this gives the impression that the Ascendant is false: a misrepresentation of the real you or a fake, contrived persona. The Ascendant may not represent *all* of you, any more than any other planet does, but this effect is not inherently due to falsity. The Ascendant's purpose is not necessarily about constructing a certain look or putting your best foot forward, although you may utilize the Ascendant when you are doing these things. When we are trying to make a certain impression on someone, we have already stepped out of the sole realm of the Ascendant because we have started to think (Mercury) about our strategy and we may have started to plan our wardrobe and the social gestures we intend to employ (Venus) and we may have even thought about the level of authority that person has (Saturn) and how to respond accordingly. The Ascendant is a seamless, natural, automatic style and approach to the world; it is not entirely by conscious design. Your hand gestures, typical tone of voice, and facial expressions can all contribute to the overall style that the sign (coupled with any planets conjunct your Ascendant) conveys.

Ascendant in Action

Someone with a Capricorn Ascendant may naturally come across more formal and reserved, preferring to put their best foot forward with dignity. Someone with a Sagittarius Ascendant, in contrast, may automatically give an impression of being more open, friendly, and energetic. A Gemini Ascendant may be talkative and engaging in general, and approach the world from multiple perspectives, ready to multitask their way through whatever they've got on the menu for the day.

SECOND HOUSE: HOUSE OF RESOURCES

The second house is known as the house of money, but is better understood when we expand it to encompass the concept of resources. While most of our resources, or assets, may be measured monetarily, not all resources are material. Resources such as skills (especially so-called marketable skills that we can list on a résumé), natural talents and abilities, and even time itself are all resources we have at our disposal. How we acquire more of them and how we utilize or spend them are the primary activities of the second house. Planets and the sign on the cusp of our second house can reveal how we act to acquire resources, what resources we tend to value more than others, and how we spend those resources.

Conventionally, the most direct way to build our resources is either by manufacturing what we need, such as a farmer growing their own food, or by trading for it, with either an object we own or through our effort and skill, such as taking a job. Any activities you undertake in an effort to bring in *more*, to increase your worth, are of a second house nature, and signs and planets here can provide insight into the means and methods by which you do so.

The questions "What do you do?" and "What do you do *for a living*?" are typically intertwined in modern society, but astrology differentiates between the two. Any professional goals we may have that highlight our vocational desires fall in the tenth house, but in the direct ways that our work provides us with the resources to live, the second house reigns.

What are we willing to trade our resources for? What we spend our resources on is influenced by any planets and the sign in the second house, as well as the way we manage them. This applies specifically, but also generally, to what we buy and how much we spend. Do we have a sense of abundance or scarcity? Do we collect objects or value experiences? Do we spend easily or haphazardly, wondering where our money goes, or do we stick to a budget and pinch pennies?

In the second house, we must measure the worth of something according to our own standards in order to decide whether we will spend our time, money, or skill (and how much of it) in exchange for the thing we want. We are also obliged to ask ourselves "What is what I have to offer *worth*?" which is subjective and may be challenging because it can get personal. Second house activities can often be traced back to our sense of self-worth. This can be as basic a principle as the way a poor or high self-esteem affects how we judge our worth and whether we think we have something to offer. Our self-esteem provides the basis for judgments of worth, both of what we're worth and what we think others are worth in comparison. The sign and planets involved with this house can also indicate the kinds of things on which we base our self-esteem, and not just whether our self-esteem is subjectively high or low.

Second house principles get even more practical: how does our own self-worth impact how we spend or acquire resources? Someone with a low sense of self-worth may have little confidence in themselves and therefore accept a lower wage for what they can offer. If the first house activities represent how we extend our personality out into the world, then the second house activities represent how we extend our *reach* into the world.

In the second house, we are asked to put our money where our mouth is, to bet on ourselves and our abilities. In a sense, we are consciously pitting ourselves against the world in an ongoing competition: will it be me or the world that wins today's battle? If we do not esteem ourselves highly, either because we don't feel we have the specific skills we need to ask for that higher wage, for example, or because we do not have confidence in our abilities, whatever others may say, we may avoid risking our current and/or future resources.

How we value ourselves in this practical, fundamental way can determine what we are willing to accept and not accept in return for our skills, time, and effort. It can also determine how much we're willing to further invest in ourselves, spending resources on improving ourselves in whatever way we choose, since we are likely to have trade resources such as money and time to devote to education or training.

While we can acquire resources in a number of ways, the second house governs the ways in which we gain and spend resources that are our own. When we sign a loan, for example, we are extending our reach into other people's resources, governed by the opposite eighth house. When we make that money our own and spend it, then it becomes ours and second house rules apply. In natal astrology, it's not so necessary to split hairs but just to remember the essence of the second house: whatever you've got going for you that allows you to survive and thrive on your own merit or ability is second house material. This explains why the concepts of self-worth and confidence can stem from beliefs and practices in the second house.

Because we can live or die by our resources, the second house activities are, at their deepest root, about survival, even if we're not always thinking that deeply when we pay the bills or go to work. The realities of what we need to do to live and sustain our body are clear, and having the resources to do that is a fundamental need. Like the first house, the survival theme of the second house activities is primal, but rather than the instinctual self-preservation of "'me first" that is the terrain of the first house, the second house represents the primal need to *sustain* life over time.

Advertisements appeal to this underlying survival theme frequently by calling your attention to what you *don't* have and what might happen if you don't get it. Whether the product they are promoting appeals to your desire to be socially accepted or physically and financially safe, your ability to survive is enhanced and made more likely with these things on your side.

Second House Emphasis

People with a significant number of planets in the second house will frequently be dealing with issues and questions surrounding what they value, what they're worth, and how their beliefs and attitudes about money affect their lives. Planets and signs here will provide clues as to whether their spending habits tend toward the lavish or austere.

Keywords Revisited

By now it should be clear that the second house is about more than just money, the making or spending of it, and is not just about the spending and purchase of material things. While these are basic and quite practical considerations that planets and the sign in the second house can address, the deepest terrain of this house lies in *worth*—the assessment of it and how it affects all the decisions we make regarding our resources: how we acquire them, how we spend them, and how we can even recognize what we've got going in our favor. The bottom line is that our ability to ensure our own survival and our sense of our own worth can feed into our feeling that we have what it takes to survive.

Second House in Action

Venus or the sign of Libra in the second house may incline a person to spend resources on things or experiences that enhance the beauty or peacefulness in their life. Putting a favorite piece of art or extra thought into the décor of their everyday surroundings can be worth the expense and effort for the calming and uplifting effect. Meaningful or marketable skills that they may have and also appreciate in others might run along the lines of an aptitude for interacting with others. Other factors in their chart may hold sway over how they choose to use these skills in a professional arena. They may have good, old-fashioned people skills, whether or not they choose to list that on their résumé and whether or not they have honed this skill to a professional asset or just casually enjoy the benefits of this unpolished but natural talent. Given the focus on relationship, they may especially enjoy spending their resources on others, perhaps with thoughtful gifts or by picking up the tab at a restaurant.

THIRD HOUSE: HOUSE OF COMMUNICATION

When we take in new information, there is the possibility that we will retain it for a long time, possibly the rest of our lives. The data that we keep long-term goes through many processes. We have to initially observe or otherwise acquire it, make sense of it, categorize it, connect it to other bits of knowledge that we have already obtained, and maybe even conclude what meaning we think it has to us. Some information we take in never makes it that far. We may discard information that we think is insignificant. Third house activities often involve a kind of "front-end" information handling. We are in a state of almost constant observation, scanning the world around us for information, and when we receive some, we tend to do some initial filtering and categorizing. Planets in the third house and the sign on the house cusp can provide some insight into the way we handle the incoming stream of data.

Before we have anything to communicate about the world around us, we have to perceive it, to notice it. Perception is not as objective as it might seem. Our eyes and brain are not simply passive recording devices, able to register and recall every detail at will. We may not see something accurately or it might happen too quickly for us to see at all, and we are also influenced by what we expect or wish to see and by what we failed to see. Illusionists capitalize on this: what we may remember seeing may be our interpretation of what occurred, but this is not a deliberate or philosophical interpretation. This happens when you are trying to simply organize your input on the ground floor.

Selective attention is a phrase used to refer to the ability to focus your attention on one particular stimulus while filtering out other stimuli. We instinctively do this all the time and simultaneously experience *inattentional blindness*: not seeing what is out of the spotlight of our attention. The third house corresponds with this idea, in that planets in this house and the sign on the cusp will not only reveal the way you handle information intake but also what you tend to see (and remember) and not see, because of what you are inclined to look for due to your interests or what you are naturally tuned in to.

Our communication style is heavily influenced by the placement of Mercury, but planets in the third house add to Mercury's function. Planets and the sign in the third house can help answer questions such as these: What do you like to talk about? What topics interest you most? How do you prefer to take in and dish out information? In asking those questions, you're also in third house territory.

Communication is a broad word that can encompass a lot of activities in the third house, not just conversation. Expressing yourself through writing, singing, or teaching, formally or informally, is possible in the third house range.[19]

Third House Emphasis

People with a planet-heavy third house tend be keen observers no matter what their preferred style or subject of observation, because so much of their attention is focused on information gathering. Their mind is always engaged; whether they like to daydream, play word games, read the paper, or surf the Internet, they are rarely idle. They tend to be busy, if not just mentally then also physically, running errands or restlessly tapping their feet. The sign at play will determine whether they are chatterboxes or tend toward more limited or strategic communication, but find the sweet spot in their list of interests and you may find yourself their captive audience.

---

19. When it comes to expressing yourself artistically or creatively, you may also be crossing into the fifth house.

Keywords Revisited

Since all of life's activities are represented by just twelve houses, the list can get pretty long for each house. Not everything seems worth discussing in detail in your average astrology book; so often when one of the more obscure topics of a house comes up, it seems absurd or out of place. Here's a keyword you may not have heard before: traffic. Traffic is one of those obscure topics for the third house, and although it may seem odd at first, it's actually an excellent metaphor for what happens in the third house. To navigate traffic skillfully, you have to be alert and attentive to a constantly developing situation. Traffic itself is an ever-changing beast, affected continually by multiple factors. Stand-up comedy should be near the top of the list of things highlighted in the third house, because to be a true comic genius, your ability to respond, adjust, and improvise has to be lightning quick and sharp. Comedian Jim Carrey is a great example of this; he has six planets and his South Node all in the third house!

Third House in Action

With Neptune in the third house, the person might be more sensitive to information seemingly received from sources outside of the five senses, such as channeling or communicating with the dead or having a highly developed sense of intuition. They may not remember details of a situation or conversation as much as the impression or nonverbal cues that they internalized from an encounter. They may have an interest in information of an esoteric or spiritual nature. Because they look to impressions first, not to abstract facts alone, they may have a vulnerability to ascribing meanings or making assumptions based on those impressions that may or may not be intended, or to missing the fine print even though they took in a general overtone of any given situation.

FOURTH HOUSE: HOUSE OF HOME AND FAMILY

The beginning cusp of the fourth house marks another angle in the chart: the Nadir. The Nadir marks the lowest point in your chart. Symbolically, it represents what is underneath you, the foundation upon which you stand. The Nadir and fourth house territory in the natal chart represent where we've come from, our beginning, the roots from which we grow. Our family shapes our life from before birth, whether it's through the influence of our ancestors on our present life or even what we experience in the womb as part of our mother.

The fourth house terrain is not the broad expanse of the worldly ninth house or the buzzing workplace of the sixth house, but the narrow and deep pool of the past from which we sprang, and that which maintains a constant presence in the present and future. This house is not necessarily the repository for every event or experience from your past, but also the ongoing presence of the people and places that have helped shape the very foundation of what and who you are.

Family

Family, in the classic, fourth house sense, is primarily defined as the family you were born into. In modern definitions, it can also include the family you create as an adult, but ancient astrology puts children and spouses in the fifth and seventh houses, respectively. Starting with your actual family of origin is fundamental to understanding and navigating the terrain of your fourth house, but in many cases it can be appropriate to extend the definition of fourth house family to those not related to you genetically. Obviously this applies in cases such as adoption or a partner or spouse, but can include those you would consider to be family. This can get confusing—we could have housemates we are not particularly familial with, and we could have a sense of "with you till the end" with our best friend. Likewise, we may have no contact with people who are actually related to us by blood.

Regardless of whether we are born into a particular relationship or create it ourselves, the fourth house represents relationships that aren't dependent on circumstances, where a deep bond exists, even beyond our understanding. It is the relationships with the people we feel irreversibly tied to, even if we didn't choose those relationships or want them, and even if we don't see those people every day or ever again beyond childhood. Family ties of all kinds are symbolized by the fourth house.

Planets and the sign in the fourth house can indicate what threads run through our experiences with our parents. Clues to the nature of our early family experiences in general, as well as the kinds of relationships that may feel like family and our attitude toward family in general, can all be traced back to fourth house placements. It is not just the familiarity of the people we grew up with, but how we respond to the feeling of being part of a clan.

Our heritage, its nature and how we feel about it, is the domain of the fourth house. What has been passed down through our lineage and its impact on us, as well as the family culture—shaped by religion, tradition, race, and nationality, for example—can be understood in the context of the sign and planets in the fourth house.

Where home and family meet is easy to see—we are dependent on our families and the shelter they provide, of which a home of some kind is a part. Powerful memories can be evoked when we return to our childhood home or even our neighborhood—we can be stirred more deeply than we can understand or express.

Home

Fourth house activities encompass not only the subjective, psychological experience of home and all the emotions the word can conjure up, but also the physical location, your literal home base. The building, the land, and how you interact with it are all fourth house terrain. The sign and planets here can indicate the kinds of things we do to make ourselves at home, the things we do when no one else is looking, in the comfort and security of our own private space. Planets here also offer insight into the kind of environment that feels like home to us, and what we would do well to surround ourselves with in order for our house to feel like a home—anything from color schemes and furnishings, to location, to the people who inhabit it.

Like the foundation of a building, the fourth house provides clues to our foundation, our *roots*—what lies beneath our lives and even our consciousness. The connotations of home in the fourth house sense can extend to our emotional foundation as well as our literal and physical one.

Astrologer Dana Gerhardt calls the fourth house our "psychic hearth." The sign and planets here describe where we long to go and what we do when we need to collapse or retreat, without the pressure of being "on" for the world. The Nadir is the only one of the four angles that does not involve the world out there but instead the world within. Home is our beginning and our end, both in the cycle of life's everyday activities and symbolically as the beginning and end of life itself. We leave its safety to step out into the world, and it is the haven we return to when the day is done. While a physical shelter is fundamental to sustaining your physical health (and, by extension, your emotional and mental health), it offers more than a roof over your head—it sustains and supports you. Planets and the sign here can indicate the things that sustain and nourish you at the deepest levels—that enable you to let out that long breath you didn't realize you were holding all day.

Fourth House Emphasis

People with a large number of planets in the fourth house may not necessarily simply be homebodies, although it's certainly within the realm of possibilities, especially with signs more geared toward solitude or introversion. Needless to say, a lot of the focus in their life may be on their home, whether it's a love of entertaining in their home, or perhaps working out of their home, or even a focus on home in the metaphorical sense such as the nature of the work they do or the things they enjoy being home-focused. They are more likely to look close to home, rather than out in the world, for fulfillment.

Keywords Revisited

Other than the core concepts of home and family, which have been discussed in detail, the fourth house, like a small handful of other astrological symbols, has been correlated specifically with one's parents or, rather, parent. Ancient traditions have assigned the fourth house to the father and his influence, while modern astrology has tended to link it more with the mother and her influence. In an attempt to disentangle parental roles from gender, the fourth house parent has been described as the nurturing parent. This is in contrast to the shaping parental role that focuses more on social expectations and preparation for entry into the world, which modern astrologers attribute to the tenth house parent. By that specific standard, the sign and planets in the fourth house would indicate the nature of the parenting you received. In general, the sign and planets in the fourth house can provide clues to your upbringing, but their influence cannot be attributed simply to one parent or the other. In actuality, the fourth house is more about how the idea of home (including all it is connected to conceptually) was and can continue to be fostered in you.

Fourth House in Action

Pluto placed in the fourth house has made many a parent fearful that they are their child's deepest fear or their wounded nightmare. To ignore the possibility that Pluto in the fourth house could indicate an early childhood fraught with fear, tension, or dark secrets such as abuse or abandonment would be incorrect, yet, unfortunately, horrors can be experienced in childhood even without this intense planet in this foundational house. More often than not, Pluto here *can* indicate some kind of sensitivity to wounds surrounding the need to feel protected or nurtured, especially when these things are lacking, but there can also be versions of wounding around smothering or overkill in these areas and the damage incurred to a child's psyche as a result.

Another possibility is a proclivity for remaining dependent. This can manifest as a reluctance to grow up and do for oneself—essentially the urge to remain symbolically a child out of a deep insecurity surrounding these issues. Even those who grew up with loving parents who did their best can be wounded by what they needed but didn't receive, because no parent can meet the needs of their child perfectly. There can be an attachment or fixation—a never-ending need to receive the nurturing that they feel they are owed or that they never received. Pluto's sign will indicate the style in which the wound expresses and is formed.

FIFTH HOUSE: HOUSE OF PLEASURE AND CREATIVITY

Many of the seemingly disassociated keywords that are associated with the fifth house (children, gambling, creativity, love affairs) can be linked through the undercurrent of pleasure or fun. Ask someone what they do for fun and you are asking them about their fifth house. When we engage in a hobby, play our favorite game, or do anything purely for its entertainment value, we are in the fifth house. If we describe someone as playful, that says something about their personality or style, but we all have a fifth house, and we all do activities that are meant purely to relax or entertain ourselves. The sign and planets in the fifth house point to the ways and style in which we play.

Like the word spirituality, creativity is a word that often seems to be applied too narrowly. Creativity is not just about art or artistic talent, but refers to the force behind the urge to make art in the first place, the urge to create. When we create, we pour something from ourselves into new form. We use our essence to give shape to something outside of ourselves. This is one of the reasons why "children" is an appropriate metaphor for the activities in the fifth house. We take something from inside of ourselves and give it a life of its own on the outside.

Creativity in the fifth house experience is also about engaging with creative acts that sustain us. To create anything requires a tremendous amount of energy, but when we are engaged in a creative act that brings pleasure and joy, we are revitalized rather than drained. As we give, we receive, because in the fifth house we are not limited by productivity or obligation in what we create but only by what our heart wants to express and only for as long as we wish.

It has been said that creativity is simply thinking outside the box or putting ideas together in an unusual way—a true sentiment since we are putting our own stamp on something, adding something of our own unique combination of abilities, perspective, and desires to whatever we place our attention on. We may engage our creative faculties when we try to think of an idea for work or an interesting topic to write about for our school paper, and even in everyday problem-solving. Yet creativity as an act of self-expression and joy rather than simply a means to an end or a mechanism to accomplish a goal is the sentiment that lies at the heart of the fifth house.

Pleasure can be differentiated from happiness in that it tends to be more momentary. When someone says they are happy, they may be referring to that very moment or expressing satisfaction about their life overall. When we say we are having fun, it is usually in reference to a definite experience or moment. Inherent in fifth house activities is the experience of losing oneself to the moment, even if *just* for a moment, allowing oneself to be caught up in the total experience of something. This is life as it happens, not life as it will be, could be, or is hoped to be. Fifth house experiences are about the *now*.

These experiences need not be trivial, but they can be fleeting. Profound joy can be experienced when we are deeply engaged with expressing our creativity, but the moments of pleasure themselves will ebb and flow. They can be relived when we repeat those or similar activities, but they are only experienced as memories of the past or craving for the next time when not *in* that moment itself.

Fifth House Emphasis

People with a significant focus on the fifth house in their natal chart will have a strong need to engage their creative side, not just as a distraction or to kill time but as an integral part of their life. Depending on the sign involved, they may be serious or lighthearted about the ways that they play and the kinds of things they like to do for fun, but it is the pursuit of these experiences that can be the most vitalizing for them.

Keywords Revisited

In traditional astrology, the fifth house has been called the house of children, and some astrologers still, in part, look to planets here to predict the likelihood of someone having children or issues surrounding the matter. In natal astrology, a more expansive and less literal perspective of this house looks at children as a metaphor for everything we do that invokes the state of being childlike and all the typical characteristics of a happy child, such as expressiveness, living in the moment, and engaging in activities we find pleasurable. We can also consider children from the perspective of a creator and what it means to give birth to something from the essence of ourselves—if not literally a child then perhaps a creative work or the things we do when we're not worried about how it looks or who it impresses but are just experiencing the moment.

Fifth House in Action

With Jupiter in the fifth house, there may be a willingness to try anything—or at least many things, if the sign is more conservative or careful. A person with Jupiter here will want to go big or go home; once they get started, they'll want to let it all hang out without restraint. Jupiter's influence is expansive and limitless, so in the fifth house, it's the pursuit of pleasure that may be unlimited, and that can be a challenging power to wield wisely. The sign through which Jupiter acts in the fifth house territory will play a strong role in determining the types of outlets one finds most enjoyable and whether restraint is difficult or extremely difficult to come by.

Saturn in the fifth house will change the tone from expansiveness to restriction, where the problem isn't letting too much hang out but learning to do so. Pleasurable pursuits that have some kind of practical purpose behind them can encourage more creative behavior, but it's likely that the pursuit of pleasure and hobbies or the expression of one's creative urge will be initiated with more purpose, restraint, and strategy rather than spontaneously or uninhibitedly. It may be challenging for this person to understand the benefits of play, and they may even have a habit of approaching play as a kind of task. They will have to practice at playing!

SIXTH HOUSE: HOUSE OF WORK AND SERVICE

The sixth house, while it is called the house of work and therefore can be a useful piece of the career profile available in a natal chart, is not a career house specifically in itself. For career or vocation, looking at the tenth house is most direct in answering the big questions. However, sixth house matters can be quite relevant to questions regarding one's career, for what you spend all day doing in paid service can certainly have an impact on career choices, just as income, a topic in its own right, can be greatly dependent on one's career path. The sixth house can tell you more about how you work, what motivates you to work, and what environments you work best in.

Whatever work you do, *how* you work is just as relevant as your job title when it comes to sixth house matters. Do you need a great deal of freedom at work or do you perform better with structure and set expectations? Do you prefer consistency in your schedule and projects or do you thrive in circumstances that promote creativity and experimentation? Answering those kinds of questions are the fundamental lessons of living in this house. While work is always work, the more we are in alignment with the agenda of the sign and planets in this house, the more work can feel like play, energizing and almost effortless rather than drudgery and toil.

While a skill possessed can land solidly in the second house of one's personal resources, the practice and application of a skill can also apply in the sixth house. On-the-job training is a sixth house matter, not only because it enables us to do our work but because an apprenticeship approach is a very real-world, hands-on kind of activity in which the sixth house specializes.

Working a lot in itself does not guarantee success, achievement, or satisfaction, of course. Whether someone consistently supports others and is always the underdog or works tirelessly to build an empire, the same amount of effort may be invested. If the sign involved or planets in other houses are focused on achievement, ambition, or the bigger picture, the sixth house activities will serve as steppingstones rather than busy work or aimless effort. Either way, the sixth house is not about taking a vacation, and indeed, people with strong focus in this house may find it difficult to commit time or resources to leisure at the expense of sixth house efforts.

Whether or not we are on someone's payroll, we work. Maintaining a life requires us to perform any number of tasks, such as running errands, taking care of household repairs, washing the dog, and so on. The sixth house represents many of the mundane activities in which we engage in order to keep our lives running more or less smoothly. Anything that we might see glossed over in a movie montage on the big screen because it's too boring to watch in real time is probably an activity that belongs in the sixth house! That's not to say the entire realm of the sixth house is boring, but only that it is very *real* and *mundane*; these are activities that ground us in the realities of everyday life as opposed to the activities represented by the opposite house, the twelfth house, which take us out of the world in body and/or soul.

Sixth House Emphasis

Because activities in the sixth house all center around work and effort, people with many planets here have a tendency toward workaholism, because they are tuned in to the never-ending list of things that must be done. The sign involved here will give clues as to the style of working, and certainly not all signs lend themselves to industrious, nose-to-the-grindstone attitudes; but if many planets are in the sixth house, much of their focus will be on these kinds of activities.

Keywords Revisited

The word service is often given in common titles of this house's activities. In some ways, this may just be a synonym for work and can be left at that, but this can also conjure up ideas of self-sacrifice. Here's another idea: service may refer to *servants*, which is an ancient association with the sixth house. Of course, most of us don't have a butler waiting in the wings, but with this house being just under the seventh house of *equal* relationships, the idea at the heart of this perspective

may be unequal relationships of many kinds. This is an idea more relatable in modern life, where we see boss-employee or teacher-student
dynamics as commonplace. This is not an observation on authority in
relationship, however, but simply an acknowledgment of the context
in which service can take place.[20]

While most of the activities this house represents are work-oriented,
the sixth house is often called the house of service and health. However,
in natal astrology, in terms of health, a differentiation is made between
wellness and illness, between overall constitution and overall health
vulnerabilities. The house of health from the standpoint of one's constitution corresponds more to the first house, which is associated with the
body and a person's vitality, whereas the sixth house can illuminate vulnerabilities in one's health, such as the circumstances that may lead to
illness of certain types. This can be a significant topic in natal astrology,
but exploring it fully involves branching out into the detailed terrain of
medical astrology.

Sixth House in Action

Uranus in the sixth house can indicate an inventive approach to work,
perhaps in an innovative, up-and-coming field or in a research and
development department where the person can break new ground
and experimentation is a job requirement. They may need a great deal
of freedom on the job and in their daily routine outside of the workplace. The sign on the cusp of the sixth house may clarify whether the
person needs that freedom for spontaneity and variety (such as Sagittarius or Gemini) or simply needs to avoid being pressed by authority
and to be their own boss (such as Aquarius or Aries).

If the rest of their chart supports it, a person with Uranus in the
sixth house may prefer entrepreneurship, where they can be free to

---

20. Ultimately the sixth house is not a relationship-oriented house, but some relationships may be inherently formed around sixth house circumstances. When considering relationships in the sixth house context, it is more focused on how that's a
means to the end or a situational necessity rather than a commentary on how two
people will get along with each other.

make up almost all of the rules in their daily routine. However, they may not necessarily want to be in charge as much as they want to be free to work independently, and they won't tend to favor an environment that is structured heavily on teamwork. Boss-employee relationships that are based on rigid ideas of authority will also be likely to provoke a rebellious response from them, although whether they rebel passively or aggressively may be dependent on the sign Uranus is in and the orientation of the rest of the chart.

SEVENTH HOUSE: HOUSE OF PARTNERSHIP

Throughout the day, the Sun burns like a bright bulb, a distinct disc against the blue sky. At sunset, the Sun seems to spread across the sky, the light spreading, refracting into multiple colors, the disc now blurred and smeared into streaks of yellow, orange, pink, and red. Important relationships in our lives affect us similarly. The seventh house begins with the Descendant, symbolizing sunset, where the distinctness of your personality meets with the horizon of the Other, where the I surrenders to the We. When you enter the seventh house, you are subjected to a reciprocal effect where the light that shines from you is bent, changed, and refracted because of the influence of another person on your opinions, beliefs, actions, and feelings.

Since the seventh house is known as the house of marriage, it seems that one's spouse is the embodiment of the seventh house terrain, and indeed, a spouse is a meaningful way to engage in seventh house activities, but not the only way in which we do so. Relationships with good friends or business partners are also the terrain of the seventh house. Essentially, any time we engage in a relationship with another who has the potential to affect us (and conversely, have us affect them), in a significant and not transitory way, we are in the seventh house. We may not make a formal pledge of 'til death do us part, but in seventh house relationships, a natural sense of obligation and unspoken commitment toward another person begins to arise. When we begin to feel that we want to and also should take into account another's feelings, needs, and wishes, we have entered the seventh house with them.

It is not long before this sense of shared space between two people brings up the issue of trust. While it may be limited, depending on the type of relationship, there is a natural vulnerability between two people who can affect each other greatly. We change and are changed by those who affect us on the seventh house level because we are open enough to them and engaged enough with them that they can have a significant influence on us. We learn about the kind of influence people can have on us in relationship and wrestle with the influence we can have over another in the seventh house.

Healthy and unhealthy dependence is also a seventh house lesson. In significant relationships, we are both supporting and allowing ourselves to be supported by another. When someone supports us, it's up to us to choose whether to accept that support, and if we do, and continue to throughout the relationship, a certain amount of dependence will tend to form. We learn whether we can depend on someone and whether we are willing to allow ourselves to be vulnerable enough to trust. Likewise, our partner is also making the same decisions and choices about us.

In the seventh house, we are walking a fine line between dependence and independence and hopefully finding the sweet spot. Too much dependence or independence can work against the balance in relationship. If we don't feel we're getting as much as we're giving, we can feel resentful and closed to that person, putting them in the childlike role of dependent rather than partner. On the flip side, if we aren't giving as much as we're getting, we aren't able to contribute properly to the relationship, which can also lead to resentment. The goal of seventh house partnerships is for two people to care for and support each other but still maintain integrity and responsibility.

The seventh house doesn't just point to the kinds of partners and partnerships we engage in; the sign and planets in the seventh house also illuminate our personal relationship lessons, needs, and hang-ups. Choices in whom we partner with matter greatly and are seventh house terrain as well. Relationship patterns can be uncovered using a variety of symbols in the natal chart, including the sign and planets involved with the seventh house. The kinds of people you find your-self attracted to or frequently drawing to yourself can reveal your re-lationship patterns, and those patterns, healthy or unhealthy, have one common denominator: you. What we learn outside of relationship (but in relation to it) about ourselves is also a valuable component of this terrain.

Equality between partners is high on the list of important factors that contribute to a successful relationship. In more formally defined relationships, such as those defined by a contract, a quid-pro-quo method may be appropriate, but often the balance can be measured much more loosely—not in numbers but in how the relationship feels to each party involved. However this balance is achieved, it is impor-tant that each partner feel that there is room enough for them in the relationship, in the space created between two people. The sign and planets associated with the seventh house in one's natal chart can pro-vide clues as to the most important needs in achieving that sense of balance, whether it's Mercury needing to be heard or Aquarius need-ing to maintain their independence. In general, a sense of reciprocity contributes to a healthy partnership, and it is in the seventh house where we engage in activities that teach us these lessons.

The path to balance and equality in relationship is not always clear. Not only do the actual specifics vary from relationship to relationship, but we are constantly bombarded by mixed messages. In one breath we are told to stand up for ourselves and in the next not to be rude and to let others go first. Which is it? Both. Equality between partners is also a flowing, living, breathing thing. Whether to ask for your way, concede to your partner's wishes, or find some middle-ground com-promise needs to be reevaluated with each new situation or problem.

Negotiation is an important principle in all seventh house ac-tivities, because we are navigating shared space and need to be made aware of our partner's terrain as well as inform our partner of our own in order to truly own the space together. Sharing cannot take place if both partners don't reveal and share of themselves. Chroni-cally taking up too little space can be just as damaging as taking up too much. When we adjust our behavior too much and alter the natural expression of our true self, we can become a ghost in the relationship, only a mirror reflecting the other and not a true partner. No true sharing, support, or openness can happen in this state.

Relationships are often compared to dance. Just as we symbolically maneuver with and around our partners in relationship, we do so literally in dance. In couples dancing, partners must maintain the proper distance and stance in relation to each other if they are to skillfully glide across the floor together. Without proper tension in each partner's arms to "hold the frame," the duo collapses, moving out of sync and/or bumping into each other. An appropriate distance must also be maintained—too far and the partners obviously can't reach each other, but too close and there is no ability to move freely together. Notice that this doesn't mean there isn't a leader; one partner must lead and the other follow, but the leader can change with the situation, and with each person contributing their part, the partnership can happen.

It is not only friends and lovers whom we encounter in the seventh house context, but also those with whom we are less than friendly. People who get under our skin and stay there form the relationships of the seventh house, and we often encounter not only those whom we like or admire but also those who are largely different from us, the yin to our yang. Opposites often do attract because the differences between two people can be what draws them together like magnets. Relationships between people who have almost everything in common may seem like a match made in heaven, but in actuality these relationships have little or no draw because there is no friction to create a spark of attraction between them. Those who differ enough from us, even if they are not exactly our opposite in every way, often have a way of filling a need or stabilizing parts of our personality in ways we may not predict or even know we needed.

Carl Jung, who had a natal seventh house Sun, was fascinated with the idea of a shadow self, a part of our identity unconsciously hidden from ourselves because it is made up of traits that either we or society do not find acceptable. Jung believed that when we encounter people who irritate us unintentionally simply because their own natural personality grates against our own, further analysis of the root cause for irritation can lead to a greater understanding of what we suppress in this shadow self.

This concept is very much alive in seventh house partnerships, for there is no greater mirror than a partner who knows us well, sometimes better than we know ourselves, and can give a different, if not entirely objective, view of ourselves from the outside. Someone's assessment of us, even if they know us well, may not be any more accurate than our own, but their view of us can call attention to our blind spots, giving us the opportunity to become more self-aware and thus more whole.

This reciprocity happens on more than one level; as we interact with a significant other, not only can they tell us what they observe about us that we cannot see objectively, but we also tend to become aware of needs and behaviors we may not have been aware of in any other context, without the influence of another person on us who engages our heart and mind significantly.

Seventh House Emphasis

Those with a significant focus on the seventh house in their chart will often be challenged with issues of perspective: learning to keep hold of their own point of view while opening up to others', either through conversation or by the impact others have on their own life. Relationships tend to be learning-intensive for us all, with seventh house people being no exception, but lessons for these people may focus greatly on how much space they take up in a relationship, whether too much or not enough. The planets and sign here, as well as the context of the rest of the chart, will indicate on which side of this balance they tend to fall and where they are pressed to stretch into new terrain through relationships. It is important to avoid assuming that a seventh house person will find themselves in a higher number of significant relationships or that their destiny is to be married or partnered, for the terrain of relationship can teach a great many things with or without the ties of commitment.

Keywords Revisited

This house has been referred to as the house of marriage, which is certainly fitting but does not present the whole picture. This house was also traditionally known as the house of open (known) enemies. Granted, not all marriages are happy, but most of us don't think of enemies and our spouse in the same sentence. The idea with the seventh house is not just those we love, but those we *tangle with* in some significant way. Learning to do that effectively and learning about ourselves in the process is the terrain of the seventh house. This can be anything from learning how to have a loving confrontation in openness and honesty with a friend or loved one to trusting the other person enough to ask for what you need to craft the terms of a fair business arrangement. This house's activities all have some aspect of negotiation between you and another in order to coexist in a relationship.

Seventh House in Action

Saturn's placement in the seventh house might indicate someone who approaches relationships with caution and seriousness. In the extreme, this may manifest as either an eagerness for a defined commitment in important relationships or a reluctance to enter into *any* commitments due to their gravity. This person will most likely be drawn to people who have an air of maturity about them, either in their demeanor, interests, or physical age. They may tend to take on a great deal of responsibility in relationships, for better or worse, or, because the seventh house can represent that which we project onto others, they may be drawn to partners who have this trait themselves. Saturn in this house has classically caused astrologers to dictate a life of loneliness for the native, but this is not necessarily the case. If loneliness does seem to be perpetual, it can often be because of the challenges involved in finding true balance and intimacy in relationship with others. Simultaneously, Saturn here can manifest as a preference for solitude and a penchant for self-sufficiency.

Because Saturn is a planet that represents both blockages and limitations as well as the work we need to do to manage or overcome those blockages, a person with Saturn in the seventh house may find close relationships to be particularly challenging. They may be vulnerable to becoming stuck in behavioral and situational patterns, which can often be recognized by Saturn's sign; for example, Saturn in Aries may indicate challenges surrounding strength, anger, or dominance in a relationship, whereas Saturn in Cancer may reveal a difficulty in opening up to another, accepting nurturing as well as receiving it.

EIGHTH HOUSE: HOUSE OF POWER AND THE PSYCHE
Just as the eighth sign, Scorpio, is compelled to dig down beneath the surface of life, the eighth house represents this underworld territory. Eighth house experiences underlie everyday life, whether it's our inner psychology motivating our everyday behaviors and pursuits, the fears in the corners of our mind that we may try to escape or ignore, or the secrets we keep about or from ourselves and others.

As with the fourth and twelfth houses, eighth house experiences often take us into hidden or private territory. This can make it difficult to clarify and understand, because it takes us out of the obvious and into the hidden, out of the literal and into the symbolic, out of the physical and into the psychological. What happens in the eighth house goes on behind the scenes, hidden even from ourselves as well as others.

Perhaps nothing tests us as much as surviving loss. Even the thought of losing something or someone precious to us can keep us awake at night, and no one is immune to the fear of losing what feels vital to us. Were we to remain constantly consciously aware of the dangers we narrowly escape in everyday life, we would surely be driven insane and would feel safe nowhere. So it is in the eighth house where we often find the thoughts and fears that we push out of our own consciousness in order to maintain normal daily life, mostly unburdened by the knowledge that life is dangerous, or that it ends, or that our lives might drastically change at any time.

Planets here represent a part of us that is always reminded of the intensity of life, whether it's the acknowledgment of what we deeply need or crave and are dependent on having in our lives or the emotional reality that we will be going to the funerals of those we love someday. It is also the part of us that is enriched by those experiences and that knowledge, even though, at best, they can be bittersweet.

Learning lessons about loss and living with the depth and intensity that is interlaced through even the most joyous and brightest of life's experiences is eighth house terrain. The sign and planets associated with this house reveal the nature and style of these lessons. While the twelfth house territory seems to house experiences that encourage us to let go and surrender, the eighth house is more real and raw, overwhelming and penetrating us with the intensity of living through the experience itself rather than the letting go and moving on that may happen alongside and afterward.

Experiences that are dramatic and crisis-oriented are often tied to eighth house symbolism because of their intensity and ability to engulf us. In crisis, we are dealing with powerful forces that threaten to overwhelm us, and we're trying to keep our head and come out alive. Acknowledging the need to let go, the death and ending of something as part of the cycle of life, is not entirely isolated to the twelfth house, however, and is also part of the wisdom that eighth house experiences can impart. This house of death refers to the familiar cycle of ending, with the thought following that a beginning is not usually far behind.[21] What lives also dies. What we gain, we also lose. Classically, engaging with the eighth house terrain is said to make one moody and

---

21. The fourth house has also been referred to as the house of endings, because it is family, hearth, and clan, the foundation of life and the cocoon we return to as we come full circle through life and old age. In contrast, however, the eighth house is more specifically where we deal with the emotional impact of endings and the realistic acknowledgment of it. We don't end, but we must endure another ending, which can be wounding and out of our control.

morose, which can certainly be the case if the focus remains on what is being lost or what is unbearable. But things grow from the rich soil of what has passed before. The eighth house experience is never light and easy, but it is meaningful and profound.

Eighth house experiences, with their depth and intensity, tend to have an overwhelming quality about them, which can make us feel vulnerable or powerless, especially when these experiences come in the form of circumstances that are beyond our control. When we reveal a secret, a part of our soul, or our physical body, we are leaving ourselves naked. Forging an appropriate understanding and relationship with powerlessness is not an easy task and is part of the eighth house terrain. When we surrender to an experience or even a person, we allow a kind of beauty and depth into our lives that is not attainable when we are fully in control.

Shared Resources

Many of the activities in the eighth house correlate with our entanglements with others, but unlike the seventh house, the eighth house takes this entanglement deeper. The eighth house is often referred to as the house of shared resources, just as the opposite second house is *personal* resources.

When two adults are in a committed, 'til-death-do-us-part type of relationship (formalized or not), there is a lot of sharing involved. Yet just as someone may take on the bulk of the household responsibilities when their partner is sick, there is not always an even balance in who gives what and when. In the seventh house, we practice equality, seeing someone as our equal (and making sure we don't forget ourselves in that picture) and allowing them into our lives in some way. In eighth house intimacy, we don't simply stop at fifty-fifty, contributing an equal share before going back to our individual corners. In the messy realities of deep love, we don't merely share, we merge. The eighth house governs the kinds of activities that we do when we are deeply entangled with another, when the two become one. Partners do this almost literally during sex, as well as legally and financially in marriage. While the eighth house isn't entirely about relationship, many eighth house activities can serve to bond us to another and also test our fears about being so dependent or entangled with another and what might happen if we lose them or they betray us.

Eighth House Emphasis

Those with a large number of planets in the eighth house may have a secretiveness or an intensity about them that lies just under the surface. Their attention is often turned inward, and they may surprise you with their depth, especially if they do not appear intense or serious otherwise. Unless the rest of their chart leans toward the gregarious, they may seem introverted or otherwise removed or quiet unless you get them talking on a subject that catches your attention with its depth or edginess. Even with more conservative or cautious signs, they will also tend to immerse themselves in whatever topic, activity, or person has caught their attention, pursuing it to an extreme degree, as if they can never get their fill. They may also be captivated by experiences and topics of exploration that are symbolic, mysterious, and/or taboo in nature, which is why sex, death, and the occult are often topics listed within this house's terrain.

Keywords Revisited

All houses incorporate an impossibly long list of topics within their boundaries. With some, it's easier to spot the underlying theme, and with others, it seems like a merry-go-round of unrelated topics, with the theme only emerging after some creative investigation. The eighth house is one that sometimes confuses astrology students with its bizarre list, with sex, death, and other people's money at the top of the list of topics. The discordant ideas here all come together under the banner of highly charged experiences, where we tend to feel vulnerable. The issues surrounding the power we have (or, more often, don't have) arise especially in this terrain. Money, sex, and death are three of the most intense areas of life, and probably the top three reasons people find themselves in divorce court, jail, or a therapist's office!

Eighth House in Action

Someone with a Gemini Sun in the eighth house will likely have a core need for finding out the kind of information that isn't obvious or easy to obtain. They may enjoy and excel at research because they are driven to find the answers—not to trivial questions but to hard and sometimes scary questions. Their inner monologue may be constantly running, often centering on the deeper motivations behind their and others' behavior and what drives them, psychologically speaking. They may have a tendency to think too much about things that may go wrong, given the intensity of the eighth house terrain and running anxiety-amplifying disaster scenarios in their mind, depending on the nature of their fears.

Depending on the position of Mercury, they may have a rather symbolic way of interpreting the world and may be able to read more deeply into the meaning of circumstances than others. Given this penchant for understanding symbolism, they may love delving into things like cracking codes and puzzles—reveling in the pleasure of finding the key that unlocks the mystery.

NINTH HOUSE:
HOUSE OF PHILOSOPHY AND EDUCATION

Education, specifically *higher* education, is often an arena aligned with the ninth house. In higher education, we are not just taught the building blocks of a topic, but we dive deeper through specialization into a specific area of study. Through this exploration we are able to see patterns and connections between what we learn, which align with entire existing systems of thought or become new ones entirely. The sign and planets in the ninth house can indicate the kinds of topics that we are interested in as well as the ideas and beliefs that we may hold regarding those topics.

The higher we go in the educational process, the more we are obliged to experiment and form our own opinions, not just parroting what others have learned but building on what we've been taught. When we learn more about something we are deeply interested in, there is usually more than intellectual interest, but a deep engagement with the knowledge we are seeking, making the ninth house experience not just one of the mind but of the total being. When we learn, we seek to integrate the information into what we already know and believe to be true. Sometimes new information breaks apart what we already know, collapsing former beliefs as we make room for new truths, but most often we try to tie new ideas into our existing worldview, the one we are already comfortable with. Gaining knowledge in the ninth house way is gaining knowledge that we use to shape our philosophy of life. We are not the sponges that we are in the third house, simply observing and defining; attaining ninth house knowledge has us seeking the underlying *meaning*. What does it mean to us that something is or isn't true? How does this knowledge affect our behavior and the way we make sense of the world? How does this add to or change the story? This is education in the ninth house.

What we learn informs our worldview, and what we believe about the world and our place in it can influence our behavior. Reciprocally, when we experience something new in the world, we read meaning into it based on what we already believe to be true. Planets and the sign in the ninth house all contribute to our worldview, that which we consciously and even unconsciously believe to be true. This is most obvious in the areas of religion, law, and politics—they are large systems of thought or belief that have been formalized by those who unite under common beliefs.

The ninth house arena doesn't just cover formal, organized religions, but also our personal philosophy in the broadest sense. One-sentence mottos, cults, corporate mission statements, political movements, words to live by, proverbs, and even the golden rule all fall into the ninth house because there is an assumption behind them, a truth that is being proselytized.

Ninth House Emphasis

Someone with a strong ninth house focus may be an armchair philosopher, often thinking beyond what is obvious and speculating on the deeper or broader implications of any situation.

Because education and philosophy go hand in hand, a ninth house person may have a strong interest in not only learning but also teaching, whether formally or informally. They may also be vulnerable to becoming too reliant on their existing beliefs, shutting out new experiences that may threaten what they feel certain of even while they hunger to experience the sense of expansion that comes with having one's eyes opened to new ways of thinking.

Wanderlust is not uncommon for these people, although the sign and planets in the mix will dictate whether this manifests as actual travel or something more symbolic. Whether they travel by couch, by imagination, or by plane, bus, or car, they are often drawn to the romance of far-off places or unfathomed mysteries.

Keywords Revisited

It has been said that education paves the way to a richer and broader life. Education does more than expand the mind, but also allows us to see opportunities and possibilities we never knew existed outside of the small world we were born into. The more we know, the bigger our world can become. No matter what the style (sign) at work, we are a seeker when we enter the ninth house, invited to discover what truths lie "out there."

Long-distance/foreign travel and education are keywords that are frequently connected to the ninth house and can seem a bit disjointed. Although it does seem to be true that people with many planets in the ninth house do seem to significantly enjoy travel, it's useful to think of travel and the ninth house in terms of what travel can do for you, which is to *expand your world*. Both education and travel expose you to new ideas, either formally through study or informally through direct experience of the new and foreign.

Ninth House in Action

With Venus placed in Pisces in the ninth house, there may be a strong interest in studying art or humanities topics. This person may be especially inclined toward study-abroad opportunities. Other fields of study along Venusian or Piscean lines may interest them as well, such as fashion, poetry, art history, religion, or mysticism, and they may be especially drawn to mystical or ancient places that have an aura of mystery to them.

Since Venus often reveals the kinds of people we are drawn to, a person with Venus in the ninth house may find themselves drawn to people who are exotic or unique in some way, who stand out from their own culture. It is not uncommon for these people to marry outside of their own nationality, religion, or culture, and with Venus in the openhearted sign of Pisces, they are likely to be very accepting and interested in all kinds of people.

From the perspective of one's worldview, Venus in Pisces combines to create a very peaceful and compassionate philosophy. Whatever this person's chosen system of formal belief, if they have one, the underlying sentiment will be one that is informed by great empathy and a tendency toward a sense of connectedness, not only with humanity but potentially branching out into belief in a sentient or benevolent universe, or a thread of destiny and meaning running through the seemingly haphazard events of everyday life.

TENTH HOUSE: HOUSE OF CAREER AND PUBLIC LIFE

The tenth house is the third of three houses that focus on a different aspect of the practical matters of survival and work. The second house highlights your resources and skills, both their utilization and their development. The sixth house highlights your routine and environment, the quality of daily life in and out of the workplace. The tenth house completes the triumvirate with a focus on your public and professional facets of life.

This is the first of the last three houses (tenth, eleventh, and twelfth) that represent life from a macrocosmic point of view: the eleventh house with its broad alliances and expansive view of the future, and the twelfth house as the vast realm of the spirit and the connected human consciousness. The macrocosm of the tenth house is illustrated in two concepts: the type of person you appear to be from afar, and the legacy of work and contributions you may make throughout your vocational life.

Vocation

The tenth house represents the activities we do to sort out and live out our calling or vocation, sometimes expressed as career if we're lucky enough to have our talents, desires, skills, and financial opportunities come together in one profession, but career is just one potential vehicle. A vocation can be described as some great work or undertaking that we feel resonates deeply with who we are and who we are called to be and is a more appropriate umbrella term for the activities we may undertake that involve contributing to the world in some way. Whether our vocation is vaguely or clearly defined, and no matter how many ways our expression of it in the outer world changes throughout the years, the tenth house terrain is the way that we put ourselves out in the world in this way. What is the nature of your unique contribution to the world? What sort of legacy do you want to leave? What things do you seem to stand for or endorse because of your actions and alignments out in the world? The sign and planets in the tenth house can provide answers to these questions.

In youth, it seems as though success is a straight line, from the starting point to the end goal, but in reality, the path is often a mishmash of various experiences and offshoots, some of which may culminate in one ultimate vocation. The sign and planets in the tenth house can indicate the kinds of qualities and interests that, when explored and developed, may lead you in the direction that is most fulfilling for you vocationally, even if it develops across multiple jobs and outlets.

The beginning of the tenth house is marked by one of the four angles, called the *Medium Coeli* or Midheaven. When the Sun is high in the sky, its light touches everything as far as the eye can see—everything is visible. Likewise, the Midheaven represents the most visible parts of you, whether you intend to be visible or not. While the Ascendant is the parts of your personality that you wear on your sleeve, the Midheaven is a bird's-eye view of your life, not necessarily personal and intimate but broad. In society, we are constantly observed (and judged) from afar. The family or place we come from, our profession, and our socioeconomic status are just a few examples of the powerful but impersonal observations people make about us on a daily basis. We may not intend to be seen or categorized in these ways, but we are often still subject to the realities that placement in these social categories impose on us.

From the outside in, the Midheaven and tenth house represent the terrain of our individual appearance out in the public sphere. From this perspective, the planets and sign here represent the kinds of things you will be known for at large, and the assumptions others may make about you from this broad perspective.

Social examples are often contradictory: society loves mavericks who go out on a limb and invent something new but looks down on irresponsible or risky behavior that is often inherent in that process; it admires those who make their mark on the world but criticizes those who step out of the norm. In many ways, living out your Midheaven in a satisfying way means knowing how to distinguish between the roles you're being pressured to play and the roles you're truly meant to play. There are roles, jobs, and promotions that we feel we *should* want, that we'd be foolish to turn down, and there are those that maybe aren't as flashy but are closer in alignment with our true path. In this way, a sense of destiny is sometimes integrated with the Midheaven. Although destiny is often something that's agreed upon in hindsight, following the guidance of the sign and planets in the Midheaven will often get us to the place we feel we're meant to go.

Tenth House Emphasis

Those people with significant planetary weight in their tenth house may be very concerned with their profession or vocation as a main focus of their personal expression. The question "what are you going to be when you grow up?" may have had a dominant effect on their life from an early age. They may have a strong sense of mission, although it is common not to see it coalescing until well into adulthood, after they've had a chance to get to know themselves.

Because the tenth house also represents the activities we do to step out into the world on our own, separate and independent from our family, upbringing, or anything else that may overshadow us, a tenth house person may find that relating to authority figures may be especially rife with intensity throughout their life as they seek to become their own authority. This does not necessarily mean there will be constant conflicts with authorities, but that they are hyper aware of the impact those deemed to be in charge can have over others, and the power that can be wielded as a result.

Keywords Revisited

Although career can be an apt term for tenth house activities, like many keywords, it can be limiting enough to be misleading. Equally confusing is the apparent redundancy: the sixth house is referred to as the house of work and the tenth house as the house of career. Just as participation in sixth house activities is still needful whether we perform them in the context of a paying job or in the daily maintenance of our lives, people who never earn a paycheck may have planets in their tenth house. The difference between sixth house work and tenth house work is often a matter of how close you want to look. The professional life of a doctor can provide a good example. The general public sees the white coat, the stethoscope, and the clipboard and recognizes that as the role of doctor. But the nitty-gritty details of the job may be closer to a routine that's something like paperwork, conversation, "turn your head and cough," paperwork, conversation, write a prescription, etc. The tasks that keep us busy in and/or out of a profession (sixth house) and the perceived role one plays in society in and/or out of the professional arena (tenth house) are different enough that they are governed by these separate houses.

Although considered less often than the Sun or Saturn, the Midheaven is sometimes used to glean information about a person's father or mother. Again, just as with the fourth house or the Moon, any clues that the Midheaven or tenth house planets can provide about either of one's parents would be more about the relationship with or perception of the parent from the viewpoint of the native, and not necessarily an objective statement about the personality or character of the parent in actuality. Furthermore, the Midheaven is less directly tied to a parent as much as it may be to any *authority figure*, as the Midheaven and tenth house planets play a role in social conditioning, and authority figures tend to be the most dominant in shaping that conditioning as enforcers of the social rules. We are taught by authority figures, beginning with a parent or guardian, how to socially integrate into the world.

Tenth House in Action

With Pluto acting in the terrain of the tenth house, we might find someone who has a deep-seated desire to make a profound difference in the world, even in cases where they are unsure exactly what impact they want to make or how. The nature of the gift they have to offer the world may reach out into topics that are not easy, lighthearted, or popular and require a great deal from them to manifest them. They may have a gift for delving deep into the inner workings of the bodies or minds of humanity, such as a surgeon or psychologist may do. They may feel called to deal with people in crisis, such as someone who works at 911 dispatch, a suicide hotline, or on the front lines as an EMT. Whatever their calling, they may find they have an inclination toward work that is taboo, dark, or difficult in nature in order to uncover mysteries, seek out truths, or heal deep wounds.

Because Pluto often represents deep-rooted fears, the tenth house journey may be particularly difficult in some ways. There may be a love-hate relationship with fame, prestige, or success as it is perceived and measured by society. The conscious fear of failure may be super-seded only by the unconscious fear of success, which can potentially cause self-sabotaging behaviors to arise from self-doubt or second thoughts about one's goals. The sign will point to the nature of these fears; for example, Pluto in Virgo may be vulnerable to suffering more from self-doubt or chronically feeling underprepared and thus not ready yet to face the world, while Pluto in Libra may have difficulty committing to one path and closing other doors in the process. The facing of deep fears and healing that the person with Pluto in the tenth house must do will lie along these lines.

ELEVENTH HOUSE: HOUSE OF THE WORLD

In the fourth house you find your family; in the seventh house, your best friend, spouse, or coworkers. In the eleventh house you find, well, everyone else. The eleventh house represents the territory in which we interact with humanity at large, such as the various communities we find ourselves in, and often specifically in the ways we find ourselves identified with social peers or groups. Any groups you may associate yourself with, whether in person or in abstract, through one or several outlets, takes you into the eleventh house terrain.

Community is not just a word for the neighborhood or town in which you live. The word community is derived from the Latin word for fellowship, *communitas*, which is in turn derived from *communis*, meaning common. When you gather together under the banner of a shared cause, interest, or even something less intentional such as a shared physical characteristic, a town in which you happened to grow up, or a school you attend, you are in the eleventh house. Church congregations, identification with a certain political party, a knitting club, a pottery class, or Alcoholics Anonymous—these and thousands of others are examples of the way we *affiliate* ourselves with others whom we may have no real personal knowledge of otherwise. Thanks to the modern technological age, communities can form easily from all over the world in a common digital space.

The eleventh house, while inherently socially defined, does not belong solely to extroverts. We all have natural membership in a variety of groups whether or not we realize or act on it. Live in a community, large or small, and you are affected by eleventh house matters. The social nature of the eleventh house isn't about enjoying company or alleviating loneliness like you would by calling up a friend for a chat, but seeing yourself reflected in the world around you, and even finding your place in it.

A sense of belonging is not just a shallow quest for popularity but is of vital importance to one's overall well-being. Humans seem to be hardwired with a sensitivity to whether we belong or not, perhaps because to be outside of the shelter of the group could be quiet dangerous in ancient times. Although individuality is praised and admired in Western society, no one is immune to the very real pressure to play by society's rules or suffer sometimes extreme consequences. Whether we personally identify with others on this large scale or not, we can still be heavily influenced and affected simply by whether we feel we belong somewhere, anywhere.

In her book *The Gifts of Imperfection*, author and researcher Brené Brown illustrates a clear difference between belonging and simply fitting in. "Fitting in is the greatest barrier to belonging," Brown says. "Fitting in, I've discovered during the past decade of research, is assessing situations and groups of people, then twisting yourself into a human pretzel in order to get them to let you hang out with them. *Belonging* is something else entirely—it's showing up and letting yourself be seen and known as you really are—love of gourd painting, intense fear of public speaking and all."

Both issues, fitting in and belonging, are the domain of the eleventh house. Whether we respond to peer pressure to avoid shame, ridicule, and exclusion by going along with the crowd or we reach out to others and contribute to the creation and sustainment of an inclusive community, we are acknowledging the part of us that is human and longs for others of our kind.

The term peer pressure may take us back to high school, but the realities of peer pressure and its potential effects exist at any age. This pressure is integral to the experience and can serve positive or negative ends. Social support groups too numerous to count are formed every day to provide information, help, and encouragement to those trying to reach their self-improvement goals, and the effect on personal success rates has been proven. Likewise, social pressure within communities to do something one wouldn't normally do is common, from the relatively small but intense scale of high school, the herd mentality, and group think to the large and powerful effect of the mob mentality and the anonymity that the cover of the masses affords. When people band together in cooperation, great and terrible things can be accomplished.

The social nature of the eleventh house and the sign and planets here indicate the kinds of groups and communities we may find ourselves most aligned with, whether by choice and intention or happenstance—the kind of people we might call "our people," identifying and allying with others in some way. The sign and planets here can also reveal the nature of the triumphs and struggles we may have with fitting in and/or cultivating a sense of belonging.

Everything about the eleventh house is broad in scope. The breadth of this terrain includes not only large amounts of people but large amounts of time as well—specifically the expanse of the future stretching out before us with its infinite possibilities.

When we think about the future, whether we are setting goals or simply daydreaming about the possibilities, we are projecting our consciousness ahead while remaining firmly rooted in the present. If we focus only on the future or only on the now, we will be unable to see where today's actions will lead, either sacrificing our future to eat, drink, and be merry today, or escaping into fantasy about a future that we may never reach if we are not on the path today that will lead us there. If we want to become an accomplished pianist, an author of a prized novel, or the parent of a happy and healthy adult, these things take time to develop and mature and are, in part, eleventh house experiences. If we want an ice cream sandwich, well, that's probably firmly in the "now" of the opposite fifth house.

From this perspective, the sign and planets in the eleventh house may, to some extent, indicate the attitude and approach someone takes toward the future, and the nature of the goals and daydreams they most often entertain.

These topics—the future and groups, time and people—are not as disconnected as they seem if we consider the scale of eleventh house matters. Beyond personal goals, the eleventh house involves activities and goals that cannot be accomplished by just one person and require cooperation not just of people but of generations of people over time, such as the collective legacy left by a generation that serves as a necessary foundation for the next generation.

Community (people) + tradition (behaviors sustained over time) = culture. The shape of the culture one lives in is deeply carved into the psyche of every individual who lives within it (even when one attempts to live outside of its grasp), and it is through the cultural context that we relate to the world at large.

Eleventh House Emphasis

People with many planets in the eleventh house are likely to find themselves called to participate in the world in some significant way. Humanitarian beliefs, social outreach, or political activism may be major arenas that motivate them, although activism is only one potential outlet and will depend on the sign and planets involved. They may also be moved toward community participation; from PTA meetings to volunteer work to neighborhood celebrations, they want to share in the community in which they live. Casual or formal studies in social work or social psychology may also interest them.

In a chart less inclined toward social input, it may be the issues and not the people that draw them out, or they may find alternative ways to engage with the collective, such as online communities. Still another possible outlet may be work that involves a lot of customer or client service. Whatever outlet they choose (or chooses them), it is the outer world and their place in it that represents rich territory for them.

Depending on the sign and planets at work here, this person may have a tendency to be constantly thinking about what's coming around the bend, whether in an ambitious, goal-oriented way or an anxiety-filled way, or somewhere in between. They may excel at seeing the larger connection between events and people, and understand better than most how one thing leads to another.

Keywords Revisited

This classic house of friends does not necessarily refer to friendship in the way we think of it in modern life. Although dependent on context, the word friendship usually refers to a one-to-one relationship that is at least personal enough to single a person out from the nameless and faceless, and that kind of relationship is governed by the seventh house, for the most part. Words like allies, peers, or social network tend to connect more with the meaning of the eleventh house. This is friendship on a larger and less personal scale, where we find connection with groups of like-minded people with whom we might share beliefs or interests.

"Hopes and wishes" is a vague but common phrase also associated with the eleventh house that needs some clarification. With its correlation to the future and things that develop over time, your hopes and wishes are about what you want in your future, and the phrase can just as easily be reworded to your "five-year plan." To some extent, when we are projecting our consciousness outside of now and into the future, we have entered the eleventh house.

Eleventh House in Action

Jupiter in Capricorn acting through the eleventh house will indicate someone who tends to be enthusiastic about the future and forward-thinking. The desire to explore new territory and reach for one's potential can easily be made into a concrete, step-by-step plan toward goals in the grounded sign of Capricorn. The person's desire to grow will be tempered, but not overruled, by Capricorn's practical style; they may frequently run scenarios in their head to see how things are likely to play out before committing to a course of action. Networking and other eleventh house social activities will typically need to have an underlying purpose to them, in a way that furthers the person's goals or fulfills an obligation.

TWELFTH HOUSE: HOUSE OF SPIRIT

Of all the houses, the twelfth house is the most otherworldly, encompassing the activities we do that take us out of the mundane world, whether it be into our minds through imagination, transcending ourselves through meditation or a search for the divine, or physically through removing ourselves from the routines of daily life. Everything from astral projection to Zen meditation can be found in the twelfth house, but twelfth house experiences have one common thread: an element of the mysterious and ethereal.

Real-world acts or rituals are often performed as symbolic representations of spiritual change or rites of passage. While in some cultures and ancient stories, grand acts can seem difficult to relate to, in modern, urban life, acts like these are still performed every day, some commonplace and some more extreme. Religious ceremonies and rites of passage like baptisms and vision quests are all attempts to acknowledge the divine and refocus our consciousness inward, upward, or otherwise "elsewhere." Even prayer, formal or informal, directs our consciousness from what is in front of us toward an intangible direction. The realm of the twelfth house often takes us deep into the surreal, symbolic, and spiritual.

Although many spiritual acts are done through rituals and rites outlined in various religious doctrines, it is the transcendent, altered state of being that is the twelfth house component. The "rules" that govern the structure of religious practices lean toward ninth house activities, and many rites of passage also involve a pilgrimage of some kind, relating to the ninth house terrain of travel. Also, many rites are performed for the dead, cross-referencing the eighth house territory, or are performed for one's ancestors, which can even stretch into the fourth house realm. Overall, the twelfth house embodies the part of these activities that *removes* us from the mundane world and offers *transcendence of consciousness.*

Remember when Alice fell down a rabbit hole and it opened up into an entire world? Removal from the world can be deliberate or unintentional, healthy or not. Sequestering oneself to gain a new perspective or to seek spiritual, emotional, or physical renewal is not unheard of. Ancient stories are full of examples where someone leaves everyday existence to enter a mystical, supernatural place, hopefully bringing something back with them, such as a gift of knowledge to share or simply a change within themselves. These experiences often go hand in hand with the spiritually motivated rites and rituals just described. When we need time away, either for rest, rejuvenation, transition, or inspiration, the twelfth house beckons.

Although the twelfth house realm can see us sequestered from our typical daily existence, we are often compelled to find ways to bring it into the ordinary world since we are physical beings living a physical life. Escaping from the world can be healthy and sometimes necessary, but when escapism becomes chronic, motivated not by a need to recharge or regroup but by a desire to avoid life's complications and sorrows entirely, haunting our own life. Ideally, removal from the world allows us to fill ourselves up when the world exhausts us, but we are also susceptible to simply drifting numbly through life like a ghost as the world passes by. Any vice that we use for pleasure can certainly be overdone to self-destructive ends, but in twelfth house fashion, a desire to retreat can lead to self-annihilating behaviors in extreme cases, such as what happens with drug and alcohol abuse. Altered consciousness isn't always necessarily transcendent or uplifting.

From time to time, we may also find ourselves in twelfth house experiences that are unlooked for, from the commonplace but seemingly outside-of-daily-reality feeling we may get when attending a funeral or during a stay in a hospital. Although twelfth house experiences do not necessarily involve death, its status as one of the ultimate mysteries often makes it ever present in many twelfth house experiences. Indeed, the twelfth house also governs paranormal experiences due to their status as unexplained phenomena, such as encounters with ghosts or sensing a spiritual presence.[22] Even the experience of our own soul, spirit, or consciousness, no matter what it is that we believe animates the core of us, is an ultimate mystery that astrology places in the twelfth house.

When we escape from the world, we typically do so alone. Solitude isn't the purpose of twelfth house activities, but it's often an ideal incubator for them. Isolation can help us focus, refresh, or commune with spirit or nature without distraction, and in that sense can be sought out and desired. Solitude may not even always be invited or desired, however, as the twelfth house experience with solitude may also be a sense of loneliness if circumstances force our withdrawal from everyday life in some way or for some time, either physically, mentally, or emotionally. However, the twelfth house does have an element of community to it that is more subtle than the obvious social implications governed by the eleventh house.

In many ways, over time, people have speculated about the connectedness of humans, not just through genetic similarities but through psychic links as well. Carl Jung proposed one such idea through his concept of the *collective unconscious*, a shared reservoir of archetypes that we all draw from and that inherently resonate inside of us because we are all human. Because of this shared inheritance, humans have access to a depth of experience and understanding that lies outside of our individual experiences, where we can tune in to primordial images that run deeper than our intellect can even articulate. There is a collective attunement and consistency that we can easily see when we consider myths, legends, and stories, and how similar characters and themes appear even if the details vary in each new tell-

---

22. Although the eighth house is often associated with death, the eighth house governs death in the sense of loss and ending, whereas the twelfth house governs the realm of mystery and experiences beyond death or outside of the strict definition of death. There is some overlap, however.

ing. Plato's concept of the *anima mundi*, the world soul, also expresses the sentiment that we are connected through unseen channels. This felt-but-unseen connection lies within the twelfth house, because of both its mysterious quality and its invisible nature.

This idea of soul unity, of unconscious connection between humans, underlies some explanations of what can prompt us to empathize with strangers or to perform acts of kindness and charity toward people we don't know. When we encounter and respond to the humanness in others, our own humanness is reflected back. Twelfth house experiences impress upon us a sense of awe at the vastness of the world or universe but simultaneously contain the sense that we are also all one. Although we may identify and attempt to define our understanding of these experiences, the conscious realization of this connectedness is not a requirement to experiencing it.

The twelfth house terrain, while encompassing a multitude of possibilities to enter a spiritual frame of mind, is not inherently divine or religious. The seeking out of God is only part of a larger scope of possibilities to encounter that which is mystical or unexplained. Presently, there seemingly exists a divide between those who look to scientific means to explain the world around us and those who seek answers from paranormal or spiritual sources. The twelfth house does not play favorites in this way, however; the experience of wonder when encountering the mysterious is just as open to the study of quantum physics and black holes as it is to unidentified flying objects and psychic phenomena.

Some twelfth house activities are not even necessarily intentional. When we dream while sleeping, a twelfth house phenomenon, it is not an act of intention, but something that happens unconsciously, which can take us into a rich experience that may be part wish, part fear, part imagination, or something else entirely. Twelfth house experiences often draw us into situations that come unbidden and lie out of our control. Any of the twelve houses can have an element of this. For example, in the second house we make and manage our money, but we may acquire money we didn't ask for or know was coming. In the seventh house, where we learn to compromise and share, we are still vulnerable to the whims of our partner to a certain extent. In the twelfth house, we are often challenged or forced to surrender to what is happening because it is bigger than us, whether it's because it's out of our control or because we must relinquish conscious control to fully experience what the twelfth house has to offer. The saying "let go and let God," although it has specific spiritual implications, is an illustration of this sentiment. There are many common experiences in which letting go is not only encouraged but is helpful in experiencing something more deeply or pleasantly. When we meditate, we must not hold on to or follow our thoughts, but let them come in and come out, experiencing what is outside or between them to fully enter a meditative state, for example; we withdraw control to experience something more fully.

Because the twelfth house contains experiences that seem to be greater than us, these experiences are often accompanied by a sense of overwhelm. Whether we are overcome by emotion or gratitude, swept up into circumstances beyond our control, or find ourselves the victim to something or someone, the twelfth house contains a theme of surrender. Sometimes surrender can be a positive experience, as outlined in some previous examples, but negative victim experiences are also unfortunately all too common. The twelfth house experience is often what we learn or experience that we wouldn't choose but that can enrich us all the same, or at least have its place among the experiences that steer the course of our lives.

Twelfth House Emphasis

Those whose natal charts have a twelfth house focus may constantly find themselves straddling two worlds. Because the physical, three-dimensional world is so immediate and deliberate in its effect on us, an intangible longing for the world unseen and imagined may be a constant companion for twelfth house people, as that world is far less represented than the physical world. They may sometimes seem distant or distracted as if part of their consciousness is focused elsewhere, and indeed it may often be, as their inner world constantly whispers for their attention. They may seek out activities and experiences that nurture that connection, either seeking escape into it and/ or outlets that enable integration of the two worlds, seen and unseen, reality and magic, united. They may seem to be overwhelmed more easily than some.

Keywords Revisited

The twelfth house boasts some ominous keywords, perhaps only second to the eighth house, whose headliner is often death. Self-undoing has been an enduring keyword, in addition to suffering, sorrows, and hidden enemies, making this house seem like somewhere you don't want to visit!

Most of these negative references stem from the idea that the twelfth house contains things that we cannot see and, by extension, cannot control, prove, or understand easily. The theme of surrender also runs through this house, as illustrated previously, and this is not often easy. We often try to avoid things that are hard to control, understand, or bear. Whether we push our needs or sorrows out of sight purposefully, out of necessity, or out of a lack of awareness, what is unseen in the twelfth house may often surface in indirect ways. Planets here must be led to healthy outlets or unhealthy expressions may tend to crop up unexpectedly, sometimes as a result of our own suppression or starvation of the planets' needs. What we ignore or deny about ourselves often comes back to bite us, and these unaddressed blind spots may occasionally be experienced in the context of fate or karma, also associated with the twelfth house.

Twelfth House in Action

Someone with the Sun in the twelfth house may seem to be a paradox. The Sun symbolizes the condensed center of self, but the twelfth house is an expansive terrain where we engage in activities that encourage us to surrender the sense of self into a whole or to expand beyond the boundaries of our individual identity. Much of what sustains and energizes a strong and united sense of self for them is not easily obtained in the everyday world. In many ways, they may often need to retreat from the world to reconnect with their sense of center and wholeness, making getting away from it all not just a luxury, but a necessity.

A person with a twelfth house Sun in the objective and independent sign of Aquarius may find that their sense of well-being is almost wholly dependent on an acceptance of themselves as a unique being—sometimes as a misfit, isolated and misunderstood, and sometimes as a pioneer, walking freely and bravely between the worlds, participating in the world but never satisfactorily defined by it. Finding their place in the world may not be easy, for they are never off-the-rack personalities.

A person with a twelfth house Sun placed instead in the grounded and practical sign of Taurus will be challenged with bringing the otherworldly and physical together, finding a real-world outlet for their otherworldly longings in order to maintain a sense of wholeness. This person is seeking a sense of peace that can only be drawn from the spiritual, yet to keep their feet on the ground they must couple it with the corporeal. Activities that are equipped to combine the two, such as yoga or nature exploration, can be clarifying and sustaining.

While the twelfth house signals the numerical end of the list of houses, a circle is unending. The twelfth house is the end of the journey through the twelve houses but also the gestation or pre-life experience before the new birth of the first house. The houses represent separate areas of life but can also be understood as a whole cycle, just as a child is born (first house) and begins relating to and participating in their small world, branching out into the larger world as they grow. This continuous cycle of houses becomes more apparent and rich when studying astrology and the future, or how we change with our charts. Consult the recommended reading section for further study sources.

SECTION THREE
CHART INTERPRETATION

CHAPTER 9
THE BASICS OF CHART INTERPRETATION

In section one, you learned how to phrase an astrological sentence, such as "Mercury in Virgo in the twelfth house." Now you will learn how to decipher the meaning of these sentences.

The most basic process of interpreting a natal chart is straightforward enough at first consideration and may look something like this:

Start with any planet in the natal chart. Contemplate the range of possibilities of that planet's meaning. What need or urge does this planet represent?

What style and characteristics does the planet's sign embody?

What is the area of life represented by the planet's house and what kinds of activities tend to take place in that house?

Integrate the meaning of the planet with the sign's meaning. What does it mean to have this need (planet) fulfilled in that style (sign)?

Integrate that combination into the house meaning. What does it mean to have this need (planet) fulfilled in that style (sign) in that area of life (house)?

Repeat this process for all the planets.

This process may be simple, but it's not always easy. Each astrological sentence is a simple statement if taken only at face value. "Mercury in Virgo in the twelfth house" is as straightforward as "Jane walked quickly to the store." This sentence gives us information, but it can tell us so much more if we are able to infer and tease out what lies behind it. Without context, we could only guess at why Jane was walking quickly to the store, what she was wearing, whom (if anyone) she was with, what she did preceding her trip, or what she intended to do afterward. However, our astrological sentences contain this depth, waiting to be laid out, and that is what you must do. You must take each astrological sentence and discover the story contained within. Sometimes leading questions, varying techniques, and examples can help you explore the archetypes and weave them together. The rest of this book will be focused on helping you do just that.

Making chapters out of these simple planetary sentences is your first step, but you'll also need to integrate those chapters into the novel that is the entire natal chart. When you begin interpreting a natal chart, you will need to consider each planet in its respective sign and house *in isolation* in order to fully explore it. Only after you have understood the range of each ingredient can you start to understand the whole, blending them together to create a richer, more subtle and complex interpretation that reflects the reality of the human it belongs to. Take them on their own at first. Complete the chapters thoroughly. Then move on.

After compiling all these planetary sentences, you'll have a lot of isolated and sometimes contradictory pieces of information. While each planet, sign, and house has its own range of meaning, putting the ideas together and letting them mix is what creates a story of a life. Each planetary voice in the chart has its agenda, but it must act within the whole. Some voices are in competition with each other, while other voices sing in chorus. If you've ever experienced an internal conflict, you have already seen this in action: you want two different things and must find a compromise if you cannot do both! In order to be sane, you must take those voices/needs and arrange them according to priority, your own personal hierarchy of needs. This is the organic (though simplified) way we all work out internal conflicts. These conflicts will be reflected in the natal chart, and you will see them as you start to integrate all the planetary sentences into a big picture.

This is the basic process to get to your goal: cohesive integration of the meaning of the symbols in a natal chart. You'll learn a variety of tips and techniques to enhance your skill and deepen your understanding from here on out. One of the most important ways to blend these planetary sentences is by understanding and using *aspects*. Aspects trace the lines of direct relationship between planets and will help tighten the threads of meaning you've begun to create.

CHAPTER 10
THE ASPECTS

Recall that the natal chart is a wheel, divided into 360 degrees, with each sign occupying a range of 30 degrees. Planets may fall anywhere in the chart, and their coordinates are defined by the degree (and minute) number with a 30 degree sign in the chart. A planet that has recently entered Virgo might be at 1 degree and 33 minutes of Virgo (1°33'). A planet that is halfway through the sign of Aquarius may be somewhere around 16 degrees and 13 minutes (16°33'). Planets that reside in the same place within their respective signs form a particular geometric angle when a line is traced between those two planets. These angles are called aspects.

Just as a two-dimensional map represents a three-dimensional geographic landscape, a two-dimensional astrology chart represents the three-dimensional sky. When we see planets and other heavenly bodies in a chart, the distance between the earth and those planets will vary, but the two-dimensional chart will not represent this. If Venus and Pluto were both in the section of sky we call Capricorn at the time of our birth, our natal chart will show Venus and Pluto seemingly very close together, although they are physically separated by billions of miles. They may even be so close together from our viewpoint that they seem right on top of each other (something we call a *conjunction*), but obviously they are not colliding in space. If we could see them both in the sky with the naked eye, we would not be able to perceive the depth of their distance from us, only the width between them.

An aspect is a type of relationship between two planets. If each planet in its respective sign and house represents a part of you, then the aspects are what connect those parts together, tracing how they interact inside of you. The type of angle/aspect between two planets will indicate how well these two planets' style and purpose work together. No matter what the aspect, two planets linked in this way will have an effect on each other that cannot be escaped, whether it's seamless and comfortable or a source of internal conflict. To understand the function of planets in your chart fully, you'll need to understand how they interact with each other via these aspects.

HOW TO SPOT ASPECTS

The aspects in a chart can be recognized simply by reading the "map" of the natal chart visually. A conjunction between two planets will visually be represented by them being immediately next to, or practically on top of, each other in a natal wheel. An opposition between two planets will be represented by them being found on opposite sides of the natal wheel. Visually, some aspects like these can be easy to spot. Others take a little more practice to pick out.

Using the basic principle you have already learned, that the chart wheel is 360° and each sign is 30°, follow one rule when determining the distance between planets and whether they are in aspect with each other: count *signs*, not *houses*. House widths can differ, but sign widths are always standard.

- Planets in conjunction are in the same sign (0°)
- Sextiling planets are two signs away from each other (60° apart)
- Squaring planets are three signs away from each other (90° apart)

- Trining planets are four signs away from each other
  (120° apart)
- Opposing planets are six signs away from each other
  (180° apart)

Work your way through a chart and compare each planet's position to the others to see if there are any aspects between them.
There is no particular planet you need to start with; just make sure
you check them all. You'll also want to include the positions of the
angles (at the very least, the Ascendant) and the nodes of the Moon.
This may seem like a big project, but you will become proficient at it
quickly, and it is essential knowledge that can take you deeper into the
chart's meaning.

1. Pick a planet to begin with, such as the Sun. Note its position
   in the natal chart, such as 22° Virgo.

2. Scan the rest of the chart and note if any planets, angles, or
   nodes are at 22° of their respective signs. Make sure to account
   for your chosen orb (we will cover orbs shortly); in this case,
   you could be looking for a planet that is 22° plus or minus 5°
   (so anywhere from 17° to 27°).

3. If you find a planet in this position, note how many *signs* (not
   houses) away it is from the first planet. If it is two, three, four,
   or six signs away, it is an aspect. Obviously if it's in the *same*
   sign, it's also an aspect, the conjunction.

4. When you find an aspect, note it in your aspect grid (which
   will be described in the next section). Remember that any one
   planet may be involved in more than one aspect.

READING AN ASPECT GRID

The aspects in a chart are usually numerous, so astrologers keep track of a chart's aspects using an aspect grid. When you compute a chart using an accurate website form or a computer program, an aspect grid will sometimes be supplied for you, but you can make your own for any chart. Figure 8 is a basic aspect grid, with the glyphs listed for each type of aspect and a few sample aspects to illustrate how the grid is used. In this example, we can see that Mercury and Mars are in square aspect to each other, and Mars and Pluto are in an opposition. As you go through a chart and make your aspect list, this grid can easily organize your work.

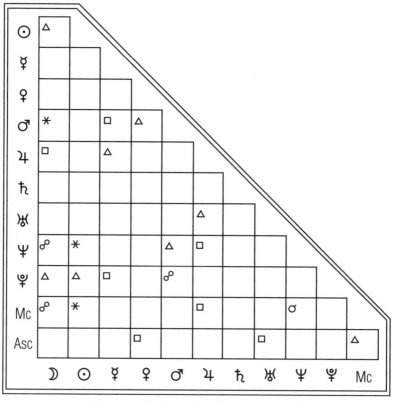

Figure 8: An Example of an Aspect Grid

ORBS AND DEGREES

Before you begin noting planetary aspects in a chart, there is one more idea that is essential to understand, and that's an orb. Orb is a term used in astrology to refer to the allowance of distance, measured in degrees and minutes, on either side of a planet before it makes an exact aspect to another planet—essentially, when two planets are "close enough" to making an aspect.

Each planet moves at a different speed, so at some point in their respective orbits around the Sun, one will pass the other, like cars in separate lanes on the same freeway. For instance, Mars takes less time to complete its orbit around the Sun than Jupiter does. Obviously Mars and Jupiter are in vastly different "lanes" and are millions of miles apart, but from our viewpoint on Earth they seem to glitter against the same flat backdrop of sky, each appearing to be a similar distance from Earth in our visual field. If Mars is moving through the sky on its way to catch up to Jupiter, it will be a conjunction when they actually do meet up. They'll both appear to be in the same place from our viewpoint on Earth, so they'll be 0 degrees apart. However, there is a time before and after that exact moment when Mars is quite close to Jupiter even if it's still technically 1 or more degrees away from it. This is still counted as a conjunction, even though it's not an *exact* conjunction. So if Mars and Jupiter are 3 degrees away from an exact conjunction to each other, then the *orb* is 3 degrees.

Astrologers vary one to the next in how much of an orb they'll allow in considering whether two planets are connected in aspect or not. The orb can also vary, depending on the planets involved or the nature of the aspect itself. Broadly, anything 5 degrees or less is typically considered an aspect by most astrologers in most cases. As you become more experienced in the subtleties of chart reading, you will probably form your own opinion about orb limits. There is one thing that most astrologers can agree on: the smaller the orb, the stronger the effect of the aspect.

ASPECTS, ONE BY ONE

Now that you know all about how to find and note aspects between planets in a chart, let's discuss what they mean.

The Conjunction

A conjunction happens when two or more planets occupy the same space in a natal chart. They are 0 degrees apart in the 360 degree wheel (give or take the consideration of the orb between them).

While each planet has its own purpose and represents a particular need to be fulfilled, planets that are conjunct each other fulfill their individual needs in the same style and with the same activities as each other. One doesn't take action without the influence of the other, for good and ill. You could say this is true for any aspect in a natal chart, as an aspect irrevocably connects parts of you together, and those parts will constantly trigger each other and partner with each other, so all planets in aspect are a package deal. However, the difference in the case of a conjunction is that the planets are made as similar to each other as possible in that they share the methods and activities that they employ to fulfill their individual purposes.[23]

If the Moon and Mercury are conjunct in a natal chart, there may be little to no separation between feeling and thought for this person. Feelings may not register in their awareness without the conscious expression or definition of them. They may not realize how they feel until they express it in words, and/or they may use words as a way to experience their feelings. They may find the most emotional support and comfort in words spoken by those they trust and love (as opposed to physical demonstrations of love or gifts, etc.). All these possibilities and more can be present with a Moon-Mercury conjunc-

---

23. Planets in a conjunction are in the same sign and house as each other in the majority of cases. However, there are instances where planets are conjunct each other but are in two different signs and/or houses. This happens in cases where one planet is near the end of a sign or house and the other planet is near the beginning of the next sign or house, technically "close enough" but crossing over a sign or house boundary. These are typically referred to as out-of-sign aspects, and their special qualities are discussed more fully in chapter 17.

tion. The sign and house will reveal more details on the specifics of how a conjunction may manifest in a person's life.

The Sextile

A sextile happens when two planets are 60° apart in the 360° wheel (give or take the number of degrees allowed for orb). Sextiling planets tend to work easily with each other, not because they have the *same* style, as with the conjunction, but because they have compatible styles that can bring out the best in each other.

Metaphorically speaking, two planets in sextile excite and stimulate each other, feeding off each other while the energy between them seems to not just flow well but escalate. If you've ever had a really great brainstorming session with a friend, where two heads were indeed better than one, you know the feeling: one suggestion sparks an idea, which sparks another idea, bouncing back and forth between each other as the ideas (hopefully) get better and better.

Mars and Jupiter in sextile with each other would create a comfortable, automatic link between the part of you that is prompted to action and the hopeful part of you that wants to reach new heights. While everyone has Mars (the urge to act) and Jupiter (the desire to grow) in their chart, when these two planets are linked in a sextile aspect, they may increase the likelihood that the person will act on their dreams and climb those heights.

The Square

A square happens when two planets are 90° apart in the 360° wheel (give or take the number of degrees allowed for orb). Two planets squaring each other can frustrate each other when their natural functions tend to get in each other's way. Sometimes planets in square aspect can bring out the worst in each other, like two people who are pleasant enough on their own but just can't get along together because they push each other's buttons unintentionally just by being themselves.

A square feels uncomfortable, like a constant internal conflict with a halting, stop-and-start feeling. As soon as part of you wants to express itself in a natural, easy way, another part of you trips it up before it can even get very far out of the gate. This may not always hold the expression back entirely, but it can result in a bumpy ride, with the actual end result sometimes looking very little like the intended action, or fraught with more detours and blocks than anticipated. This constant friction can be wearing and distracting, sometimes making the situation worse, but it can be used to polish the parts of ourselves in question, encouraging them to act consciously and strengthen their expression out of necessity.

If the Moon and Mercury are in a square relationship in your natal chart, this aspect can represent a challenge in expressing your emotional state in a satisfactory way, perhaps prompting a feeling of always being vulnerable to being misunderstood or rarely being able to clearly express your feelings without a lot of rephrasing or restarts. It may be easier for your mental processes to feel clogged or flustered when emotions are running high, making it even more challenging to communicate clearly. It may require you to take a break and calm down before communicating or perhaps take more time to work through understanding your emotional needs before your can communicate them.

The Trine

A trine happens when two planets are 120° apart in the 360° wheel (give or take the number of degrees allowed for orb). When two planets are trine, you enjoy a sense of easy flow between these two parts of you. They make sense to each other and fit nicely, like a tool fitting comfortably in your hand because it is the right size and shape. The two planets don't operate in the *same* style, as with the conjunction, and this aspect differs from the sextile in that it is not as excitable but is so comfortable it's hardly noticeable.

Because humans seem to be more motivated to take action when tension needs to be relieved versus when they're comfortable (the saying "if it ain't broke, don't fix it" being one of many examples), trines can be looked at as natural talents to enjoy and not think further about.

Acknowledging the trines in your chart can help you acknowledge talents that you may take for granted or assume that everyone has. Recognizing areas of natural ability gives you a head start in developing a general affinity for something into a full-fledged, polished skill. Nevertheless, left unchecked, a trine will continue to work for you.

It can be especially helpful to take this talent "inventory" because an awareness of your natural abilities can help you play to them and make you consciously aware of your internal natural resources when you need them, such as in situations or during periods of time when life isn't running so smoothly. Yet two planets working easily together doesn't always translate into beneficial things. Should you need to go outside of your comfort zone in the areas of life these planets touch for some reason, it can be difficult. Like grooves worn in a dirt road, it's very easy to slip into what you're used to. A trine aspect simply means there's less friction between the two planets, which can manifest as attaining desired results effortlessly or a resistance to walking off the beaten track.

If Mercury and the Moon are trine to each other in your natal chart, there will be an easy flow between the mind and heart. You may experience less trouble and even be somewhat gifted in your ability to express your emotional state, or any emotional topic, eloquently and precisely, and be more naturally able to find the right words. A person with a highly developed Moon-Mercury trine might develop and refine vocal, writing, or dramatic skills, should that be a chosen outlet for them.

The Opposition

An opposition happens when two or more planets occupy the exact opposite space in a natal chart. The two planets are 180 degrees apart in the 360 degree wheel (give or take the consideration of the orb between them).

Two planets opposing each other represent two parts of a person that may feel at odds with each other, contradicting each other or battling each other, each one sometimes trying to gain dominance but frequently caught in a tug of war or stalemate. This feels internally tense, and we may often feel indecisive or stuck in the area of our life that our opposition affects most directly.

This tension may be worked out in a number of ways. One way might be to try stifling one of those urges in favor of the other until the person can't manage to do that anymore and the other side erupts out of its suppression. Frustrated, the other part of them may flare up even bigger, overcoming the opposing urge by suppressing *it* and unwittingly repeating the pattern, just like a driver in a car swerving to miss hitting an animal in the road and then overcorrecting only to land in a ditch. After doing this a few times, the person may realize that this pattern is neither successful nor satisfying, but still feel the urges battling it out. Rather than acting them out blindly, they may decide to try to rein them both in, perhaps paralyzing themselves in indecision or hopelessness, stuck in a pattern that seems without a resolution after so many attempts resulting in disillusionment. In the example of Mercury opposite Mars, it could play out in one way as impulsive, trusting leaps of the heart that may take us off the sensible path, followed by attempts to get back on track and be a grown-up rather than fall prey to the whims of our heart like an impulsive child. Neither urge is wrong; they are simply at odds with each other.

Rather than pitting two sides of you against each other in a head-to-head fashion, an opposition can also reveal itself in the representation of two opposing needs that feel so vastly different that never the twain shall meet. The situations are essentially the same, with a feeling that resolution *seems* impossible, but rather than having a feeling of warlike internal conflict, it may have a tone of longing, maybe for an unlived life. Some of the gentler-seeming planets, such as Venus, Neptune, and Jupiter, may be experienced in this way when involved in opposition.

While it is not easy to manage the energy of an opposition, there are advantages to this aspect as well as ways to work with it. With an opposition you may feel as though you are constantly divided, yet it is this division that allows you to find a balance between the two urges that each side represents. The tension between the opposites is your clue. When you are indulging in or acting on a planet's need that happens to be in an opposition, the other part of you can start to feel deprived. When that part of you starts to become resentful or starts to long for that greener grass on the other side, the internal tension may rise. Resolution lies not in trying to resolve the conflict by silencing one of your internal needs but in recognizing that you need *both* in your life, even if *not simultaneously.*

An opposition we all partake in to some degree is the opposition between our Ascendant and our Descendant: the self and the other. We've all felt the tension between knowing what we want and wanting to please ourselves but also feeling an obligation to consider the desires of a person we care about. This is the very definition of compromise: we get a little of what we want, and the other person gets a little of what they want. When we have two planets in opposition in our natal chart, an *internal compromise* must be reached and continually revisited throughout our lives. It is the only way to ease the tension: by realizing that the tension is not the problem, but is only the warning signal; it warns us when we are out of balance, when we are favoring one side over the other a little too much (overcorrecting), and simply need to balance ourselves out again.

The Myth of Good and Bad Aspects

It's easy to think of aspects in terms of good and bad. Sextiles and trines make the good stuff happen, and squares and oppositions make the bad stuff happen—nice and simple. However, any planet-to-planet action, whether a trine or a square, represents two parts of you that trigger each other one way or the other, and to maintain sanity, you find ways to make that as comfortable and natural as possible. There is no use in saying you have a "bad" aspect, which only leaves you feeling like you are stuck with some kind of bad luck, or a "lucky trine," which robs you of the credit for your hard work or initiative.

Instead, think in terms of aspects that are comfortable or uncomfortable. This is not a misguided publicity campaign for the "bad" aspects, nor is it an effort to sweep any negativity under the rug; it is a practical suggestion. The comfortable aspects, such as the trine or sextile, feel good, and represent parts of us that work so well we don't even have to think about it. They are natural talents and easy alliances among internal parts of us. The uncomfortable aspects, such as the square and opposition, don't feel so good; they represent parts of us that are at odds with each other, egging each other on or tripping each other up.

Challenging aspects are sometimes easier to see in our lives because they represent a problem for us. We have to think about and pay attention to what is in conflict, at the very least so we can relieve the tension and feel better. With trines and sextiles, because there may not be any tension, it can be hard to see their effect because they don't need our attention; they work just fine on their own.

The comfortable aspects may seem more desirable, but a life of nothing but trines is a boring life, one with minimal challenges and minimal triumphs. The comfortable aspects are rife with undeveloped potential, maybe because it's typically only the squeaky wheel that gets the grease. It is human nature to ignore or take for granted what doesn't hurt or bother us. The uncomfortable aspects, while they don't feel good, are more likely to compel us to action than the comfortable ones.

Psychologist Carl Jung presented a framework of consciousness in a conflictual model that aligns with this idea nicely. He postulated that consciousness arises mainly when there are problems to solve, because they produce a tension in the psyche, which in turn generates creativity in an effort to solve the problem and relieve the tension. By the same token, if there is no problem to solve, no intrapsychic tension, then we act quite easily according to natural instinct, with no conscious thought required, which would interfere with or cause us to hesitate and second-guess the natural process. Therefore, according to this idea, it is conflict, with its tendency to generate creativity and create consciousness, that drives our evolution, whereas instinct keeps things running smoothly but somewhat passively overall.

As always, the sign and house that a planet resides in will be where the details and nuances lie; planets in aspect to each other will also bring their sign and house into the mix. The aspect will tell you how well these planets naturally work together in a natal chart, but the way the signs and houses mix will give you the full details about how and why.

Revisiting the earlier example with Mars and Jupiter in sextile to each other, consider a potential sign and house combination for each of these planets in a natal chart. Sextiling planets are always two signs away from each other,[24] so we could imagine these planets in Scorpio and Capricorn, respectively. A sextile will tend to bring out the best in these planets, so focusing on the way these signs are compatible can illustrate the ways a connection between these two planets are likely to play out. Mars in Scorpio represents a desire nature that is focused and tenacious, whereas Jupiter in Capricorn represents the urge to grow through practical means, by setting and achieving goals. Not only do these two signs share an ability to focus (although motivated by different reasons), but they can actually help each other: Scorpio providing the intensity of desire and Capricorn providing a strategy to turn deep desires into concrete realizations.

Grounding this example in houses, we might imagine Mars in Scorpio sextiling Jupiter in Capricorn from the second and fourth houses, respectively. The motivation to put oneself totally on the line when it comes to gathering and managing one's resources may work well with big, Jupiterian dreams of owning a home of one's own, for example.

ASPECT PATTERNS

Aspects are frequently connections between only two planets, but sometimes more than two planets are connected in a chart. This may be something as simple as a conjunction of two planets where both trine a third planet, for example. An aspect *pattern* involves three or more planets where each makes multiple aspects to other planets in the chart. They form a pattern, a circuit that goes further around the chart, one feeding into the next in a loop. These configurations can seem to dominate the chart because they tend to cover more territory

---

24. Not without exception. Read more about out-of-sign aspects in chapter 17.

visually and involve more planets. Some are rarer than others, and not every chart has a configuration, but to find at least one in a natal chart is not rare. As with aspects, a variety of potential configurations have been conceived. A few major aspect patterns are the T-square, the grand cross, the grand trine, and the stellium.

The T-Square

A T-square is made up of two squares and an opposition, which are all interrelated by involving the same three planets. Two planets oppose each other, and a third planet squares them both. The T-square is named because it makes a "T" across the chart. The top of the "T" is represented by the opposition and the leg by the squaring planet.

An opposition represents two parts of a person that are somehow in a stand-off or a push-pull pattern. This dynamic is also present with the T-square but the squaring planet adds to and simultaneously tries to release the tension that builds up between the two opposing planets. Just as with a typical square, lots of energy may be released with a T-square, but much of it may be released in futility, burning off the frustration in an attempt to relieve the internal tension. With an opposition, you can get a seesaw effect: the energy can only go to one side or the other. With a T-square, the stuck or frustrated energy of an opposition may be channeled out of the squaring planet, like lightning striking the highest tree because it was the easiest target.

The Grand Cross

A grand cross is made up of two T-squares involving four planets. All four planets square each other, and there are two oppositions between two sets of those planets, forming a cross through the chart when you trace the lines between each planet through the middle. The foundation of the oppositions can create a chronic core feeling of stuckness, where the tension is so balanced that it doesn't easily release but can crystallize and perpetuate itself in one's life. The conflicts can be intense, but so can the success of the results when one learns to harness and channel the energy effectively.

The Grand Trine

A grand trine is made up of three planets, all trine each other, which then form a big triangle across the chart when you trace the lines between each planet around the circle. Like the trines of which its composed, the grand trine harnesses the energy of each planet into a repeating, harmonious loop, which astrologer Noel Tyl refers to as a "closed circuit of self-sufficiency." The planets in a grand trine function so well together that they can bring a lot of benefit in the areas of the life in which they are active (via the signs and houses), but like the trines, they are also a grooved track on which the planets are used to expressing themselves. One may be skilled at thinking or acting inside that "box" but be averse to straying outside of those lines.

The Stellium

A stellium is composed of a bulk of planets (at least three) that are in conjunction with each other. Like a conjunction on steroids, planets in a stellium will tend to be powerful because they concentrate a lot of energy into one outlet: the sign and house in which they are found, uniting each planet involved as much as possible. A powerhouse of energy, for better or worse, may dominate the chart depending on how many planets are involved, making a strong mark in the life.

There are many more aspect patterns that have their own individual meanings, such as the kite, the grand sextile, and the yod. Entire books have been written on elaborate ways to interpret them (see the recommended reading for further resources on aspect patterns such as these). However, the important thing to remember is that each complex aspect pattern is truly understood by first breaking it down into its simpler components. A grand trine is made up of three individual trines between two planets. A T-square is two squares and an opposition.

Don't agonize over the complex patterns in a chart. While they are interesting, the core of interpreting them lies in the individual aspects that make up the larger configuration. Once you understand the pieces, you'll more easily make the leap of understanding into how they might all feed into (or fight against) each other.

CHAPTER 11
CHART THEMES

Interpreting planetary aspects is a fundamental technique for learning to blend and integrate isolated planetary sentences and chapters into a more complex story, but there's more still to consider.

ASTROLOGICAL THEMES

Humans can be quite complex and varied in the details of their individual stories, but humankind tends to play out and repeat a small number of issues as a whole. There's the guy whose life is shaped by the pressure he's felt all his life to live up to his father's expectations. There's the woman who is learning to find herself amidst all the cultural pressure about what it means to be a woman. There's the person learning the real value and meaning of friendship or love, and the other person who is learning to follow their spiritual purpose even at the sacrifice of their material comfort. A person's life is not meant to be devalued by such reduction, and these stories certainly don't reveal everything there is to each individual, but the human plight is the same at its core for us all and it shows up thematically. These stories reveal a theme—a central need, method, or purpose that seems to drive someone and that the person seems specially equipped for, both in their talents as well as the nature of their trials and lessons.

It is themes such as these that you are trying to uncover with astrology. A natal chart has many components and combinations, all of which can seem to have their separate meanings, isolated islands of planetary needs all jumbled together in one person. *A natal chart theme is a central idea of core importance that many of the individual islands of planetary meanings support and contribute to.* There can be more than one theme, but typically only one emerges—two at most— often one being a lesser or "sub" theme of the other.

IDENTIFYING THEMES IN A NATAL CHART

As you go through interpreting each planet, in its sign, in its house, you will understand one planetary need and how and where that person typically will get that need met. But it will be isolated, only telling you one tidbit of meaning about a person. Everything in a chart has multiple layers of meaning when you put them in the context of the rest of the chart.

However, each planetary island of meaning is not as different as it might first appear. As you compile and interpret these islands of meaning, eventually you may start to notice that you've repeated yourself. This is not likely to be a literal, word-for-word repetition as much as you'll notice you've expressed a similar idea in a few different ways or ideas that piggyback on each other. This is the first sign that you are uncovering a theme in the natal chart, which will start helping you tie ideas together.

An additional way to recognize a chart theme will occur as you gain a deeper understanding of each individual component in a natal chart and start to get an idea of how the components might amplify something else in the chart, causing it to be more extreme, or how it might cause an internal conflict.

Training yourself to think more deeply about the *why* behind each astrological symbol is the first step in training your brain to think more deeply about the connections between them, the ones that aren't as obvious, such as an aspect between them. If you know that a Virgo Sun's identity is based on feeling like they are useful and serve a purpose through offering their skills and that a Gemini rising's approach to the world is constant curiosity played out through asking and answering and asking more questions, and Mars in the ninth house reveals a motivation to learn and explore, then when you contain all of that in one person, it makes sense that one possible theme that begins to emerge is one of pursuing (Mars) learning experiences (ninth) in order to become more versatile (Gemini) and skilled (Virgo) at whatever one wants to become (Sun), and that drive will be of primary importance to the individual.

A theme can come from any combination of things in a chart and cannot necessarily be found by following the same formula every time. No one planet combination holds the key in every instance, but there are many techniques to help you uncover a theme, wherever it is found. The rest of this book will focus on techniques to do that and more.

What you learned in section two will provide you with all the building blocks you need to get started interpreting charts. In section three, you are taking the leap into advanced territory, but until you've mastered your knowledge of the basics, the complexity of a natal chart may continue to overwhelm and confuse you. Persist. Map out and analyze a lot of natal charts. Test what you know about a chart against the way people are living their lives and let it enhance your thinking. Although you may know the basics, you'll find yourself learning more and more about the components every time you work with them in a new way, and although the components are always essentially the same, every natal chart is an entirely new puzzle.

CHAPTER 12
CHART INTERPRETATION TECHNIQUES

The following techniques illustrate a variety of methods to use to begin analysis of a chart. These methods are starting points to help you begin to build a foundation of understanding about something essential in the natal chart from which to build the rest of your analysis.

Not all of these techniques will carry you all the way through the chart. Some are just leaping-off points, some more complete than others. Combining two or more techniques may seem overwhelming at first, and if doing so seems to lead to more confusion or contradiction, take a step back to keep from losing your way. When you are ready, combining techniques can yield a multifaceted view of a natal chart that will enrich your interpretation and offer a more complete picture.

It does not matter which technique you use, other than the importance of it being sensible and meaningful for you, given your personal philosophy and style of thinking. All techniques are simply different ways to start building an understanding of the chart as a whole rather than a mishmash of individual parts. Some will provide better support at helping you get at the theme of a chart; others may simply help you get your feet wet or discover a particularly important part of a chart.

There are a few factors that are high priority no matter what chart interpretation technique you use. It's important to keep these in mind,

but rest assured that you'll end up covering all of these once you delineate a natal chart to completion (assuming they are present in the
chart—not all are):

- The placements and aspects of the Sun, Moon, and Ascendant.
  These typically make up the bulk of one's personality.

- A stellium, if present. So much planetary focus on a sign or
  house will make that sign or house energy more dominant in
  a natal chart than that sign or house might otherwise be, especially if it's the Sun or Moon.

- Any planets conjunct the angles are often considered more po-
  tent than they might be otherwise.

- Any planet that is involved with a large number of aspects
  may have a dominating influence on the natal chart and in
  the personality.

WEIGHTS AND MEASURES

Typically, the deeper you dig in a chart, the more you are able to uncover the things that really matter in understanding someone. However, it's easy to get lost in too much detail by jumping in right away.
To gain perspective, sometimes a broader view (rather than a deeper
view) can help you spot significant patterns in the overall bigger picture of someone's personality. Taking stock of how a natal chart is
"weighted" can sometimes provide an overall picture that you can
keep in mind as you dig deeper into interpretation. This technique
is often a good one to start with no matter which method you use to
fully interpret a chart.

Without considering each planet in its individual sign and house,
think of their placements scattered across the chart like dots on a map
and observe the patterns they create. Are there more planets in one
quadrant of the chart than the others? Are there many planets in fire
signs but hardly any in water? These types of questions can be the broad
strokes when painting a natal chart picture. Understanding the weights

in a chart doesn't usually uncover the entire theme, but it can be a good foundation on which to build your interpretation going forward.

Each sign and house has an individual meaning but also shares some broad, simple things in common with other signs and houses. These commonalities are organized into categories listed as follows.

SIGNS

Dualities

The dualities divide the signs into two categories, which have had many different names over the years, such as masculine and feminine, positive and negative, or projective and receptive. The projective signs are Aries, Gemini, Leo, Libra, Sagittarius, and Aquarius. The receptive signs are Taurus, Cancer, Virgo, Scorpio, Capricorn, and Pisces. The projective signs have a more outgoing energy expression. They are more likely to *project* their energy outward into their environment than their receptive counterparts, which are more likely to draw energy inward (*receive*).

This is a very simple concept, offering only a broad baseline of a sign's natural energy flow, and is not to be confused with whether someone's overall personality is friendly or hostile, social or withdrawn, etc. Rather, the receptive signs are more likely to recharge their energy with experiences that are contained and focused, usually in environments that are more quiet and stable. The receptive signs are more likely to feel emotionally drained by noisy environments with too many people or too much activity. The opposite is true for the projective signs, which are more likely to be energized by environments that are stimulating and active.

Elements

The four elemental divisions are fire, earth, air, and water. Although each sign within these groupings has a different style, there are similarities that shine through their variances. Elements speak to the overall quality and tone shared between the signs.

The fire signs are Aries, Leo, and Sagittarius. While each of these signs has its own way of going about things, they all share a tendency to approach life with enthusiasm and very little hesitation, with the direct energy of *yes!* They navigate life with openness to new experiences and want to feel unencumbered, free to respond to whatever feeds that feeling of being alive inside of them. Aries likes to charge right after what it wants, Sagittarius lets the spark draw them wherever it will, and Leo lights its own fire, attracting others to its light, but they all draw on their passion to navigate life.

The earth signs are Taurus, Virgo, and Capricorn, and they share a common desire to keep things practical. They orient themselves around making and following through with plans and are more comfortable dealing with the management of resources and time that are a part of everyday living. Taurus likes to keep things simple and stable, Virgo likes to get into the details to keep everything working efficiently, and Capricorn likes to see and plan out the big picture, but they all navigate the material world sensibly and with fortitude.

The air signs are Gemini, Libra, and Aquarius. The air signs all share an orientation toward an information-seeking way of life. Their mind is their greatest asset, focusing their intellectual capacities through creative thinking and gathering multiple perspectives. Libra wants to know the other side's perspective, Gemini wants to know a little bit about every perspective, and Aquarius wants the unique perspective, but they all like to step back and think about things rationally and dispassionately.

The water signs are Cancer, Scorpio, and Pisces, and they share an emotional, subjective orientation to life. They navigate intuitively, sensing what's going on around them and inside of them, and acting on what they feel. As water shifts and flows in its natural direction, so do the moods of the water signs shift and flow as they respond to their environment. Cancer operates with a keen intuitive awareness of its internal tidal shifts, Scorpio reads between the lines to see what lies beneath the surface, and Pisces absorbs the emotional waves around them, but they all respond to the nuances of the unseen world, a vast well of information that lies outside the conscious realm.

Modalities

The three modalities are cardinal, fixed, and mutable. Modalities speak to the nature and rate of the energy moving within similar signs.

The cardinal signs are Aries, Cancer, Libra, and Capricorn. Cardinal signs are groundbreakers and initiators. They want to keep things moving forward, through the innovation of Aries with its eagerness to charge ahead, Capricorn's continual striving toward achievement, Cancer's urge to care for and establish shelter for itself and those it protects, and Libra's ability to reach across gaps and build a bridge between ideas and people.

The fixed signs are Taurus, Leo, Scorpio, and Aquarius. Fixed signs like to sustain what has been established, whether it's the security from a predictable routine for Taurus; the self-possession of dignified Leo, who will not be thrown off center by the demands of others; Scorpio's tenacious, single-minded focus on whatever draws its gaze; or Aquarius's ability to hold true to its own ideals, even against the tide of popular opinion.

The fixed signs excel at maintaining a status quo, whether material, emotional, or otherwise, to take the new growth that the cardinal signs create and give it form, stability, and a chance to plant roots. Their persistence allows them to achieve things and reach goals that other signs may not simply because they are willing to continue to build on something every day.

The mutable signs are Gemini, Virgo, Sagittarius, and Pisces. Mutable signs prefer to always be in some kind of motion, whether it's Gemini's shifting flow of thought, Virgo's striving to gain new ground through growth, Sagittarius's restless search for new experiences, or Pisces' intuitive and fluid adaptation to the emotional environment around them. The mutable signs are flexible and adaptable, yet, because of their need for movement, they tend toward restlessness and like to liven things up with change when they feel stagnant.

Although the houses also partake in these elemental and modal groups, it is the signs' natural membership in these groups (dualities, elements, and modalities) that tend to be more significantly applicable. Signs have a distinct style and tone to them, whereas houses encompass a category of activities that could embody any style and are essentially neutrally charged, without the overlay of a sign to determine the attitude with which those activities are undertaken.

HOUSES

Hemispheres

A natal chart can be divided into halves in a couple of ways, into both an upper (southern) and a lower (northern) half, or a left (eastern) and right (western) half. When a high proportion of planets are placed in one of these halves in a natal chart, certain overall tendencies may emerge.

If a natal chart shows planets placed predominantly in the lower half of the chart (including all the houses *below* the Ascendant/Descendant axis), it can indicate that, overall, this person's focus is more narrow and immediate, with their interests and meaningful activities experienced in their own corner of the world, so to speak. For them, fulfillment lies just outside (or inside!) their doorstep, with things like family, home making, creative pursuits and self-development occupying their days. When the upper houses are predominantly occupied, it can call a person to become more involved in activities that feel "out there in the world," with things like travel, social networking and activism, or professional development taking them far from home, sometimes literally.

Certainly this doesn't mean that someone with a majority of planets in the upper hemisphere isn't interested in their family, or a person with many planets in the lower section will never venture from their home. These groupings speak to an overall, general tendency, so the more heavily the planets are placed in one hemisphere over another, the more these differences become clearer. The signs involved in any of these cases will also have a lot to contribute in understanding how these hemisphere weights manifest specifically in one's life.

Similarly and just as subtly, a majority of planets placed in the western hemisphere is more indicative of someone who leans toward more adaptive behaviors, adapting to their environment and making the most of what they have to work with. Eastern-hemisphere predominance is indicative of someone who, overall, is more inclined to shape their environment to suit them. Again, the signs involved will have a lot to say in shaping how this reveals itself.

House Elements and Modalities

Elemental groups can be applied to the houses as well. The first, fifth, and ninth house activities have a fiery quality to them and are concerned with activities that are spontaneous and provide one with a sense of personal freedom. The second, sixth, and tenth houses have an earthy feel to their activities because they're concerned with practical, worldly, or material activities. The third, seventh, and eleventh houses resonate with the air element, being connected with activities of a socially connecting or intellectually stimulating nature, and the fourth, eighth, and twelfth houses resonate with the element of water, encompassing activities that deal with inner life on emotional and non-conscious levels.

Modalities also apply to houses, although they are often known by different names: angular, succedent, and cadent. The first, fourth, seventh, and tenth houses are angular (cardinal) and are concerned with activities that initiate, create, and direct. The second, fifth, eighth, and eleventh houses are succedent (fixed) and revolve around activities that are stabilizing and sustaining, with little fluctuation. The third, sixth, ninth, and twelfth houses are the cadent (mutable) houses, whose activities are more about growth or the influx of the new that enables a continual shift in perspective and experience.

Many other weight and measurement systems have been utilized by astrologers, including the Jones patterns and quadrant divisions. These are all attempts to define broad, overall strokes in a personality and gain a sense of the big picture about someone. Their importance can easily be overestimated, however, because while they can provide some overall color, you still need the fine lines and details of the specific planet-sign-house combinations to really see a true picture of a person.

APPLYING WEIGHTS AND MEASURES

Understanding each sign and house's membership in these categories can give you further insight into the style or behaviors of each. Knowing that Sagittarius is a projective, mutable fire sign can tell you that Sagittarius is energetic, flexible, and ready for new experiences. To apply these categories specifically to a chart to gain an overall personality perspective, count how many planets someone has in each of these categories.

It is important to remember that all the signs and houses are represented within *every* natal chart, even if there are no planets there. Everyone has access to these energies, but a person may be more highly attuned to one type of energy than another if they have a large number of planets placed in one more than the other. Therefore, using these groupings to understand the broad dynamics of a chart is typically most useful when there is a *deficiency or a predominance of any one particular grouping*. Someone who lacks any planets in the fixed houses might find routines and predictability in their lives difficult to maintain, preferring to start projects and finish or even abandon them when they start to feel too bogged down by them. Someone with a predominance of planets in fixed houses would be more likely to *want* that kind of predictability and to be nurtured, rather than stifled, by a predictable routine and seeing things through to their conclusion.

When there is a lack or predominance of planets in any of these groupings, the negative side effects, as well as the positive, are also likely to be more prominent than in the personality of someone whose chart is more balanced. A person with a predominance of fire signs may live life on the edge, with enthusiasm and confidence, but may also potentially experience backlash from naive or impulsive actions.

Understanding how each category interacts with the others can increase the effectiveness of this method. Any given sign, for example, is in three categories at once, and the combination tells its own story. Sagittarius, for example, is a projective, mutable fire sign, restless, dominant, and living on the edge of their seat in some fashion, whereas Taurus is a receptive, fixed earth sign, gentle, practical, and constant.

Questions arise almost immediately when compiling the weights and measures in a chart: does everything have an equal weight? What components should get measured? Although opinions vary, it's typical to consider just the planets (including the Sun and Moon), leaving out any non-planetary objects or calculated points, such as the angles or nodes. This will give you ten objects to measure. It is sometimes suggested to count the luminaries as a double weight because of their importance in a natal chart. If your intuition prompts you to do so, go ahead and experiment with it. Don't worry too much about which one is right. If changing methods tips the numbers slightly from one side to another, then it's likely that the chart is mostly balanced anyway and you may not get a lot of insight from it. If the difference between the numbers is vast, then it's likely that fact will shine through, even if you change methods and end up making that gap wider or smaller.

THE BIG THREE

The big three technique uses the Sun, Moon, and Ascendant as the foundation for the rest of the natal chart interpretation. Once you have a sense of the essence of these three planets in a natal chart, interpreting the rest of the planets can be easier, as they can be understood in the context of what you know about the big three already.

Begin with the Sun and think about its essential, neutral meaning. What human need does this represent? Then consider the sign the Sun is in. How does this person build a strong sense of identity? What types of characteristics are central to their personality? Next, consider the house the Sun is in. What activities foster and reinforce a strong sense of self? How does the sign's style factor into these activities? Get an in-depth understanding of the core meaning and needs of the Sun via its chart placement.

Repeat the process with the Moon. As you do this, keep the core meaning of the Sun's interpretation you just completed in the back of your mind. The importance of the Moon's individual meaning in its sign and house is significant, but it will also fall within the context of what you already know about the Sun. As you delineate the Moon's meaning, you'll start to become aware of the ways that the Sun's needs may cooperate or conflict with the Moon's needs, and how it might be to live with these two strong influences on the inside.

Finally, repeat the process with the Ascendant, keeping the essential meanings you've already interpreted of the Sun and Moon in the back of your mind, or, if that is overwhelming, revisit the whole after completing each piece's interpretation.

Once you have these three individual components, think further about how they might interact with each other, even if there are no specific aspects between them to force the question. How might someone with this sort of core personality (Sun) and that sort of emotional disposition (Moon) interface with the world most comfortably (Ascendant)? If there are aspects just between the three of them, fully consider the aspect and its nature, as this can be helpful to understanding the ways these three interact more fully.

Integrate these meanings as much as you can. Since there are a number of ways to express a planet in a sign and a house, think of multiple ways each of them might manifest; this can give you more to work with when you are integrating the Sun, Moon, and Ascendant together and starting to get a picture of the things that are essential to this person.

From here, extend what you know about the Sun, Moon, and Ascendant by considering planets that are in aspect with them, not just among the big three but throughout the chart. Sun trine Pluto? Moon square Mars? Consider the planet's placement itself as well as its impact on the Sun, Moon, or Ascendant. This will deepen what you have just learned and connect you to the rest of the chart. Once you have done this (or determined there are no aspects to the big three, a rare occurrence, but possible), you can pick any other planet or even angle in the chart to continue your chart interpretation.

Applying the Big Three: A Walk-Through

Consider this combination: Sun at 21° Aries in the third house, Moon at 4° Scorpio in the twelfth house, and a 19° Sagittarius Ascendant.

First, bring what you know about the Sun in general to the front of your mind. Write it down if necessary. The Sun is the central sense of self. The sign and house in which the Sun lies are the traits and activities that are of central importance for this person to build and reinforce a strong sense of identity. These traits and activities are, at least in part, what a person's self-confidence is built on.

Repeat this process with the sign in which the Sun lies: Aries. Aries as a spectrum of characteristics represents the power of assertion and drive, the instinct to discover new territory and to push oneself beyond what's safe. Competitiveness, impulsiveness, and impatience are all possible side effects of these traits.

Finally, review the types of activities in the third house experience: communication and learning by asking questions, absorbing information through a variety of sources, and a tendency toward lively activity—both through the Aries passion and the curiosity-quenching activities of the third house. This house encompasses the continual process of observation and integration of what one observes into what one already knows about the subject matter.

Integrate these ideas by connecting each of the dots in a variety of ways: This person's central identity (Sun) is built on the confidence that comes with conquering new territory, pushing and proving themselves to themselves and/or to others, to *act* in life rather than wait or stand back (Aries). These behaviors and needs may manifest most obviously in the way they communicate and learn (third house) and may indicate a high level of activity in general in their lives, especially since they tend to act with immediacy (Aries) on what they want. Potential pitfalls might include a tendency toward impatience and impulsiveness, especially focused on speaking (third) from the hip (Aries) before they've fully thought about what they want to say or how it might impact their audience. There is a potential that this person may lean toward argumentativeness or debate. Like most everything else, the likelihood of this argumentativeness potential manifesting will depend on the rest of the chart's disposition (such as where Mars, the planet ruling conflict, and Mercury, the planet of communication, are placed). There is no need to fully interpret these other planets now, but a quick glance at Mars and Mercury in the chart will help you determine whether their condition reinforces or disputes that conclusion. You can also leave this idea out as a potential and refute or corroborate it later when you begin integrating the rest of the planets into your interpretation.

Notice that the process of integration automatically narrowed down the possibilities in each spectrum. For example, Aries encompasses a wide range of possible expressions, from competitiveness, to a love of physical activity, to a courageous sense of adventure, to direct and sometimes brash expressiveness, to argumentativeness … the list goes on. But when we narrow the playing field to the terrain of the third house, we can see that most of the Aries expression is going to channel into behaviors that have to do with learning or communication, so while it's possible that this person likes to run the marathon every year or has made a career of mountain climbing, the third house placement presses you to narrow your consideration to things like the style of speaking, a potentially ambitious and off-the-cuff style of observing new information and forming opinions, and so forth. This narrowing process will be exponential as you integrate new symbols from the chart into what you've learned so far.

Moving on to the Ascendant, consider the function and role of the Ascendant in a natal chart. The Ascendant is the way one interfaces with the world at large and the people in it in a way that is most natural and instinctual.

The sign of Sagittarius represents characteristics that encourage expansion, whether of mind, body, or experience. Not just Aries, but all fire signs, seek the experience of feeling alive, and Sagittarius feels enlivened by new adventures; embracing the unknown is the best way to expand one's view of the world. Sagittarius's projective nature tends to encourage one toward casual friendliness.

The Sagittarius Ascendant person views the world in the sense of what is possible, with each day representing an opportunity to experience something new. They may not always be cheerful, but they lean toward the optimistic and positive and their flexible nature (being a mutable sign) helps them roll with the punches of whatever comes their way. They tend to appear friendly and easygoing to others overall.

Finally, consider the planetary need and role of the Moon. The Moon represents our need to feel emotionally safe and protected. The experiences that nurture us and, in turn, how we nurture others are represented by the Moon's location in the chart. The flow of our moods and the kinds of experiences that trigger mood changes are also governed by the Moon's placement. The Moon is our most vulnerable, private self and our most unconscious instincts.

The sign of Scorpio has a need for an intensity and authenticity of experience—nothing must come between it and the raw truth of something, even if it reveals something unpleasant or frightening about a person, experience, or life itself. It seeks depth over breadth and longs to be overwhelmed by experience while it also seeks to empower itself through raw strength and emotional courage.

The twelfth house realm encompasses that otherworldly terrain: when we dive into our imagination, get away from it all, or seek out experiences that take us into a spiritual or fantastical frame of mind.

Combining these symbols, the Moon in Scorpio person would especially have a depth of *feeling* that can be too intense for some, even themselves at times. Their *emotional* instincts are strong, sensing truths that are unsaid or ignored in polite society, and they may long to bring out in the open what they know lies beneath. To build trust with someone, they need to be assured of that person's loyalty and honesty, and will return it in kind; however, it can be difficult for a Scorpio Moon to be vulnerable, so they may be more focused on getting rather than giving the raw truth about themselves sometimes. With this Moon in the remote twelfth house, they may feel things deeply, but the ability to identify and express those feelings may be challenging, not just because they are self-protective but because their emotional responses may be an enigma even to themselves, which can lead to feeling emotionally isolated. They long for deep and transformative emotional experiences that cannot easily be experienced in everyday life. They will require a lot of solitude and periodic withdrawal from the noise of the world to stay attuned to their emotional body.

Not only have we integrated each planet in its respective sign and house, but now we have enough material to consider how these combinations combine with each other, further clarifying how each symbol combination is likely to express itself.

The Sun in Aries and a Sagittarius Ascendant are in a trine with each other. This gives us a head start on integrating these two symbols to form a cohesive interpretation. They both have a fiery way of approaching the world: in a direct manner, with enthusiasm, drive, and a sense of adventure. There is probably an overall vibrancy and action-oriented tendency in their personality.

The Moon is strikingly different in its style from these two, being in a water sign and house. Instead of the outwardly directed energy of the Sun and Ascendant, the Moon in Scorpio and the twelfth house are more concerned with the inner, private realm, such as the imagination, heart, and psyche. While it's an understandable idea to conceive that one's private or inner life and public or outer life are often in contrast, it is not always extremely so, as it seems to be in this case. This person may find it difficult to reveal, even to themselves, how they are truly feeling about something, because the subconscious nature of the Moon itself, further emphasized by the protective or secretive element of Scorpio and the removed terrain of the twelfth house, might make it easier for this person to express the obvious, outgoing elements of their personality because they have an immediate and direct way of expressing, whereas their true inner feelings may take time to rise to the surface. Those who know them may find it difficult to get close to them or know how they are truly feeling because of this "smoke screen," even if it's unintended. Their private emotional nature in contrast with the rest of a strong, outgoing personality may make it difficult for them to recognize when they need to retreat to recharge.

Note that in utilizing the big three technique, you don't have to review these three symbols in any rigid order. If it makes more sense to you to start with the Ascendant, do so!

The big three technique can provide you with a good understanding of the most fundamental parts of any natal chart. From here, you'll want to look for planets in aspect to any of these three symbols to continue your analysis. Begin by choosing which planet you'll analyze next. Then contemplate what it represents and how it expresses itself in this natal chart given its sign and house placement. Then *add that layer* to what you've already discovered so far about the chart. Is it similar to the theme you've started to uncover so far or vastly different? How does it "get along" with the Sun, Moon, or Ascendant that it's aspecting?

FOLLOW THE RULER

Every natal chart interpretation technique ultimately seeks to aid your discovery of the dominant themes in a natal chart, either by teasing out repeating patterns in a chart or by determining the strongest influences in a chart. The weights and measures technique sought to discover the dominant element, modality, and duality in the chart overall. Chart interpretation techniques that focus on planetary rulerships work by trying to establish a planetary hierarchy. One such method is featured here, but before we can get more deeply into these hierarchal methods, we'll need to fully understand rulerships.

Introducing Rulerships

Each sign has a designated planetary "ruler," a planet that is said to be able to perform its function with more ease when placed in the sign it rules, such as a king rules comfortably and confidently in his own kingdom.[25] You were briefly introduced to planetary rulers in the sign sections, which described correlations between planets and the signs ruled by them. Now we'll learn more about rulerships and their function in interpreting an astrology chart.

Although planetary rulerships started out as planet-sign correlations, rulerships have been expanded to include houses in modern use. The *astrological alphabet* pairs a planet, a sign, and a house together, as some of their meanings correlate with each other. For instance, Mercury, having to do with the mind (learning, thinking) and the voice (communicating, expressing), has a similar theme and motivation to Gemini, which wants to acquire and share knowledge. Together they share these things in common with third house activities, some of which are studying, communicating, and observing.

Here are the astrological alphabet combinations:

- Mars, Aries, and the first house share topics in common such as drive, self-focus, and initiation.
- Venus, Taurus, and the second house share topics in common such as comfort and pleasure, and a focus on worth/value.
- Mercury, Gemini, and the third house share topics in common such as communication, observation, and curiosity.

---

25. Although meaning has been drawn and synchronicities observed, the original designation of planets into the signs they ruled was not so oriented on the meanings of each matching up, so to speak, but set in a pattern of distribution, starting with the Sun and Moon and branching out from there. When planetary rulerships were distributed, each planet, aside from the Sun and Moon, ruled two signs, one diurnal (day) sign and one nocturnal (night) sign. For more on ancient astrology and rulership, see the recommended reading section at the end of this book.

- The Moon, Cancer, and the fourth house share topics in common such as home, nurturing, shelter, and the inner, emotional parts of life that stem from formative early experiences.

- The Sun, Leo, and the fifth house share topics in common such as self-expression, creativity, and playfulness.

- Mercury, Virgo, and the sixth house share topics in common such as a focus on the minutiae of life, whether it's analyzing an idea or working industriously on daily chores.

- Venus, Libra, and the seventh house share topics in common such as partnership and social awareness of the interpersonal variety.

- Pluto, Scorpio, and the eighth house share topics in common such as fears and wounds, issues that arise from our "psychic basement," and power (im)balances.

- Jupiter, Sagittarius, and the ninth house share topics in common such as expansion, far-reaching enthusiasm, and big ideas/experiences.

- Saturn, Capricorn, and the tenth house share topics in common such as duty, structure, and how one is seen by and participates in society.

- Uranus, Aquarius, and the eleventh house share topics in common such as working out belonging vs. individuality, recognizing and sometimes standing against the status quo, and the individual's role in the social world and community.

- Neptune, Pisces, and the twelfth house share topics in common such as the mystical realm, otherworldly experiences and desires, and spirituality.

You'll notice that some houses and signs share a ruling planet. Remember that before Uranus, Neptune, and Pluto were discovered and integrated into modern astrology, there were only seven heavenly bodies to divide among the twelve signs. This is another example of the multidimensional nature of these rich symbols to represent more than one idea. Some astrologers have suggested that some of the asteroids would be appropriate as rulers for some of these signs, such as utilizing Chiron as the ruler for Virgo rather than Mercury, for example. Only time will tell if this catches on in the astrological collective.

Using Chart Rulerships to Establish a Theme

The concept of rulership can assist in recognizing the themes in a chart. Everyone has only one Mercury, one Gemini, and one third house in their chart, but there are ways that these three components each might feature prominently in a chart, providing us with a potential natal chart theme. If Mercury is conjunct the Midheaven, for example, or Gemini is the sign on the Ascendant, or the third house is packed with five planets, we take note of their individual meanings. However, if *all* of these things are present in one natal chart, the astrological alphabet would help us to recognize that the common mental and communicative theme of Mercury, Gemini, *and* the third house would be dominating the entire chart, even though they would all retain their individual meanings as well. No matter what method of chart interpretation you utilize, recognizing these threads running through a chart whenever they are present is a key part of determining the overall themes present in a chart and is a hallmark of chart synthesis.

The astrological alphabet is powerful but must be used with care because an assumption can be inferred that each component of an astrological alphabet combo is fully interchangeable. While they share traits in common, Gemini is *not the same* as the third house, nor is Mercury placed in any house the same as having Gemini there. Recall the neutral nature of planets discussed in section two. Mercury wants to think, learn, and communicate, but it's not going to be inherently attached to a certain *style* of doing so until it's placed in a sign and takes on the agenda and characteristics of that sign, which may not be Geminian in nature. Mercury naturally rules Gemini, but if it's placed in Taurus, for example, this learning style wants to stay with a topic and work with it until it understands it enough to put it to practical use, possibly needing to be shown a hands-on example rather than just entertaining an abstract concept. This style is very different from the Geminian style, which would be more than happy to quickly absorb the concept and then move on.

Applying Rulerships: The Chart Ruler

Determining the chart ruler is fairly simple: the planet that rules the sign on the Ascendant is considered the ruler of the chart. Mercury rules a Gemini Ascendant, so Mercury is the chart ruler. Libra or Taurus rising? Venus is the chart ruler.

Because the Ascendant represents what you *lead* with, how you receive, respond, and act upon the world, the planetary ruler of the Ascendant is considered to be the ruler of the entire chart because it adds to the presence with which you approach the world overall. Our response (and the world's response) to our Ascendant can, in many ways, make or break the way we are received by the world, influencing things like the opportunities we are offered and the contacts we make. While the sign on the Ascendant informs your overall style of approach, the sign and house in which the chart ruler is placed can give additional information about the nuances of that tone and style, providing insight into the energy you seem to *embody*.

There is one exception to this method of determining the chart ruler, and that is a planet in close conjunction to the Ascendant itself. A planet conjunct the Ascendant is always clear and apparent in its influence on the way we instinctively present ourselves to the world. Although the planetary ruler of the sign on the Ascendant may be important in the chart hierarchy, it is typically the planet in conjunction to the Ascendant that takes center stage. However, the chart ruler can be in debate in some circumstances. If the planet ruling the sign on the Ascendant is a powerhouse in the chart, such as the Sun or Moon, and a planet conjuncting the Ascendant happens to have a wide orb, perhaps it would be more difficult to determine the chart ruler. It may be easiest to consider them both of elevated importance. Of course, if a planet conjunct the Ascendant also rules the sign on the Ascendant, then it's no contest!

One nuance to this condition, where the chart ruler is a planet conjunct the Ascendant, is whether the planet conjuncting is doing so from the first house or the twelfth house. It can be subtle, but if the ruler conjuncts the Ascendant from the twelfth house, the effect it has on the person's demeanor and style may not be as conscious as it may otherwise be, with the chart owner potentially less aware of how that planet colors how others respond to them. If the conjunction has a small orb, this differentiation may be too subtle to matter.

The Significance of the Chart Ruler

The importance of the chart ruler comes into play when you blend the meaning of the ruler with the meaning of the sign on the Ascendant. To begin, start with the sign on the Ascendant. Familiarize yourself with what it means and how it might look on a person who "leads" with the energy of this sign. Remember that the Ascendant symbolizes the need to present a face to the world that is a reflection of who we are, even if not in totality. It is our everyday socialized persona, the characteristics we embody and the techniques we employ when interacting with the world that allow our interface to be as comfortable for us as possible.

Think about the chart ruler's meaning and its core functions. Then think about how those functions are carried out via the agenda and style of the sign that the planet is in. Then layer on the possible behaviors and activities of the house that the planet resides in. When you have located the planetary ruler of the sign of the Ascendant and have integrated the meaning of the sign and house it acts through, add that to what you know already of the chart, which at this point will just be the nature of the Ascendant. Integrate its own meaning with the meaning of the Ascendant. What might it mean to have Virgo rising with Mercury, Virgo's ruler and therefore the chart ruler, in Libra in the second house? The Ascendant has its own solid meaning, but the nuances of your understanding of the chart will shift when you add different chart ingredients to it.

Consider the previous scenario, with Virgo rising and Mercury in Libra in the second house. This is someone with a no-nonsense manner who feels most comfortable with a sense of control as they approach the world. Inherent in Virgo is the need to grow and improve as well as the humility to recognize where they have room for improvement, so this person may have a modest or even self-effacing demeanor, not necessarily shy but preferring not to call attention to themselves needlessly. Virgo is also motivated by being useful, so they will feel most comfortable in new situations when they can figure out a way to put themselves to work and contribute in some way rather than just idly observing. They will want to be seen as competent and helpful. Virgo's critical eye for detail makes them good at problem-solving and spotting what needs to be fixed, so they may feel like they are constantly seeing and measuring the world by its flaws, which can bring out a critical, negative face and/or have the person feeling overwhelmed in situations where too much is going on, where there's too much potential for something to go wrong, or where it's too hard to control what's happening and how it happens. This can especially be true if they initiated the situation.

Mercury is Virgo's planetary ruler, so let's consider the possibility of Mercury in Libra in the second house. Mercury represents the function of communication and thought, the need to gather knowledge as well as express and share it, the way we learn and think, including the things we like to learn and think about most often. With Mercury placed in Libra, this person would gravitate toward a communication style that constantly adapts to consider the nature and personality of the listener. Someone may do this by inviting feedback and checking in frequently to see how the person listening is responding to the information as well as by taking care not to offend or discount the listener's point of view. A person with Mercury in Libra may be instinctively more aware of the social niceties and cues that go into a refined social interaction and will be more inclined to take the time to observe them with others. In their thought processes, this person would not tend to jump to conclusions too quickly, but would be more inclined to weigh different points of view and understand that there is always an alternative to every definitive opinion, even their own. With Mercury placed in the second house, there would be an emphasis on seeing the ability to think and/or communicate as a valuable asset, perhaps even naturally finding a vocational outlet for these skills. This person may find themselves frequently thinking about their financial situation and how to improve it or how to put assets to good use.

How does this fit in with what we already know of our Virgo Ascendant person? We know that the tendency toward thinking in utilitarian and practical terms may be further emphasized with Mercury in the second house of worth and resources. Virgo rising already has a desire to be useful in general, but with the chart ruler in the second house, there's even more emphasis on making the most of what they've got. There would be an enhanced desire to communicate ideas that are of worth and use in a mutually beneficial way, being in Libra, a sign focused on cooperation and teamwork. We can also see how the tendency to interact with the world in that no-nonsense manner, which can sometimes be off-putting to some if it seems too abrupt, might be softened by the Libran influence, with an aim toward considering how they are coming across to others and not necessarily always sacrificing amiability for efficiency.

Keep in mind that the chart ruler can add an interesting perspective to your overall interpretation of a natal chart, but as with the weights and measures technique, even at its most helpful it's only one component and will never supply the meat and potatoes of your interpretation on its own, as techniques such as the big three can do.[26]

---

26. Other techniques not mentioned here utilize this system of rulerships, such as tracing dispositorships to determine a sole or final dispositor, if any. It is the author's opinion that these techniques, while time-honored and worthwhile in their own right, often prove to be overly complicated for beginning students in comparison to the relatively small value they provide in chart interpretation from a psychological and spiritual perspective, so they are not included in this book. See the recommended reading section if you are interested in these topics.

FROM THE TOP

This technique is helpful in that it provides an orderly and thorough method of chart interpretation. To utilize this method, simply begin at the beginning, with the first house. The cusp of the first house is an important angle, the Ascendant, so start with developing a detailed understanding of the sign on the Ascendant and the role it plays in a natal chart when it's the style of energy a person leads with.

Next, consider any planets aspecting the Ascendant. To keep things orderly, isolate what you understand about that aspecting planet to the sole way it influences the Ascendant, rather than considering the aspecting planet in its entirety and the meaning of its own placement in sign, house, etc. Don't worry, you'll eventually come back to it.

From there, consider any planets in the first house (if a planet is conjunct the Ascendant, you may have already entered this step). What is the nature and purpose of the planet? How does it act through the sign and house? Then consider planets that aspect this planet.

From here, move on to planets in the second house and repeat the process through all the houses. If you feel so inclined, you can consider the sign on the cusp of each house if it contains no planets, but don't overestimate its importance in comparison to the planetary placements; planets are where the action really is. It should go without saying that you'll eventually come to the house and sign of planets that were aspecting planets you've already covered. When this happens, interpret the new planet thoroughly and then revisit its relationship to the planet you've already interpreted to get a solid and integrated understanding of the way these two planets interact.

If you are able, consider how each step is informed by and can be integrated into the meaning of the previous step. If that threatens to overwhelm you, keep these nuggets of interpretation isolated and work on blending them at the end of the process.

A pitfall in this technique is that it won't necessarily assist you in finding the chart's theme in a hurry. You can be sure you won't miss anything with this method, but you'll want to keep a diligent eye on overkill, so you don't start to succumb to the pressure of building an exhaustive encyclopedia from the chart, losing perspective and potentially missing the theme among extraneous data. It's only because of the thoroughness of this technique that you almost won't help but stumble upon a repeating pattern that leads to a theme, eventually.

NARRATIVE

If you prefer to just jump in and freestyle things, this method may be for you. In some cases this may seem like a more advanced method to utilize, not because it yields better results than the others necessarily but because there's less structure to depend on. This is essentially the method in which you follow your train of thought, skipping from one place to another in the chart in a way that intuitively makes sense to you.

Obviously, there's not a lot of detail to the "technique," here as each chart will lead you on a different path, but there are a couple of essential guidelines to this method that can help you get started. First, start wherever you feel most moved to begin, which may be different from chart to chart. What catches your eye? A stellium in a certain sign or house? An Ascendant whose sign you understand more easily than other signs? A planet on one of the angles? Start wherever that is, working with the planet, sign, and house. Then ask yourself what makes sense to address next. What kind of topics and characteristics have you been musing on and what topic (and its corresponding planet, sign, or house) does that naturally lead you to next? Think of crafting a narrative, the story of the person's life to whom the chart belongs, maybe not necessarily plot-driven, but character-driven. What makes the most sense to talk about next in the story?

While the narrative technique can be a way to start, it's an even more helpful way to end. No matter which of these techniques you use, you may have to catch the planetary stragglers that didn't make it into one of the technique "nets." Although this method seems like less of a method and more of a free-for-all, it's still important that wherever you start and wherever you go next, you continue to build on what came before to avoid a jumbled mess of disconnected, abstract ideas. Each step must provide a foundation or a context for the next step to rest on in order to yield an integrated, meaningful interpretation.

THE NODAL FOUNDATION

The nodal foundation method [27] of chart interpretation begins with the South Node of the Moon as a foundation for the rest of the natal chart interpretation and the North Node as a guiding principle that can help to balance the excesses of the South Node by learning new ways of perceiving and responding to life. Any planets in aspect to the nodes are also integrated into understanding the entire nodal structure. This structure puts everything else in the chart into a new perspective, highlighting the lessons and skills to be learned and practiced to enable someone to live their life to the fullest, and pinpointing behaviors and attitudes that might hinder growth. The nodes "bookend" the chart, providing a starting point (the South Node) and an endpoint (the North Node), with the rest of the natal chart territory between them, revealing how to get from A to B. This method will usually uncover the theme of the natal chart more thoroughly than any of the previous methods on their own; therefore, we will go into this method in great detail and keep a running example as we follow each step in the process.

Dual Aspects of the Nodes

This method analyzes the North and South Nodes, as well as any planets in aspect with them. Because the nodes don't stand alone, but lie on an axis, any planet aspecting one of them will actually always be aspecting

---

27. Although any astrologer who employs this technique must work with and add their own flavor to it, as I have done, the underlying structure of this nodal analysis technique has been largely pioneered by astrologers Steven Forrest and Jeff Green, under the banner Evolutionary Astrology, or EA (with individual variances). As the practice of the evolutionary astrology paradigm continues to grow, it has begun to represent more than an idea or philosophy, but also a set of techniques and procedures, some of which I've employed here. However, this book is not a definitive work on EA. Check the back of this book for extended reading on these methods.

both of them, even if it's not the same aspect; a planet trine the South Node simultaneously sextiles the North Node, for example. This method begins with a full, layered analysis of the South Node *before* any analysis of the North Node. This means that although a planet will be aspecting both nodes simultaneously, you will be working *only* with that planet's impact on the South Node first. Later in the method you'll revisit the same planet, but in the context of its effect on the North Node.

Any planets that aspect the North and South Nodes will have a dual or multifaceted purpose in the natal chart. Along with their typical, individual function in the natal chart, they will also represent a step in the process of the soul's journey from South Node to North Node. The technique of analyzing the nodes in a natal chart and using it as a foundation before beginning the rest of the natal chart interpretation has been referred to as the "chart within the chart" or the "chart behind the chart," because of the multiple layers of interpretation that any planet involved with the nodes will have.

When using this technique, focus on any planets in aspect to the nodes in the role they play solely for the nodes first and foremost. Later, after you've done the full nodal analysis, a planet whose relationship to the nodes you analyzed will have its own meaning on its own terms, in addition to its role in the nodal story. For example, if the planet Mercury is aspecting the nodes, it will have a straightforward meaning about the style and arena in which this person learns, communicates, and perceives that can be derived from the sign and house that it's in. It will *also* have a dual or broader meaning, playing a part in the overall pattern that the entire nodal story illustrates, perhaps functioning as a life lesson that can serve as a catalyst or steppingstone toward North Node goals. Focusing on the role a planet plays with the nodes will help you lay out the nodal foundation, and give more meaning and background to its straightforward interpretation later on.

South Node Sign and House

To begin, focus on the South Node's placement in the chart you are analyzing. Remember that the South Node represents a comfort zone, a habitual approach to life, or an automatic way of thinking and/or responding to life. Think of it as the bottom line or the entry point of the natal chart. The South Node can be thought of as what this soul would bring to the chart from its "past," as if it were trying the natal chart on for the first time.

Start with the South Node's sign. What characteristics does this person have more than enough of? What ways of thinking and responding to life underlie the rest of their personality? What are the potential pitfalls of this sign? Then look to the South Node's house. What behaviors are habitual, comfortable, and easy for them? If they were applying for a job, what sort of experiences would already be on their résumé? The South Node represents what they already know and are already good at, but it can also represent a limitation in the way they perceive and respond to life, preventing growth or risk by clinging to habit. What activities might they be *too* good at and what side effects or blind spots might there be from being too good at them?

In Action: A Gemini South Node would present possibilities such as the person being a great communicator and a quick thinker and having an aptitude for handling lots of data and a naturally curious orientation to life. This same person may also have an inclination to move on quickly from something when they get bored without seeing something through to completion, an inherent restlessness that too easily disperses their energy or attention, or a blind spot when it comes to trusting their own experience versus official or secondhand information.

Place this Gemini South Node in the twelfth house and layer in the terrain of behaviors and circumstances this house represents. Since the twelfth house represents activities that take us out of the everyday world, this may be a person who has a knack for understanding abstract or broad concepts relating to things from the out-of-the-ordinary or fantastical realm, anything from quantum mechanics to the paranormal to Jung's collective unconscious. They may tend to retreat into their own mind and away from the world, perhaps too often, without putting their ideas out into the world or testing them in a real way.

With each example there are a multitude of possibilities that could be explored. These few have been highlighted to demonstrate the method. Also, when beginning the South Node analysis, you'll only have the sign and house to work with, so come up with a broad expanse of possible ways the planet might express itself through sign and house and be patient with all that you *don't* know about the chart yet. As you move further into the nodal analysis, you'll start whittling away at these broad ideas, refining and defining them, and the broad picture you painted in this step will become more focused and distinct.

When a Planet Conjuncts the South Node

After analyzing the South Node by sign and house, look to the planet(s) that conjunct the South Node, if any. Usually a planet conjunct the South Node will also be in the same sign and house as the South Node,[28] so focus mainly on the nature of the planet and how that contributes to what you already know about the South Node's sign and house. What fundamental human needs might dominate their underlying response to life? How might those needs express themselves in a predominant way through the South Node's sign and house?

In Action: Saturn conjunct a South Node may represent ways this person wants to be an authority figure or naturally embodies a sense of authority or wisdom. It may also represent a potential to avoid circumstances that feel risky or out of control to such a degree that they can get and stay stuck in situations or attitudes for a long time rather than risk change. There may be a natural inclination to melancholy

---

28. If a planet conjunct the South Node is not in the same sign and/or house as the node itself, you will need to integrate an understanding of that planet in its own sign and house into what you know of the South Node you've interpreted already. See the "Out-of-Sign Aspects" section in chapter 17 for further insight.

or depression, or a pessimistic approach to life—too quickly jumping to the "can't" or the "shouldn't" perspective. They may be great at disciplining themselves and reaching their goals but, as a side effect of their self-possession and discipline, have difficulty living in the moment or letting go and relaxing. They may have an instinctual tendency to take on (or have been saddled with) too much responsibility for their age or life circumstances.

With Saturn conjunct a Gemini South Node in the twelfth house, rigid thinking or clinging to a certain perspective even in the face of new evidence may be a possibility. They may be vulnerable to trusting information (Gemini) that comes from a source claiming to be an authority (Saturn) rather than seeing for themselves. With Saturn's inclination toward solitude in the already removed twelfth house terrain, their tendency toward withdrawal or feelings of isolation may feel overwhelming or imprisoning.

When a Planet Opposes the South Node

Next, consider any planets opposite the South Node. For the sake of organization, ignore the conjunction to the North Node for now and concentrate only on the planet's opposing effect on the South Node. The North Node will get its turn. A planet opposing the South Node may feel like something that's thwarting or blocking you, a part of *you* that gets in your own way as represented by an ongoing internal conflict. Because the South Node is often strong and so inherent to our personality, a planet opposing the South Node can feel foreign and difficult. Because it's *also* a part of us but perhaps not as dominant as the South Node habits, it can be difficult to embody if the strength of the South Node overwhelms the desire that the opposing planet represents. Although they may represent two needs or voices inside of us, they are in conflict with one another, and a planet opposing the South Node can be an additional challenge because we have to overcome the ease of the known to venture into what may be underdeveloped parts of ourselves in order to harness the power of the opposing planet.

At various times or in various circumstances in our lives, a planet opposing the South Node may actually be projected onto a specific person or type of person whom we encounter in our external lives. If we disown or disassociate ourselves too much from the opposing planet's nature, it can show up as people in our lives who embody the opposing planet's energy, to serve as an example (or sometimes a target!). Conflict or frustration with that person can be a reflection of the internal issue that this opposing planet represents in your life. This is often (though not always) more easily seen with planets that represent edgier or harsher issues, such as Mars, Saturn, Uranus, or Pluto.

While a planet opposing the South Node can be viewed as blocking the South Node, it also happens to be the planet farthest away from the South Node and therefore may simultaneously represent something that you want but can never have. This may be because we don't think we've got what it takes to acquire it, or because it's so different from who we think we are that we doubt we could ever embody it. It may even represent something we are almost too afraid to acknowledge that we want, and feelings of longing may be obscured by defense mechanisms such as resenting or judging those who *do* have what it represents. This may sometimes (though not always) be the case with gentler planets such as Venus, Jupiter, or Neptune.

It may be difficult to tell which of these possible interpretations may apply in a natal chart at this point in the nodal story. As you weave the story, adding in new pieces, what you know so far will narrow and refine itself at each step, moving from a wide spectrum of possibilities to a more likely scenario given all the components. If it's not apparent which (if not all) of these potentials are manifesting with the opposing planet, keep them in the back of your mind as you move forward and it may become more clear as you go. It's also possible that more than one interpretation of the opposing planet may apply.

In Action: Mars opposing the South Node may present a block or problem with handling anger or conflict appropriately. Additionally, a person with this natal chart placement may have trouble revealing or acting on what they *want*. Because Mars is *opposing* the South Node and not conjunct it, the person may be more likely to disengage from or avoid Mars energy and therefore *underutilize* it, *refraining from* acting on what they want or avoiding conflict; but ultimately, the context of the rest of the nodal story and the entire chart will reveal which way this imbalance may manifest. In a chart with strong or dominant personality overtones, the person may manifest a Mars opposing the South Node with an exaggerated response to conflict rather than an avoidance of it, for example.

Whether a person tends to over- or underutilize their Mars energy due to this opposition, if Mars energy is disowned and projected onto the environment, they may seem to encounter more than their share of aggressive or dominant people. Until they can claim this part of themselves as their own and direct the Mars energy appropriately, they may find themselves too frequently in conflict or feel that their life is dominated by their efforts to avoid it, and wonder why. They may have a conscious or unconscious desire to be able to embody the Mars energy but feel that they are unable to for various reasons, perhaps out of a fear that they may become the type of aggressive or dominating person that they dislike or fear.

Working Mars into the ongoing example puts Mars in Sagittarius in the sixth house, opposing the Gemini South Node in the twelfth house conjunct Saturn. Mars acting through Sagittarius embodies the desire for adventure and learning via new experiences. There is a natural desire to act spontaneously and without reserve. In the sixth house, Mars in Sagittarius may manifest at work or in work- or task-related projects, with a willingness to take on new projects and tackle them with gusto and optimism and a need for a lot of freedom and flexibility in how they go about their work. If a person disowns this energy, they may be judgmental or jealous of, frustrated by, or surpassed by people getting things accomplished in this manner and wish they could be as carefree or adventurous.

Internal conflict may arise because this Mars part of them has the aptitude and desire to act in ways like this but the comfort zone of the South Node is dominated by Saturn, so they may be more comfortable (though not necessarily happy) with a controlled and realistic or cynical approach, and may be reluctant (Saturn) to reveal their ideas (Gemini) or feel incapable or unqualified to put them into action in the real world (twelfth house = removed from the world). If this person does act out the enthusiasm and assertiveness of this Mars placement, there may be a vulnerability to letting the Saturn agenda unconsciously drive their actions, perhaps out of trying to prove something or needing to establish themselves as an authority by dominating a situation, even if it's with an innocuous air of Sagittarian enthusiasm and vigor.

When a Planet Squares the South Node

Next, consider any squares to the nodes. A planet that squares one node will be squaring the other, as it is roughly equidistant from both. Astrologer Jeff Green coined the term "skipped step" for a planet that squares the nodes, meaning, in part, that since the planet is halfway from the South Node to the North Node, it can represent something that needs to be worked with before the North Node can be fully embraced, a gateway that must be passed through and integrated. It can represent something that habitually provides a stumbling block in a person's life, especially if they continue to respond to and deal with what it represents in the same way. The planet may represent something of a "can't go forward, can't go back" paradox, where it seems like every method taken to escape or overcome the internal conflict loops right back around to it. As the person learns the best way to work with the squaring planet's energy and release some of the South Node behavior patterns that continue to frustrate the squaring planet, they can more easily reach for that North Node perspective (more on that soon).

When analyzing a planet squaring the nodes, you'll want to consider the planet's essential meaning in its sign and house as an integrated whole, so follow the same process of interpreting a planet in a sign and a house. Consider the basic range of needs the planet represents, the style in which it will express and meet those needs (sign), and the activities undertaken to meet the planet's needs (house). Then consider how any frustration might develop between what the comfort zone of their South Node represents and the squaring planet, potentially sending the person through a repeating loop of growth (movement toward the North Node) and setback (frustration of the squaring planet kicking them back into relying solely on South Node behaviors).

In Action: To our ongoing example, add Uranus in Pisces in the ninth house squaring the South Node. Uranus represents the desire to individuate so as to be free to express the authentic self. This often takes the form of separation from or rebellion against the status quo. With Uranus in Pisces, this may be done through gentle methods, with a desire for peaceful freedom, rather than riotous or aggressive methods, and the nature or style of authentic self-discovery may be through an inclination toward things that are fantastical, spiritual, or mystical. The activities of the ninth house encompass the things we do to try to understand the world at large, making sense of it and our part in it, largely through education of a formal or experiential sort. There may be a desire and a tendency to seek out alternative (Uranus) education experiences and to branch out from status-quo thinking inherited from their own culture.

How might the person's natural Uranian outlet thwart the South Node comfort zone? Every time they reach for this urge to think and learn outside the box, the level of internal conflict that comes from challenging their safety zone may pull them back into the known territory of established beliefs and ideas. This may manifest in a number of ways, from following their interest in pursuing alternative education (formally or informally) only to back out or not follow through in fits and spurts, to encountering people from other cultures or backgrounds who challenge their way of thinking, exposing them to new ideas but also pushing against their boundaries and maybe causing them to push back if the tension gets too extreme. They may also encounter experiences where a flash (Uranus) of intuition (Pisces) affirms something to them on a gut level that the construct (Saturn) of their mind (Gemini) can't make sense of or validate on an intellectual level. They may find a recurring conflict (square) between what they think should be true or what they can prove is true (Saturn in Gemini) and what they sense (Pisces) through personal experience (ninth house).

When a Planet Sextiles or Trines the South Node

Finally, look for planets trining and/or sextiling the South Node. Planets trine the South Node will be sextile the North Node, and vice versa. A planet that trines or sextiles a node provides a natural outlet for and assistance to the node and what it represents. This may be a planet that's in cahoots with the South Node, because it works easily with the South Node's agenda. This can be helpful and provide an additional layer of natural talent and ease but, like the South Node, can also be used to keep repeating behavior patterns that are comfortable but stagnant. A planet acting in the South Node's best interests in this way is not bad, it's just *easy*.

In Action: Mercury placed in Libra and in the fourth house would be in a trine to the South Node. Perhaps this person's mode of thinking would be greatly informed by the viewpoints that they inherited from their family (fourth house). Mercury in Libra can be a balanced thinker, weighing different points of view and holding opposing ideas simultaneously; however, with the South Node in the hidden twelfth house, and Saturn, a planet of restraint, conjunct it, they may have a tendency to keep their ideas to themselves. Mercury in the peacekeeping sign of Libra, then, might easily be in cahoots with that South Node agenda, potentially avoiding bringing up conflicting points of view (Mercury) or not allowing themselves to fully entertain those points of view in order to remain in harmony (Libra) with their family (fourth house). They may have especially done this as a child, as both the South Node and the fourth house can point to childhood/foundational programming.

Since we also know that Mars is opposed the South Node, we know that embodying Mars's energy (confidence, will, assertiveness) is somehow challenging to this person, so we can see how that might be further incentive to avoid conflicts that may arise through offering an opposing viewpoint. All this does not mean that this person *will* encounter conflict every time they offer a viewpoint, but that they are sensitive to that possibility and it's easier to avoid it rather than risk it.

The North Node Sign and House

After fully analyzing the South Node, consider the North Node. You'll be going over much of the same territory when it comes to the planetary aspects involved with the South Node, but you'll see and integrate them from an entirely different perspective. The North Node represents something that might be unknown or underdeveloped, an opposite perspective from the well-known and comfortable South Node. By developing the characteristics and behaviors suggested by the sign and house of the North Node, the person can maximize their growth, integrating new, liberating habits and perspectives into the old, comfort zone of the South Node. What new approaches and traits might feel foreign to them but, if embraced, can open up a whole new way of perceiving and approaching life? Look to the North Node's sign for insight. What behaviors can they start to "try on," even if they feel awkward at first, to help them start to gain a sense of their own potential? The North Node's house placement can provide clues to this.

At this point, you'll probably start to recognize how the meaning of the North Node is in direct opposition to what the South Node represents, just as they are literally found opposite each other in the chart. You may be able to use this perspective to refine your understanding of what you have already deduced about the South Node. What might the sign or house of the North Node have to "teach" the South Node sign and house? How might it be a sort of antidote to the excesses of the South Node behaviors, bringing them into balance?

In Action: Recall that the South Node in our ongoing example is in Gemini in the twelfth house, so the North Node lies in Sagittarius in the sixth house. Gemini itself is not all bad habits, nor is Sagittarius all good ones, but in order to gain an understanding of how this person might want to grow, focus on the North Node sign and house as an antidote to the negative or excessive side of the sign and house of the South Node.

Sagittarius can teach Gemini that there is more to knowing than just facts and abstract applications; there's also the wisdom and knowledge gained through personal experience. Where Gemini disperses its energy through pursuing a variety of ideas to briefly satisfy curiosity, Sagittarius unifies and concentrates it through passion and enthusiasm. Sixth house experiences encourage real-world, practical activities through work, while the twelfth house experiences are mostly removed from the world. Therefore, the North Node in the sixth house in this case encourages this person not only to put their ideas out there by giving them form and voice but also to put them to the test.

When a Planet Conjuncts the North Node (Opposite the South Node)

Most of the time, planets conjunct the North Node will be in the same sign and house, so consider the nature of the planet itself as the primary new component. As mentioned earlier, this planet has its own specific meaning in the natal chart, but another perspective on it is that it can represent a kind of energy that the person may not be as comfortable working with or a need that they are not inherently sure how to fulfill successfully. Planets conjunct the North Node can sometimes feel like they require extra effort to integrate into one's life, but they can also provide a head start or additional motivation to fulfill the North Node intention. The North Node is not loaded with experience, habit, and comfort like the South Node is. However, with a planet's energy focused in the same place as the North Node, the North Node will naturally get the person's attention more often in life than if it were on its own, as the person works on fulfilling the conjuncting planet's need through their lifetime.

In Action: Mars is conjunct the North Node in our ongoing example. In general, Mars represents our will: action, motivation, passion, drive, and how we act on all of those things. Our reaction to and style of handling conflict is also governed by Mars. We already learned that Mars opposing the *South Node* can indicate the likelihood of a pattern of avoiding conflict, a difficulty handling anger, or a difficulty in acting on their desires, sometimes finding themselves repeatedly encountering more than their share of aggressive or dominant people. Now we can add this background understanding to the interpretation of Mars in service to the North Node.

Learning to handle and express one's own drive and passion is of prime importance for North Node work. This would cover territory such as learning to be more assertive and confident, standing up for oneself, and not shying away from necessary conflict (rather than avoiding it, backing down, or overreacting to it). In a sense, Mars represents our very right to exist, live, and thrive, and advocating for ourselves or acting on what we want is an extension of that.

We already established the meaning of the North Node's sign and house, so by adding Mars to the mix, we can understand that the drive to *act* is what will carry this North Node lesson forward. With Mars in Sagittarius, cultivating a style of action that is spontaneous, freely expressed, and confident is a healthy expression of this planet. In the sixth house, work may be a learning-intensive arena for this lesson. Learning to act on and follow through on one's desires and not just contemplate them or remain in endless "someday" preparation for them is another way this Mars can spread its wings.

When a Planet Opposes the North Node (Conjunct the South Node)

A planet opposing the North Node is obviously also conjunct the South Node, but from the North Node perspective, the challenge lies in being able to extract what a person inherently knows and has experienced in utilizing this planet's energy and repurpose it to integrate into the North Node aim, to identify and experiment with another way in which the need that a planet represents can find a way to express itself.

In Action: Saturn is opposing the North Node in our ongoing example, from Gemini in the twelfth house. We learned before that this may lead to habitual behaviors that center around limitation or solidification to the point of being stuck or stagnant (especially of ideas or beliefs in Gemini) and a potential toward pessimism and/or holding back of oneself from the world. A tendency to carry the weight of the world on one's shoulders may also pervade.

In service to the North Node aim, this person may be learning to draw from the natural ability to handle responsibility and to think critically and realistically while not letting themselves fall into the trap of avoiding risk or growth altogether in an effort to maintain control. The Sagittarius, sixth house North Node experience is about engaging in life with confidence and enthusiasm, putting oneself to the test and experiencing new adventures. Such a person is learning to have faith in the possibilities and in themselves and what they can do, so embodying a sense of personal authority (Saturn) instead of waiting for permission from others is another way they can bring Saturn's gifts forward.

When a Planet Squares the North Node (and South Node)

As illustrated, a planet squaring the North Node represents a kind of blockage, and engaging with what that blockage represents can provide a steppingstone toward the North Node. When dealing with the *South* Node, we try to understand the ways that this squaring planet, through its own nature as well as its sign and house, gets us frustrated along the way to our North Node and loops us back into comfortable South Node behaviors.

When analyzing the effect of the squaring planet on the *North* Node, we must understand that it thwarts the North Node too. It's a rock and a hard place, the "can't go forward, can't go back" paradox. The frustration of dealing with the squaring planet can lock a person up and make it difficult to move forward. But like all squares, the pressure it symbolizes will keep that person continually wrestling with the issues as they seek a solution, a relief from the pressure. A common paraphrasing of a quote by Albert Einstein expresses the sentiment that a problem cannot be solved with the same mind that created it—a new way of thinking must be employed to see a way through. A planet squaring the nodes represents that which blocks and frustrates us *as well as* the method through which we must creatively engage with the fundamental problem to rise to a higher level of thinking. Whether it's a fundamental change in behavior or perspective, or both, a planet squaring the nodes represents a pivotal passage to nodal evolution.

You've already analyzed the planet that is squaring the nodes, but consider what you know about it in the context of how it, or the struggle surrounding it, can move one toward the North Node.

In Action: Uranus in Pisces in the ninth house is the squaring planet in the continuing example. In the greater context of what we've already discovered about the nodes, Saturn, and Mars, there are several layers. In a sense, this person is moving not only from the South Node to the North Node, but also from Gemini to Sagittarius, from the twelfth house focus to exploring the sixth house potentials, and from Saturn in its most rigid expression to Mars in its healthiest one. Plug Uranus into each pathway and you'll be able to get a well-rounded idea of how it may represent a steppingstone in these processes. Uranus goes beyond Saturn boundaries to break up rigidity and break through fears or insecurity that embody the South Node face of Saturn.

With Uranus in Pisces, this may be done through an intuitive or feeling faculty as opposed to an abstract or intellectual style alone, and through allowing oneself to become friendlier with the mysterious, the unknown, and the unexplained, which Saturn tends to shy away from. With Uranus in Pisces in the ninth house, education and exposure to alternative (Uranus) ideas can provide a platform, voice, and consciousness to what may have been unconsciously assumed (twelfth house) and unchallenged about the world and their part in it. Education and the mixing of ideas challenges one's view of the world openly like no other way, so seeking out new ideas can allow them access to arenas where they can test and expand their ideas, ultimately enriching their beliefs and showing them the personal truths behind their convictions as they allow themselves the openness of these experiences, even ones that challenge their traditional ways of thinking. If the person goes so far as to teach (ninth) from their unique perspective, sharing their beliefs and ideas in a variety of potential ways, that may also allow them to become more comfortable and confident in what they have to offer (Mars).

In a nutshell, Uranus in Pisces in the ninth house can be a steppingstone because it provides an outlet and an urge to break up potential stuck (Saturn) or hidden (twelfth) thinking (Gemini) that can provide one with a sense of security (Saturn, South Node) but can isolate (twelfth) one from the hands-on (sixth), sometimes messy and challenging but wonderful experiences that can enrich and sometimes outright change one's thinking entirely. Pursuing (Mars) those hands-on experiences can allow one to put ideas to the test in the real world (sixth) and allow one access to a deeper sense of personal truth (Sagittarius).

When a Planet Trines or Sextiles the North Node (Sextile or Trine the South Node)

A planet trine or sextile the North Node can be looked at as an assistant, one who may find it easy to work for the South Node boss but who can be summoned and redirected to North Node ends as well.

In Action: In our running example, Mercury is in Libra in the fourth house, and we have seen how it might support the South Node behaviors through a trine. Mercury is also simultaneously in sextile with the North Node. Now we can see that although this person may be at risk for trying to keep the peace by keeping their ideas to themselves, they are acutely aware of imbalances (Libra), especially in ideas and communication (Mercury), and in situations or with people they trust (fourth house), they may be inclined to summon the courage to share their point of view, even risking conflict in the process.

In this way, Mercury can be the assistant to the North Node, not only providing an incentive to speak up in an effort to relieve the inner tension they feel whenever there is intellectual conflict but also helping the person move away from siding with authority (Saturn) or letting intellectual authority or tradition overrule their own instinctual knowing (Mercury in the fourth house). The Sagittarius North Node in the sixth house, while not necessarily about ideas or speaking up in itself, is about engagement and enthusiasm (Sagittarius) in a hands-on, real-world way (sixth house). Being willing to speak up about what they think and/or believe is one way they can do that.

More on Planetary Duality: Squares, Trines, Sextiles

Because the North Node and South Node are always in exact opposition, any planet that makes an aspect to one of them automatically makes an aspect to the other and must be understood in both the context of the North Node and South Node. A planet that squares, trines, or sextiles the nodes can be thought of as potentially serving two masters. Its energy can be used to do what we know and are good at, a valuable resource but a potential place of stagnancy and frustration, or it can be used to venture into developing new soul growth, which is satisfying but can feel awkward and uncertain.

More on Planetary Duality: Conjunctions and Oppositions

Oppositions and conjunctions to the nodes can seem a little trickier at first when attempting to understand their dual role. Within the nodal analysis process, a planet conjunct the South Node will have a role to play in the larger picture of this person's spiritual foundation and habitual comfort zone, and it will have another role as a potential opposing force to the North Node's efforts. The reverse is also true: a planet conjunct the North Node will have a role to play in assisting the North Node work and another role as an opposing force to the South Node's stasis. Don't panic! Just layer the separate meanings one by one and watch the chart come alive.

Again, we see how important it is to understand the flexibility and complexity in the astrological symbols when we consider the duality in planets that aspect the nodes.

South Node Bad, North Node Good?

Due to the nature of the common interpretation for the North and South Nodes of the Moon, it seems as though, overall, it's good to move toward the North Node behaviors while minimizing the South Node behaviors. But what does it say about a natal chart, then, when planets are found in the same sign or house as the South Node? Are we to leave them behind? Likewise, if natal planets are found in the same sign or house as the North Node, it may seem that the interpretation of the North Node being unfamiliar energy isn't so applicable.

Planets that reside in the same sign or house as the *South* Node are still relevant; these planetary needs are just as significant as any other need. To work out this seeming contradiction, consider that each planet in its sign or house has a spectrum of possibilities in how to express itself. If a person with a Virgo South Node also has Mars in Virgo, this could indicate (among other possibilities) that it's very easy for this person to react too quickly or with anger (Mars), especially when they feel triggered by situations out of their control (Virgo). However, learning to use their anger in productive ways, to take organized action on matters that are important to them and work through instincts that have them tripping themselves up by trying to exert too much control over matters that are out of their hands, are all healthy lessons that fall within the spectrum of possible manifestations of the Mars in Virgo energy. This will be true of any person with Mars in Virgo, even if their South Node is not also in Virgo. The key is to watch the *habits* and *intent* that surround their typical Mars behaviors, as they are vulnerable to falling in line with South Node behaviors that can be destructive or undermining to growth.

In the opposite case, when a natal planet is in the same sign or house as the *North* Node, learning to provide for the needs represented by that planet can also help further one's soul growth overall. Depending on the rest of the natal chart placements, this person may have a sharper learning curve than some when it comes to meeting the need that this planet represents in a healthy way. While the North Node "carries no inherent energy at birth but is simply a good idea," as astrologer Steven Forrest has described it, the planets represent a variety of powerful needs inherent in life and are not easily ignored. Having a natal planet in the same sign as the North Node can therefore be a powerful motivator toward embracing North Node lessons, even though it may seem as though that planet has its work cut out for it!

Once you have a good sense of the nodal story after going through these steps, you'll have an entire foundation on which to overlay your natal chart interpretation. After analyzing the nodes and their aspects, you'll have uncovered the prominent theme of the natal chart. Every planet in its individual sign and house will be understood within the context of the nodal story, and the pieces will fall into place. After completing the nodal analysis, it may be useful to continue with any of the other chart analysis techniques, such as the big three technique.

Revisiting Planets in Aspect to the Nodes

As you've seen in the examples, it's likely that an analysis of the nodes will lead you to analyzing at least one or two planets in the natal chart because they lie in aspect to the nodes. This is not true in all cases; obviously there are exceptions, where no planets aspect the nodes. However, when you analyze planets in the natal chart that aspect the nodes, you'll be focusing on their meaning solely in that context. How does that square from the Sun in Leo in the third house deepen your understanding of the nodal story? How about that trine from Mercury in Sagittarius in the seventh house? And so on.

When you have completed your nodal analysis, you'll be moving on to analyze the rest of the chart, with the foundational meaning of what you've learned about the nodes now on the back burner, informing what you learn about the chart from this point on. Remember that even if you already analyzed some natal planets, you did so primarily with their impact on the nodes in mind. You will likely want to revisit those planets to construct a full analysis of their meaning in their *own* right, with their own sign, house, and aspects taken into consideration. Look at each natal planet with the understanding that these are the tools one has come to develop, the building blocks of personality with which to explore the world. Their history (South Node) and their future (North Node) will certainly illustrate why those tools are so important, but let your analysis take you beyond the nodes once you've laid the foundation.

CHAPTER 13

THE NODAL FOUNDATION CHECKLIST

This technique is not complicated, but you'll want to keep the steps clear and separate to create layers of understanding rather than a muddled stew. Here is an outline of the steps of the nodal method of interpretation in order:

1. South Node sign and house
   a. What is this person (too) good at? What attitudes or behaviors might be too comfortable? Where are their inherent blind spots as a result of their natural orientation to life?

2. Planets conjunct the South Node
   a. What need does this planet represent and how does it contribute to this person's comfort zone?
   b. Like the South Node itself, what does this planet represent in terms of what they are good at that they might be able to utilize as a natural talent or skill?

3. Planets opposed the South Node
   a. How might this planet, via its sign and house, represent an obstacle to overcome, either as an internal block or an external personification? What kinds of experiences, people, or ways of life might seem inherently too far outside of

their realm to encounter, whether because they personally reject those experiences or they simply can't see a way to them?

4. Planets square to the South Node
   a. What kind of stumbling blocks may occur in repeated patterns, turning them back toward South Node behaviors until they are able to break through this loop?

5. Planets trine or sextile to the South Node
   a. What part of them flows naturally with the innate skills and attitudes of the South Node? How might that end up conspiring to keep them in their comfort zone too easily?

6. North Node sign and house
   a. What experiences and perspectives might this person reach for in order to grow? What area of life or viewpoint might they have little experience with or be naive about?

7. Planets conjunct the North Node
   a. What might this person resent or, conversely, long for? What might they think they don't have or can never have? What (planetary) need are they learning to fulfill in a healthy way, leading them toward growth? Given the urge or need that the individual planet represents, what idea or area of life do they need to rethink or form a new relationship with in order to experience it fully in a new context?

8. Planets opposed the North Node
   a. What planetary need is this person already comfortable fulfilling but may want to expand? How can they take the impulses and needs this planet represents and move beyond the one-track or automated ways they express it?

9. Planets square to the North Node
   a. What kind of stumbling blocks tend to hang this person up? What kind of behavior patterns or situations might recur in a loop as they move toward growth? How does this

planet represent a gateway that they must pass through in order to move toward the North Node?

10. Planets trine or sextile to the North Node
   a. How might the inherent ease of using this planet be re-routed or repurposed to additionally serve the North Node purpose?

Regardless of the technique you use, any time you begin a natal chart analysis, you are working with a blank slate. As you create meaningful interpretations for each planet-sign-house combination, you will begin to know more and more about the nature of the chart you are studying, providing yourself with more context as you go, which will in turn help you narrow down the vast potential of interpretations into the more likely or meaningful outcomes. In other words, the more knowledge you gather about a chart, the easier the interpretation can eventually start to become. However, initially you will have no context in which to work, so remember these two things: first, be prepared to start with a wide set of possibilities as you begin your first planet-sign-house interpretation, and second, don't be afraid to go back and modify your original thoughts as you get more contextual understanding through the rest of the interpretation.

CHAPTER 14

ONE CHART, MANY METHODS: STEVE MARTIN

It's time to put these methods to work on the natal chart of Steve Martin, comedian, writer, and self-proclaimed "wild and crazy guy." Like a mirror ball, each technique will provide a different perspective, sometimes yielding insights other techniques didn't and other times repeating and reinforcing the core themes. You may not utilize every method for each natal chart you analyze, but it can be helpful (though potentially overwhelming) to do so in the beginning if you are not sure which methods work best for you or if you want to get a more complete picture.

First, we'll concentrate on drawing out the astrological symbolism of the chart with each technique and organizing what we find out. After the natal chart analyses, we'll look to Steve's biography to see how he has played out the influences in his chart through some of his choices and life events. We'll be using a 5° working orb for this example, the Porphyry house calculation method, and the true node.

WEIGHTS AND MEASURES

Dualities

Steve's chart is perfectly balanced, with five planets in projective signs and five in receptive signs.

Element Balance

Steve has two planets in fire signs, two in earth, three in air, and three in water, providing an almost perfect balance among all the elements. He has potential access to all styles of energy expression on this basic level.

Modality Balance

Steve has three planets in cardinal signs, three planets in fixed signs, and four planets in mutable signs. Once again, this is as perfect a balance as possible. Having one extra planet in one category, in this case mutable, is not enough to tip the scales significantly. Overall, we can note that he has access to a variety of different styles of approach, which can, in theory, provide overall flexibility in his character. The actuality of this potential will become more realistic and nuanced when we leave the realm of categorical interpretation and get into the specifics.

Hemisphere Balance

Here the scales tip significantly, revealing nine planets in the eastern hemisphere and only one in the western. This reveals a general tendency toward orchestrating events and influencing people in a way that encourages them to bend to his agenda rather than him bending to theirs. This doesn't necessarily mean that he is a dictator but that he has a way of subtly dominating his environment; through charm, presence, or will, he can get the water to part around him.

THE BIG THREE

Sun

Steve's Sun is in the sign of Leo. It may not seem surprising for a comedian and actor to be born under the sign of Leo, but as we saw in the description of Leo, not every Leo wants to be center stage, literally or otherwise. At the heart of Leo is the desire to experience and give birth to the self, through creativity and *engagement*, not finding the self but making and discovering the self as they go through life. Steve's *essential self* is based on this need: to discover himself through play and engage with life by letting it draw him out into experiences that reinforce a strong sense of self and that provide a sense of dignity as well as joy.

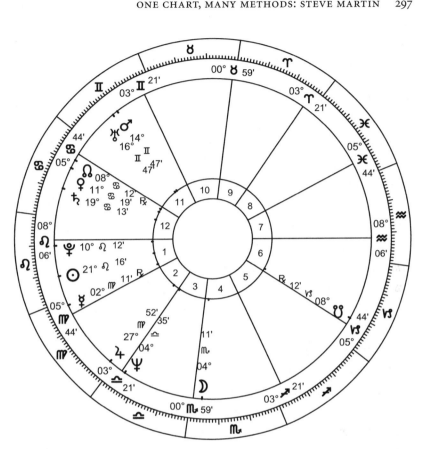

Figure 9: Steve Martin's Natal Chart
August 14 1945 / 5:54 am CWT +5:00
Waco, TX / 31°N32'57" 097°W08'47"
Porphyry Houses

Steve's Sun is in the first house. The first house represents the terrain of the self, meaning the immediate, automatic way we project ourselves onto our environment and are shaped by it. In the first house we are not crafting or thinking about self but simply *being* in an unplanned, instinctive way. Because the Sun's placement in a chart tends to reveal what characteristics we identify with and the activities that reinforce a strong sense of self and empowerment, the Sun in the first house of self can represent someone who thinks and acts with the immediacy of instinct and what feels good and right to themselves and themselves alone.

Moon

Steve's Moon is in the sign of Scorpio. Since the Moon represents our instinctual and emotional orientation, a Scorpio Moon would give Steve an instinct to sniff out untruths, to just "get a feeling" when there's more to a situation, story, or person than appears on the surface. He's not likely to accept things at face value very easily and will have an instinctual sense about things, people, or places; therefore, he's not easily fooled. He instinctively trusts people who aren't afraid to tell it like it is, not out of brashness or a desire to be outrageous but because they are brave enough to say out loud what they see. He is not likely to think people are saints or sinners, but are simply human, flawed and real.

Although seemingly contradictory, Steve may feel most safe when acknowledging the intensity or danger inherent in life, rather than trying to ignore it. He may not always be challenging himself to live on the edge at every minute, but his emotional awareness of the subtle "underbelly" of life means he'd be *more* uncomfortable in situations where he's called to put on a happy face and make small talk, although he may easily compensate with an outgoing Leo Sun in the visible first house. He's most emotionally authentic when he can be real and raw, and when others he's with can appreciate or at least handle that part of him. He's not likely to reveal it to just anyone, however, with a strong sense of privacy and self-protectiveness.

Steve's Moon is in the fourth house. His celebrity status notwithstanding, with a fourth house Moon placed in Scorpio, he may lean toward keeping his private life private. He feels things very deeply even if he doesn't show it. A nurturing home that feels like a haven can keep him emotionally fed and grounded in a way little else can, even if he lives alone. He may especially enjoy homemaking activities, such as gardening or home improvement, or even involvement in the real estate market. Not every person with the Moon in the fourth house longs to settle down and have kids, nor are they all close to their family of origin, but a sense of shelter, togetherness, and comfort in a family (blood relation or otherwise) can be emotionally centering and healing for them.

Ascendant

Steve's Ascendant is in the sign of Leo. With Leo being the method through which he greets and is greeted by the world, he is likely to have some kind of magnetism that others are drawn to immediately, even without his fame. He is likely to be someone you notice, whether intentionally or unintentionally, and not just because of an extroverted or over-the-top persona but simply because there is a *presence* in his demeanor. He can be as self-conscious as the next person but never reveals it, and is likely to project himself in a more brassy or bold way the more insecure he feels, never letting on that he is quite sensitive to how others respond to him. Like all fire rising signs, he may tend to show a happy face to the world, even at times when his inner world feels like a mess.

Summary

With a Leo Sun and Leo Ascendant, Steve projects a confident persona, and the depth of his Scorpio Moon is often obscured by that bright light (something a Scorpio Moon would prefer anyway!). He may surprise others with that sharp Scorpio edge, and with all the charisma of Leo, he can carry it off. He may have a love-hate relationship with the spotlight, being energized when performing though he could very well self-identify as shy in his personal life.

We can take this much analysis further with the added integration of any and all planets in aspect to the Sun, Moon, and/or Ascendant.

Steve's Sun Is Sextile Uranus (and Mars)

His creative and dramatic flair will always tend toward the unique or different, with a desire not to just show off his stuff but to really stand out because of what he does that no one else thought of. He'll always have a little spark of weirdness that is core to how he expresses himself.

Although Mars technically lies outside our 5° orb, its close conjunction with Uranus obliges us to pull it into the sextile. Remember that when planets are in conjunction with each other, they act in a unified way. The Mars function and Uranus function are triggered together in Steve, so to separate them here in order to maintain our orb cutoff is impractically rigid. With Mars entwined fruitfully with the Sun, the self-motivating and self-interest drives of the Sun in the first house are amplified by the Mars action-oriented agenda. Although Steve is not immune to laziness, procrastination, or insecurity, this connection indicates it may be easy for him to keep on his toes, always pursuing what he is passionate about and acting in his best self-interest.

Steve's Moon Is Sextile Mercury

An electrified link between his heart and his head may make it easy and exhilarating for Steve to express himself. His Moon is in Scorpio, a sign that is able to observe and note unspoken subtleties in the environment and others' behaviors, so having it teamed up with Mercury in this way makes him a keen observer and gives him the ability to articulate what he observes. The amount of detail he observes with this analytical mind may be vast; however, he may not express or reveal everything he observes, since his Mercury is in controlled and deliberate Virgo, so he might restrain himself if expressing his observations might confuse or belabor an issue beyond helpfulness or efficiency.

Since the symbol of the Moon itself is related more to our subconscious and emotional life, Mercury can play the role of articulating what we're feeling both to ourselves in organizing our thought processes and to others by expressing our feelings aloud. A cooperative aspect between the Moon and Mercury may make that process a bit easier for Steve. The link to Mercury also gives him an outlet to express what his instincts tell him, and this certainly shows up in his instinct for comedy. While a well-told joke can make us laugh where a poorly delivered one cannot (Mercury's role), what we find humorous feels like more of an impulsive, instinctual response (Moon), so the connection between these two planets in Steve's chart may represent, in part, his ability to feel and express humor in a natural way, and his comedic instincts.

Steve's Moon Is Square Pluto

Pluto can represent a place in us that is capable of great empowerment but is often wounded and fearful. With Pluto placed so publicly and obviously in Steve's chart, being perched right on the Ascendant in Leo, he may be especially sensitive to negative feedback in response to his personal style and may feel like his insecurities are all too visible. Simply the way he *is* or *seems to be* may often seem to trigger negative responses in others. Much of this may not be something he intentionally projects, but those with Pluto conjunct the Ascendant sometimes radiate an intensity or overwhelming energy from them that others find reason to be uneasy with, even if they can't put their finger on it. This can be a subtle undertone or vibe that the Pluto-Ascendant person may feel consciously or not throughout their lives.

A square between two planets indicates that they have difficulty working together, often bringing out the worst in each other or combining in painful or frustrating ways more readily than in helpful or cooperative ways. We already know that his Scorpio, fourth house Moon has a strong streak of depth and privacy, but now we may be alert to some of that being in response to insecurities or woundedness, especially centering around vulnerability or nurturing, the Moon's domain. Difficult or neglectful experiences with a parent in childhood may be especially impactful for him, and there may be defense mechanisms he's created to prevent others from seeing his vulnerability or ways he avoids letting others care for him as if he's always got his guard up. He may simply be so self-sufficient that he's used to living without needing that from others.

Again, because Pluto is placed in a very expressive sign and in a very visible house, this may be a clue to the method of his self-protection or response to his wounds being triggered. While he may be prompted to push back, it's likely that the dignity of his Leo Sun and

Ascendant will not allow him to stoop so low, but may occasionally take digs at others, couching it in raw, edgy humor or delivering it otherwise indirectly. Another possibility may be the reverse, where the best defense is to play dead, or laugh at yourself first so the power of others' ridicule is undercut.

Steve's Moon Is Square His Ascendant/Descendant, Opposed the Midheaven, and Conjunct the Nadir

The Moon's placement happens to put it in aspect to all four angles, squaring his Ascendant and Descendant, opposing his Midheaven (tenth house cusp), and conjuncting his Nadir (fourth house cusp). This may seem overwhelming, but in fact, all are saying the same thing, at least in part, and it's something we've already discovered: he has a need for privacy and a safe haven in which he can feel protected, often in solitude or with someone he trusts and may even call family. The Ascendant (our public interface/projection of self) and the Descendant (our reception toward others and relationship) both take us into the realm of people and the world, and the Moon is hunkered down in a private sign and house, making the tension between the two realms obvious. The Midheaven, also a point of public interface, opposes the private Moon, again revealing the obvious tension of the vulnerability of the private self versus the showmanship or the career man who has it together at all times. And the conjunction to the Nadir is a reinforcement of what we already know about Steve's Moon acting through the fourth house.

Steve's Moon Is Trine the North Node and Sextile the South Node

Steve's North Node is in Cancer in the twelfth house, and his South Node is in the opposite location—Capricorn, sixth house. While the nodal analysis technique will take us deeply into understanding these two symbols on their own, the fact that the Moon is linked in this way to the nodes can reveal the importance of Moon-centered lessons in his life and how they may serve as mileposts in his evolutionary growth.

Steve's Pluto Is Conjunct His Ascendant and Opposite His Descendant

In addition to what we already learned about Pluto when focusing on the Moon-Pluto square, Pluto can represent ways we are able to claim our own power if we can bypass our fear of it, identifying and facing what is frightening as much as we are able. Finding ways to maintain a sense of confidence but not arrogance or superiority as compensation may be the journey toward a healthy use of Plutonian power with it right on the Ascendant. Breaking taboos can also be a powerful way to utilize Pluto—not being afraid to call attention to what others try to ignore because of collective fears, and being willing to take the heat for doing so. Because the Ascendant also tends to describe, in part, our overall outlook on life or instinctive approach to it, the intensity of Pluto at the helm of one's life in this way can create an all-or-nothing style of navigating the world, for better or worse.

The Descendant is always exactly opposite the Ascendant, so whatever is conjunct the Ascendant automatically opposes the Descendant. With Pluto opposite the Descendant, relationships can be powerful catalysts for Steve, but only when they are able to capture him with an intensity to match or overpower his own intense desire and habit of moving through the world according to his own agenda and will.

Steve's Neptune Is Sextile His Ascendant and Trine His Descendant

Neptune symbolizes magic and fantasy and is in an easy relationship with Steve's Ascendant, through which first impressions are made and taken in. His way of looking at the world is colored by the ability to see whimsy in anything. His Pluto rising can give him a hard edge, so he's not easily fooled or inherently naive, but with Neptune in cahoots with his Ascendant, he can be won over by what he *wants* to see.

The Neptunian influence is also something people may observe about him, since it's in alignment with the Ascendant, which is how a person seems to others, and it's also in a trine to his Descendant, the angle of relationship and the type of people you are drawn to. Neptune's positive influence on the Ascendant may soften some of the Pluto intensity and turn up the gentle, kind, and charming levels on his persona. Obviously the performer and entertainer in him benefit by Neptune's grace, adding that touch of magic and enchantment. As for Neptune's influence on the Descendant in Aquarius, Steve may appreciate people who are confident in their individuality and always seem cool and collected but at the same time have a sensitivity about them.

Summary, Expanded

Adding to the integration we worked out before by adding in the planetary aspects, a theme seems to emerge already with Pluto prominently placed on his Ascendant and the Moon placed in Scorpio, the sign Pluto rules. The Moon is also in a square to Pluto itself. Emotionally speaking, then, Steve's need for privacy seems to come from many sources, which means it's likely to be a more prominent trait than it would be in the chart of someone who had just one of these configurations. Because the Moon is involved in so many planetary aspects, its importance begins to elevate as we understand it has a far-reaching influence on many parts of him.

Note how the expressive Leo tendencies of his Sun and Ascendant may incline us to think he's quite outgoing, but he's not laying everything out in the open like he seems to be with Pluto bringing a sharp edge to it and Neptune softening the whole thing and couching it in a bit of mystery and sensitivity; not to mention that Pluto is drawn into the Moon's agenda through the square, and the square between the Moon and the Ascendant—both powerful reasons that the extrovertedness that seemed easy to assume now seems more subtle.

FOLLOW THE RULER

Steve's Ascendant is in the sign of Leo. We've already covered the essentials of Leo rising in depth, so we'll reiterate the highlights here. Steve greets the world with a natural charisma and magnetism that is hard to miss, even when he's not performing (in any sense of the word). He has a fundamental approach to life that is motivated by self-expression and exploring personal creativity, with the world as his canvas.

In Steve's chart, we immediately see a competition for chart ruler. The Sun is the planetary ruler of Leo, but Pluto is in close conjunction with the Ascendant, with only about a 2° orb. Considering both planets as equally important is probably our best bet at thoroughness; however, we may note that the Sun is quite powerful in this chart, considering it's the Sun and therefore one of the fundamentally important planets in any chart, and it's in its own sign, Leo, as well as ruling the Leo Ascendant.

The Sun as the chart ruler is powerful, but nothing much is added by its placement, since it simply repeats and amplifies the Leo, first house qualities of the Leo Ascendant. With Pluto as the chart ruler, this would emphasize qualities of intensity and tenacity in his approach and response to the world. Pluto represents ways and areas in our life through which periods of great transformation can deeply change us, for better or worse, so with Pluto functioning as the overall chart ruler, these periods of life can be even more profound, changing his entire outlook in dramatic and irreversible ways. Pluto as chart ruler may increase his magnetism, although determining whether his charisma stems from the intensity of Pluto, the bright glow of the Sun in this house, or the charm of Leo seems difficult (and unnecessary).

In Steve's case, as helpful as the chart ruler can be, the importance of it here is minimal as it's lost in the wealth of insight we would already attain by simply interpreting these planets at face value in their sign and house.

FROM THE TOP

Because this technique begins at the first house, a territory we've explored well in other examples due to the wealth of planets in Steve's first house, applying this technique to Steve's chart will take us into familiar territory. To avoid needless repetition, we'll simply remind ourselves of the important highlights before moving in deeper.

Steve's Ascendant is in the sign of Leo. His approach to the world is expressive and creative, projecting a charismatic persona to others even when he's trying to play it cool (*especially* when he's playing it cool, in fact, as Leo Ascendant likes to come across as effortlessly cool).

Looking to aspects involving the Ascendant, Pluto immediately jumps into view. Working his way through his fears, even when they threaten to overwhelm him, is par for the course with Pluto in the front seat. The fire of Leo coupled with the intensity of Pluto may manifest as an all-or-nothing approach to the world. A dynamic and engaging Leo Ascendant coupled with a potential insecurity that feels as though it's on your sleeve can make for a complicated persona, making him somewhat enigmatic.

Further aspects to the Ascendant take us to Neptune sextiling the Ascendant, adding to the magnetism and mystery Steve projects as well as how he sometimes prefers to see the world: as magical.

The final aspect to his Ascendant is his Moon. The Moon represents our private, emotional, and subconscious self. With his Moon in tension with the Ascendant, Steve may find that he projects a very different image to the world than the way he feels inside, and he does not like to feel like his private self is exposed to just anyone.

Now on to the next planet in the first house: Steve's Sun in Leo. Steve's essential self is based on the need to express himself, discovering himself in the process. Playfulness and engagement with life can reinforce a strong sense of self and provide essential dignity and joy. With his Sun in the first house, Steve acts from a self-oriented center, following his instincts and drive along his own agenda.

The Sun is sextile Uranus and, by association, Mars in the eleventh house in Gemini, adding not only a desire to be different to his essential makeup, rather than just doing what he sees others doing, but also a tendency to always be active in his pursuit of self-expression and what interests him.

Now we continue with the final planet in the first house, Mercury, retrograde in Virgo. Steve articulates his ideas with precision and detail and will learn that way too. The retrograde influence and Virgo's inherent humility may incline him to think and observe longer before offering his opinions or coming to conclusions, as the energy makes an internal loop (the retrograde effect) before expressing outward or consciously. With Mercury in the first house, even though this planet is in a careful sign, Steve tends to lead with his mind and ideas.

We've completed the interpretation of the first house. Moving on to the second house, we see Jupiter in Virgo. Jupiter's location in our chart tells us where we will benefit most in operating from a place of optimism and hopefulness. Jupiter is in the deliberate and conscientious sign of Virgo, so even when Steve is going for it, he'll do so with a plan and technique, not wanting to take leaps of faith empty-handed or totally unprepared with unrealistic expectations. In the second house, Jupiter is continually pushing him to bet it all, to go big or go home.

And so on through the remaining houses!

NARRATIVE

Keep in mind that the narrative technique is based on your intuitive style, so you may not start in the same place or leap to the next place as in the following example; it will just give you a sense of the potential of a narrative flow.

The most noticeable characteristic in Steve's chart seems to be the weight of planets on the left side, the eastern hemisphere, which emphasizes the tendency to have a strong impact on the environment around him, as we already established in the weights and measures method. Any of these planetary groupings on this side can serve as a starting point, but Pluto on the Ascendant and the Sun in the same house and sign seems like a good place to zero in.

If starting from scratch on a chart using this technique, obviously we would need to go deeply into the Sun and Pluto and Ascendant at this point, but because of the nature of Steve's chart and his first house planets, we've gone over these energies enough that you can refer to previous sections for interpretations of the Sun, Ascendant, and Pluto.

From there, we might feel compelled either to discuss Mercury, since it's in the same house as Pluto and the Sun, or hop to planets involved in aspects with the Sun, Pluto, and the Ascendant, such as the Moon's square to Pluto and the Ascendant, Neptune's sextile to these two, or Mars and Uranus in Gemini in the eleventh house also in a sextile. Any one of these would be just fine; for this example, we'll segue to Mars and Uranus.

Steve's Mars Is in Gemini in the Eleventh House

Mars represents the way we take action on what we want and defend against what we don't want. Its sign and house placement represents our style of action and the kinds of things we are inclined to be attracted to pursue. With Mars in Gemini, there's a desire to pursue anything that sparks the curiosity. Questions drive answers, which drive more questions for Mars in Gemini. Mars in Gemini is a pretty openminded and experimentally inclined kind of style—it may be safe to say Steve is willing to try anything once. Mars also has a lot to do with our physical drives and instinctive, immediate responses to stimuli. Quick-wittedness, cleverness, a sharp mind, and fast reflexes could all be gifts of this Mars placement.

Mars in Gemini alone could be vulnerable to a lack of focus, either skipping from task to task or spreading oneself too thin. This problem may crop up for Steve, but further investigation of the chart may reveal just how much or how little of a problem it really is. We can already see that Mercury in Virgo and Pluto on the Ascendant both assist Steve in maintaining focus through the deliberateness of Mercury in Virgo and the passion of Pluto on the Leo Ascendant.

With his Mars acting in the territory of the eleventh house, Steve may be excited by the idea of seeing how far his ideas can take him, learning from peers and those he admires as he goes—mainly out of a curiosity to see how the other half lives. What lies in the world beyond his little community is where his passions will ultimately drive him— to go far in life and probably far from home in the process.

Steve's Uranus Lies in Gemini in the Eleventh House

Uranus represents the desire to individuate, to follow your own path, whether or not it aligns with the path laid out for you by society, family, peers, etc. With Uranus in Gemini, Steve will be especially rebellious when it comes to his right to think, read, learn, and express what he wishes. Freedom of speech and expression could be an important component to how he expresses and discovers his individuality. With Uranus in the eleventh house, distinguishing himself from his peers while finding a place among them may be a fine line he always walks. Since the eleventh house also represents what develops over the long term, it is likely that decisions and goals that reflect his authenticity may often take him off the beaten path more and more as he gets older.

Add the influence of Uranus in conjunction to Mars in the same house and sign, and we get a more specific flavor. Not only is Steve likely to be quick-witted and instinctually sharp in mind and reflexes, but he may also have a particular interest in the absurd, the unique and different, the offbeat, which would be reflected in his style of action. As Mars represents what we are driven to pursue, Uranus will add to not only his style of doing so, but also his reason for doing so. To pursue what is unique and original, outside and inside of himself, is a strong motivation.

And so on! Because we were discussing communication, a good place to go next might be Neptune in the third house of communication, or Mercury, the planet of communication, in Virgo in the first house. Wherever your instincts take you next, they will eventually carry you through the chart.

THE NODAL FOUNDATION

South Node

Steve's South Node is in Capricorn. His basic orientation toward the world will be through setting and achieving goals, both in the short and long term, and sticking with them until the end. In typical Capricorn fashion, he'll instinctively organize his activities around reaching whatever goal is top priority. He could be quite the responsible type, even from an early age, taking responsibility for himself and potentially others, such as siblings or classmates.

Self-sufficiency and solitude go hand in hand for a Capricorn South Node person. Steve knows how to take care of himself and was probably quite independent from an early age, not relying solely on others to provide his entertainment, shelter, or care as a child typically might. Sometimes this can arise out of necessity if an early childhood situation of distant, absent, or busy parents forces the issue. In any case, Steve knows how to buckle down and just get things done when a situation calls for it, in some cases whether it's his responsibility or not. He is used to viewing life with a sense of stark proficiency and pragmatism. There is a stoic quality underlying everything in his personality, a fundamental expectation and understanding that no matter what you believe or want to believe about life, you can only take it at face value and keep on keeping on. Whether he greets life's adversities with elation or frustration, he moves quickly to the bottom line of "and now what am I going to do about it?" He tends to commit to things for the long haul, whether by default or intention.

Steve knows that if you want something done, you've got to do it yourself. He would automatically approach his desires with a willingness to work hard and steadily to achieve what he sets his mind to accomplish, and have little problem taking on additional responsibilities toward that end.

A potential pitfall of a South Node in long-suffering Capricorn is a tendency to always act from the perspective of one's duty and obligations—what one *has* to do rather than what one *wants* to do. This gives Steve the ability to put off his momentary desires to avoid being waylaid from his goals, but may also have him discounting his feelings when they interfere with the plan or shutting out experiences that don't fulfill a practical purpose. He tends to excel at things that require commitment or a dutiful approach, easily taking on the responsibilities he feels he must even if it's with a pessimistic or stoic attitude.

Steve's South Node is in the sixth house. Strong sixth house energy indicates someone who tends to work hard, whether by choice or out of necessity, so with a hardworking, dutiful sign like Capricorn in action here, it's easy to see how these dovetail with each other. Capricorn can be a take-charge sign, but in the servile sixth house, this tendency is likely to play out not as the boss but as the right-hand man, the one who holds down the fort, whom you can depend on to take care of things.

Also accompanying a sixth house South Node can be a tendency for the person to see themselves as an underdog in life. This can go toward the extreme of feeling like a victim if the sign or other planets emphasize it, but in Capricorn it may center on feeling like he is the one who gets the short end of the stick, having to hold down the fort or take care of the nitty-gritty things while the bosses go out and play. While he has no problem working hard, he may be vulnerable to embodying a kind of slave mentality, doing more than his share or feeling like he's got to make it to the top the hard way, with a willingness to put in his time at the bottom.

Through the unequal relationship angle of the sixth house, mentorship or apprenticeship can be a theme with a sixth house South Node. His life may have been influenced by one or several mentors. There is also the potential of the flip side too, that Steve, himself, is a natural at mentoring others, although he has to be careful regarding the level of personal responsibility he is willing to take on in order to do so, as he may be likely to automatically take on too much.

Following the steps in the nodal analysis process, now we check for any aspects involved with the South Node.

Planets Conjunct the South Node

There are no planets conjunct Steve's South Node.

Planets Opposite the South Node

Venus is opposite Steve's South Node. When a planet opposes the South Node, there may be a personal sense that the experiences and characteristics represented by that planet are elusive, unobtainable, or undesirable. Venus opposing the South Node, a planet most straight-forwardly representing relationship, friendship, healthy dependency, and love, could indicate that Steve has a sense that love and/or friend-ship can be difficult, elusive, or simply absent for some reason. We can speculate what the reason for that may be with the signs and houses involved.

We've already delineated some meanings of the South Node Cap-ricorn and the sixth house combo as hardworking, long-suffering, and responsible, with a tendency toward pursuing objectives over goofing off or wasting time, and taking care of oneself in a self-suffi-cient manner. Relationships by their very nature incorporate interde-pendence, sharing, cooperation, the giving and receiving of support, intimacy, and vulnerability, so through contrasting these two, we can speculate that perhaps his Capricorn South Node makes it easy for Steve to stay too busy or focused to take time out for relationships, or maybe his inherent self-sufficiency and love of solitude make it easier to just take care of himself rather than adding the complexity of en-tanglement with another, no matter how enjoyable.

Venus is in Cancer, the opposite sign of Capricorn. While this has its own straightforward interpretation, we are only concerned now with understanding how it could be problematic to someone who identifies with a Capricorn South Node. In this context only, we could see that

Venus in Cancer is a combination that, at the positive end of the spectrum, works from the heart, motivated by kindness and the giving and receiving of loving attention. On the negative side, there may be a tendency to give too much or to be easily overwhelmed by sensitivity and have a difficult time overlooking or forgiving slights from a partner.

With Venus being *opposite* the South Node, Steve may disown and project these characteristics onto other people in his life instead of learning to embrace the part of him that wants and needs these traits in a partner and even *has* these characteristics, or at least the potential to develop them as part of his own personality. He may see certain relationships or people whom he's attracted to as needy or eventually needing too much from him. With Venus in Cancer in the *twelfth* house opposing the South Node in the sixth, there's also the potential that the "perfect" loving relationship seems unrealistic or unobtainable, not just because it's opposite the South Node but because the twelfth house has an otherworldly component to it, and when we experience the twelfth house, we are outside of the regular hindrances and realities of everyday life (sixth house). His expectations may be "out of this world," setting him up for disappointment in real life.

While we probably have the themes right, it's important to note that we don't know how *Steve* has explained these relationship challenges to himself or to what extent and in what context he recognizes them—whether he's decided he doesn't want a relationship or just chalks it up to bad luck, shyness, the wrong partners, or any other number of possibilities. If he were our client, we'd share this perspective and then talk to him to find out how he's framed this in his life experiences. It's also important to note that this doesn't mean he would *never* have relationships, but only that we might be alert to a theme or pattern that reveals an out-of-reach quality to relationships throughout his life, whether it's in the types of partners he attracts or the marked absence of meaningful relationships either in the short or long term, or other possibilities. There isn't always necessarily a dark or terrible reason in these cases; sometimes it's simply the side effect of something that is otherwise good and desirable (like how being self-sufficient in the extreme can lead to isolation).

Saturn is well outside of our working 5° orb, far enough into Cancer to be outside the boundaries of the opposition to the South Node and technically not even close enough to Venus to pull it in by association. Realistically, however, the fact that Saturn is in the same house and sign as Venus and the North Node makes it likely that it's influence will be a relevant factor when it comes to Venus and North Node work for Steve, so we can afford to insert a quick aside on Saturn here.

Where Saturn is in our natal chart points simply to something we might find difficult, because we either don't like it, don't understand it, or don't want to face the realities necessary in order to harness Saturn's energy for our benefit. With Saturn in Cancer, Steve may have difficulty getting in touch with or expressing his vulnerability or more tenderhearted feelings. Nurturing others or receiving that nurture himself may not come easily. With Saturn in the hidden twelfth house, it may be even more of a challenge to clearly identify any emotional blockages or reservations he may have here; he may have to have the patterns in his life and relationships reveal it to him over time. He may not hesitate to be serious, with a Capricorn South Node and Pluto on the Ascendant, and he may easily fall into the role of the comic with slightly caustic and detached humorous observations, but to surrender to softness and wonder may take practice. It may be his own hidden resistance to intimacy and vulnerability that may play out in the Venus opposition to the South Node, him holding others at arm's length rather than the reverse, or circumstances, or idealism. There is no doubt this terrain will be part of the overall picture when it comes to working toward his North Node.

Planets Squaring the South Node

Neptune forms a square to both the North and South Nodes in Steve's natal chart. Concentrating on this square from the South Node perspective first, we want to look at the ways this planet's natural expression may be discordant or cause tension with his South Node orientation to life. One thing a Capricorn South Node can lack is flexibility, both in perspective and in routine. It sees the route and makes a plan, and it wants to follow the plan through to its end. Where Neptune resides in our chart is a place where we need to cultivate the ability to step into the flow of whatever we're feeling or whatever situation we're in, which may change from moment to moment, to psychically feel our way through it and respond in that rhythm. Neptune is also not about concrete, defined reality but about feeling and living many potentials at once. Where Capricorn requires boundaries, Neptune is boundless, dissolving boundaries and finding its way through the seams, as water does to rock.

With Neptune acting through his third house, Steve will be cultivating his ability to tap into and respond to the flow through his perceptive abilities. He'll practice having a flexible perception rather than a fixed, predetermined one, but also be able to see multiple layers of truth and possibility at once in each situation he's in. Because Neptune takes us into a dimension beyond the five senses, Steve will likely be able to perceive things that others may miss altogether in any situation, perhaps noting a certain subtle undertone to a situation that isn't obvious to the casual observer. This ability won't come from his knack for perceiving detail, which his Mercury in Virgo will certainly allow, but from the ability to sense subtle nuances that won't show up in a factual account of any given event. Subtlety is the word to emphasize here. He'll be good at sensing the vibe—something difficult to explain in factual, objective terms. Much of the way this reveals itself will probably happen in the context of relationship, with Neptune in Libra. Steve not only will be cultivating an ability to tune in to another person and respond to them on these subtle, unobvious levels, but will also have a knack for perceiving when any situation feels off-kilter or out of balance, and be able to gently nudge it back into harmony with something simple like a word or a facial expression, with most people being none the wiser.

The challenge in embracing Neptune will be to his Capricorn South Node, which will want to deal more in terms of measurable, objective reality, so he may doubt his own perceptions, second-guessing himself. If he doesn't doubt them, he may actually instead try to force them to fit into a rigid paradigm, insisting that what he sensed is exactly true and attempt to assume and impose facts over the vibe he sensed, trying to make the subjective objective. He'll have good intuition when it comes to situations and people, but that doesn't necessarily mean he can read their minds. The difference between *what* he senses and the logical explanation he tries to come up with after the fact will be vastly different and will be of key importance for him here. Even if he can sense vibes, he can't read minds and he may struggle to realize that difference so he can use the information he gleans from his intuition in an effective way, without leaping to conclusions.

In the meantime, this ability may often backfire on him in a couple of ways: either he may be unable to prove the assumptions that he so adamantly insists are true and/or he may get such negative feedback from others in trying to use this internal barometer and force what it tells him on other people that he'll continue to loop back into self-doubt and denial of what he perceives. This won't work, because everyone has their own internal barometer and if what he senses is not what they sense, they will resent it.

Planets Trine or Sextile the South Node

The Moon forms a sextile to the South Node.[29] We've seen that the Moon in Scorpio and in the fourth house creates an emotional nature that is deep, private, and focused, so we can see how it easily fits in with Capricorn's desire to work single-mindedly toward a goal and the love of solitude. We could even see how working from home, a creative combination of the fourth and sixth house terrains, might be an ideal setting for him in some ways.

---

29. To keep this chart delineation example clear, I've outlined a 5° orb, so with Mercury in a sextile to the North Node and trining the South Node with a 6° orb, it is outside of these guidelines. However, in practice, the decision to incorporate this into the nodal analysis would not be wrong by any means.

North Node

Steve's North Node is in the sign of Cancer. Cancer serves to balance the stoic, self-sufficient pragmatism of his Capricorn South Node by considering where his heart weighs in on any given matter, and learning to integrate the emotional flow of heart-centered desires into whatever plan he's made, even to the point of altering the plan if the goal no longer serves his highest good.

Steve's North Node is in the twelfth house. Due to the otherworldly nature of the twelfth house experience, his journey toward the North Node will encourage him to step out of the minute-by-minute mundanity of the sixth house South Node experience and into the timelessness of the twelfth house. Serving the needs of his inner life and not just the day-to-day practicalities that demand one's attention will propel him forward on his North Node journey.

Both Cancer and the twelfth house experience encourage him to become more intuitive and centered on the emotional, subjective experience of life to balance the extremities of the practical and realistic experiences of his South Node that have been second nature to him on a soul level.

Planets Conjunct the North Node

Venus is conjunct Steve's North Node. We have already established how it fits into the story as an opposing force on the South Node, Steve's comfort zone. Now we have to understand it as part of the way going forward. Venus's lessons and experiences most often center around relationship, both by way of the concepts and preconceived notions we have about what relationships should be like as well as what we learn and experience from the specific friends and partners we encounter.

We have to be careful in assuming that Steve's greatest mission in life is to get married, as that's only one of several possibilities with Venus conjunct the North Node. The form of the relationship is not as important as what it allows Steve to do: trust and share himself with another person. In order to do this, Steve may have to come to terms with any judgments he may have about relationships in general. We wouldn't know what those were without talking directly to Steve, but we might speculate it could be things like social norms and expectations about marriage, or that he might lose his independence, or that his love of solitude is too great, or any of the reasons we outlined previously.

Any relationships—romantic, business, or friendship—that he establishes in which he feels a sense of family, trust, and a long-term sense of good will can help him move toward that North Node Venus. We may find he experienced a lot of trial and error in relationships earlier in life, whether romantic, friendship, or familial, when it comes to trust, because these early experiences would help to provide grist for the mill when trying to move forward with relationships and a relationship outlook that is a fit for him.

Perhaps his journey will involve not only meaningful relationships but also something as simple as recovering an ability to believe in love and be less rigid about what package it might come in, or allowing himself to reveal his tenderness to another when so much of what he's comfortable with lies in being the strong, stoic one. Or the challenge may be not only to show tenderness but to allow himself to *receive* it. There may also be an element of challenge to turn the potential of unrealistic expectations and disillusionment in partnership around, not to become more cynical but to find a way to still experience the magic of love without having it based only on infatuation before that first fight or before unrealistic expectations set in.

We've probably hit the theme already, as most Venus issues correlate with standard one-on-one relationship themes, but another, albeit more abstract, possibility may be found with Venus in the twelfth house, which could also be interpreted as a sense of spiritual love—not just for one person but an all-encompassing love or divine, compassionate love for God or humankind (agape as opposed to eros). This could also be part of that journey toward the opening of the heart and the embracing of the vulnerability that is inherent in love. Along similar conceptual lines, this may also represent something along the lines of reclaiming the feminine in oneself.

Planets Opposite the North Node

There is no planet opposing the South Node in Steve's chart.

Planets Square the North Node

Now we need to look at Neptune as it relates to the North Node, as a gateway or a conflict that, as Steve attempts to resolve the tension in his psyche and life that it may represent, can open him up more to his North Node work. In the South Node, we discussed how the planet (Neptune) will naturally express as part of Steve, and the internal conflict that may cause for him. This pressure will force a conflict, where the resolution lies either in enforcing the comfort and perspective of the South Node and denying the Neptunian part of himself (something that is unsustainable in the long term) or integrating new potentials that take him out of his comfort zone but expand his view and allow him to incorporate these parts of himself.

As we grow up, the well-meaning world usually tries to dampen our idealism, to get us to think more realistically in order to save us from disappointment and disillusionment. But a Capricorn South Node comes pre-disillusioned, in a manner of speaking, and with Neptune at this halfway juncture, part of Steve's passage involves becoming a bit more idealistic, or at least becoming friendly with that perspective and all that can accompany it: hope, a willingness to try even when risking failure, cultivating imagination, and seeing the possibilities. Astrologer Richard Tarnas has said that Capricorn tends to lead with the "no," with the "can't." This serves Capricorn very well, but in Steve's case, it can be taken to excess and inhibit his North Node path from developing. He can learn instead to say "it has possibilities!"

Learning to surrender more to the energy of a given moment rather than sticking rigidly to what he planned on happening or wants to have happen will also be a useful lesson that his Neptunian side will push him to integrate. This will allow Steve to experiment with allowing himself to feel vulnerable, to be moved by his environment and what he learns from it through interacting with it, instead of trying to be the unmovable, reliable Capricorn.

Our perception of time already bends and flows whenever Neptune is involved—it encourages timelessness, surrender, and flow, not clock-watching or checklist managing, and with Neptune ruling the twelfth house, there is a link there that already pushes him toward the twelfth house lessons. In the movie *L.A. Story* (written and directed by Steve), one of the biggest messages of the movie is "let your mind go and the body will follow," with an emphasis on trusting what's happening in the moment and surrendering to it. Sounds like good advice here! In a way, escaping the mundane of the everyday (sixth house) in healthy ways *more*, not less, as is usually the advice if one wants to be a "responsible adult," may be just what he needs.

Planet Trine or Sextile the North Node

The Moon is trine the North Node in Steve's chart, which is no coincidence since anything sextiling the South Node must trine the North Node. The twelfth house, Cancer agenda of the North Node can easily integrate with the water sign and house nature of the Moon's placement, and the Moon naturally rules Cancer, so there is a lot of common ground here. Trusting his emotional instincts and pursuing what moves him is a start, but learning to do it without the enforcement of only the practical and sensible Capricorn goals and to let it be more heart-centered can push it toward the North Node agenda.

Summary

You've learned a number of techniques to give you some ideas on approaching chart synthesis and could employ even more should you be so inclined. How about laying a foundation with the four angles? Or maybe starting with the area of life you want to know most about, such as career, love, or family? Essentially, all techniques can get you there; all roads lead home. If you use the method that makes the most sense to you to begin the journey and then keep going, you'll make it through to the heart of the chart every time.

No matter what the technique, it will not help you if you do not integrate and compare what you are finding out about a chart with what you have already discovered about it. Nothing stands in isolation—each symbol is reinforced, redirected, or reduced by the context of the rest of the chart. Taking each step in context, either as you go or after completing your initial analysis of the symbols, is where astrology gains relevance and depth.

CHAPTER 15

STEVE MARTIN'S LIFE NOTES

It can be a blessing and a curse to know somebody, whether only a little or intimately, when trying to analyze their natal chart. It can be difficult to interpret their chart without drawing your conclusions based on what you know of them instead of letting the astrology speak, which can create blind spots and false assumptions. That drawback aside, comparing what you know of someone's biography and getting their personal feedback is an excellent way to see astrology come to life in a realistic and not just conceptual way, and there is no substitute when it comes to putting a chart interpretation into the context of a real life.

From his bestselling autobiography *Born Standing Up: a Comic's Life*, Steve shared parts of his life from childhood to the end of his stand-up comedy career. Using these revelations, we can speculate about how he's living his natal chart, as it unfolds throughout his own discoveries about himself and life, bringing astrology and biography together. However, it's important to keep in mind that in a public autobiography, a celebrity will probably be strategically selective in what they reveal, so we cannot assume what we do see is all that there is.

A BRIEF BIOGRAPHY OF STEVE MARTIN
Steve Glenn Martin was born in Waco, Texas, in 1945, to parents Mary and Glenn Martin, with one older sister, Melinda. His relationship with his father was especially tense throughout most of his life.

He grew up watching B westerns and comedy shows on television from age five, and would memorize comedy routines he saw the night before, performing them the next morning during his grade school's sharing time. His interest in magic started at an equally early age with storebought magic tricks and sets that were gifted to him by family members. He would practice performing the tricks intently and ended up performing them semiprofessionally in his teens.

Raised in Southern California, his first job was to hand out programs at Disneyland, which he began doing the year it opened. He took great pride in being "self-reliant and funded." Having free rein of the park after he had fulfilled his duties, he spent most of his time at Merlin's Magic Shop and the Golden Horseshoe Revue, both places where he watched magical and comedic performances, captivated. Over the years at Disneyland, he became an assistant to these performers, ultimately ending up splitting his time between the two magic shops at the theme park until he left Disneyland at age eighteen. Eventually, performing comedy outwon magic overall as he pursued his career.

Steve enrolled in college to study philosophy, although he eventually changed his major to theater and decided to drop out at age twenty-one to commit to an opportunity to write for the *Smothers Brothers Comedy Hour* television show. Over the next decade, he wrote for television and performed stand-up for audiences on shows such as *The Steve Allen Show, The Tonight Show Starring Johnny Carson,* and *Saturday Night Live.* He also released comedy albums during this time and wrote and starred in *The Jerk* in 1979. It was around this time that his leanings changed from stand-up to film, as he started to feel that his stand-up career had become "like an overly plumed bird whose next evolutionary step was extinction." Steve abruptly quit stand-up in 1981, after which his film career became his professional focus.

Steve was married to actress Victoria Tennant from 1986 to 1992. In 2007 he married Anne Stringfield, who gave birth to their first child in 2013, when Steve was sixty-seven years old. Steve is also a skilled banjo player, an avid art collector, a playwright, and an author.

CHAPTER 16
STEVE MARTIN:
THE CHART AND THE LIFE

CAREER

Knowing that Steve Martin's long and successful career has centered on performing, it is easy to see his Leo Sun and Ascendant at work. From an early age he was not just enjoying the shows he watched on television, he was memorizing (a little Mercury in Virgo precision there) and performing them (Leo) to an audience of his peers the very next day. Through his childhood and teens, he realized on more than one occasion that it wasn't the material he was performing that he loved as much as performing itself. In his autobiography, *Born Standing Up*, he called his first sight of the stage during a school assembly, with its grandeur and dramatic lighting, "the face of God."

Although he had a thirst for performing, he insists he is shy and gets embarrassed when he receives too much attention. His self-proclaimed shyness may be derived from Pluto on the Ascendant, which lends an attraction-repulsion reaction to attention and being seen, and/or from that private Scorpio Moon, which is in tension through the square to Pluto and the Ascendant. One way he may have coped with that was something that is a staple to his stand-up comedic style: he would make himself the subject of his own joke while pretending that there was nothing funny going on, taking himself totally seriously or with a sense of mock self-importance.

"I gave myself a rule: Never let them know I was bombing....It was essential that I never show doubt about what I was doing. I would move through my act without pausing for the laugh, as though everything were an aside...another rule was to make the audience believe that I thought I was fantastic, that my confidence could not be shattered."

This style may have arisen not only to adjust for shyness but also as a helpful way to cope with the vulnerability of putting himself on the chopping block and risking rejection show after show. Maybe it was a way of making himself bulletproof, a "fake it till you make it" kind of bravado, through his Pluto in Leo Ascendant. In making fun of himself, he also seems to step outside of his own act, detaching from himself as well as the audience. His Mars-Uranus conjunction in the eleventh house reveals this instinct to engage in his playful social style but remain simultaneously at a distance.

His goofy and offbeat comedy style arose, in part, from his careful observations about what was truly funny and why. Just as he memorized routines as a child, he would continue through his youth and early adulthood to methodically scrutinize other performers of all kinds, using that Mercury in Virgo to cultivate his skill. One profound realization manifested over several months that would define his unique style and lead to what his friend and colleague Rick Moranis called "anti-comedy." As Steve studied what seemed to make audiences laugh, he was struck by the somewhat mechanical rhythm of a conventional joke being told and its ensuing laughter, almost as if it were simply an automatic or polite response, such as applauding after a performance.

Steve had an instinctual understanding of the physical and mental rhythm between the punch line and the laughter, the symbiotic relationship between performer and audience, and he decided to experiment with it. Not satisfied with inauthentic or unearned laughs, he wondered what would happen if he didn't follow the formula. Instead of the punch-line-pause-for-laughter method, he kept the ball rolling, seeming to ignore the audience's laughter (and frequent bewildered silence) so that when they did laugh, it would be more spontaneous and authentic.

Leo's natural sensitivity to an audience is certainly instinctual to Steve, but this discovery in particular and how it permeated his "act with no jokes" from then on also highlights his Mars-Uranus conjunction in Gemini in the eleventh house. The combination of Mars, one's instinctual and visceral responsiveness, coupled with inventive and unconventional Uranus in the sign of curious and experimental Gemini, naturally led him to ask the question "What does this button do?" If Mercury is sometimes known as the "trickster," then Mars and Uranus acting as a pair through Mercury's sign, Gemini, begets the "prankster": he who understands the vigorous response elicited when combining the absurd with the unexpected. Because Mars is a planet that is connected with our physicality (stamina, overall constitution, physical responses, etc.), Steve had not just an idea of this but an instinct for it, especially apparent in his physical comedy, which became more and more ingrained in his act, helping him hone that instinct even more on the stage of the eleventh house.

Mars and Uranus in Gemini is a triumvirate that combines to create the quickest wit and a sense of sharpness in the ability to judge timing, something great comedy hinges on, not only because of the Geminian versatility but also because of the way Uranus represents that which happens suddenly, seemingly without warning. For all his precision and note-taking preparation, Steve's instincts were always one step ahead of him:

"My most persistent memory of stand-up is of my mouth being in the present and my mind being in the future: the mouth speaking the line, the body delivering the gesture, while the mind looks back, observing, analyzing, judging, worrying, and then deciding when and what to say next."

While the absurd and instinctual may come from Mars and Uranus, Neptune certainly lends a hand placed in the third house of perception, with a sense of whimsy in the way he expresses his ideas, which is added to an already charming and dramatic Leo Ascendant through a sextile between the two. It also contributes to his love of magic and his enchantment with not only the ability to put on a show but also the ability to deftly deceive through illusion and sleight-of-hand. Neptune is where we love a sense of mystery and enchantment, where we don't want to see too clearly but could use a little soft glow, a little softening; it's where we long to be amazed with a child's innocent belief that something impossible could be real. When speaking of the time spent learning and practicing card tricks, Steve says:

"A magician's hands are often hiding things, and I learned that stillness can be as deceptive as motion."

When observing magicians, he was very tuned in to the way a magician employed subtle manipulation on the audience to get them to focus their attention on one particular place when the real action was taking place almost imperceptibly, an example of Neptune (the subtlety and illusion) in Libra (receptivity to the other) in the third house (perception, expression).

But most of all, he loved having the inside scoop, being the one who knew how the tricks worked, being let in on the secrets that only the privileged few know.

This enchantment ties in to the heart of his Scorpio Moon, and enjoyment of the powerful feeling one gets when knowing something others don't, as well as tying back in to Pluto on the Ascendant, approaching the world always knowing that there's more to anything than what is shown. While most of the time Steve would prefer to keep that power and those secrets, putting on the show with only half his hand showing, he probably loved to burst innocent bubbles now and then with a Plutonian edge to his wit; case in point—one of his famous closers to a show was, "Well, we've had a good time tonight, considering we're all going to die someday."

When his stand-up career was reaching its height, coupled with the frenzy and the toll it took on his act and his life, he experienced firsthand the way that his Leo shine would precede him. He was expected to be exactly like his onstage persona, offstage, and to be "on" constantly. Steve has expressed how his shyness conflicted with his fame when strangers acted like they knew him and seemed to expect his familiar attention in return.

Steve's life becoming bloated and overrun by the domination of his success probably provided a significant lesson along the lines of just how far (and only so far) a hardworking, ambitious Capricorn, sixth house South Node could take you. The influence of the South Node can be quite strong throughout the life due to the comfort of ease and the sheer familiarity of what it represents, but it is especially strong in youth before experience teaches us the cost of its convenient but deadening effect on our lives. Steve had been ambitious from a very early age, working at Disneyland from age ten, and was thrilled by the opportunity to feel the sense of responsibility and self-sufficiency that working provided, even feeling superior to others his age who weren't gainfully employed.

Steve also worked long and hard, with steady commitment toward achieving success at what he set out to do. He put himself on the line more than once in his all-or-nothing Pluto Ascendant style and with his Jupiter in Virgo willingness to bet big on his skill. Yet he was suffering from years of puzzled audience and critic responses to his off-the-wall comedic style as well as anxiety attacks brought on by hypochondria and a nagging anxiety of not being able to rise to the demands of himself and others. These are all classic sixth house pitfalls, especially when coupled with Capricorn's desire to be well thought of and always above reproach. His Mercury in Virgo could also contribute to an overactive self-criticism and chronic worrywart thinking. He could never let the attacks get the best of him or prevent him from getting the old job done (Capricorn), however. When experiencing his first anxiety attack (before realizing what was happening), he didn't check into a hospital because he was afraid he would miss work and lose his place in line, so to speak, if he did.

When his success and status started to reach monumental levels, soul dissatisfaction set in. The motivation to keep the grind going, to continue to climb to the top, loses it momentum when you get there and realize it's not enough (or rather, it's too much, depending on your point of view). He had done his South Node to death in this respect; he developed his skill (sixth house) and worked with diligence, but the need to feed and engage his creativity, to seek out inspiration, play, and experimentation, was replaced by an act that was unfolding by rote. Something had to give, as he was "exhausted, physically and emotionally," with sold-out shows still ahead of him. He describes an uncharacteristic rage coming upon him on the night of his last stand-up show when he returned to his dressing room, packed his magic act away, and never went back to stand-up.

His Mars-Uranus and Pluto Ascendant may have had a hand in the seeming abruptness of this development. While in truth, hitting the top and the toll it was taking had been building to a change that needed to happen for a couple of years, the sudden (Uranus) action (Mars) itself seems quite impulsive but fitting for his style of action, which isn't hesitating. Also, with Pluto in such a prominent and influential location in his chart, that old Pluto keyword *transformation* comes into play more than once in major developments in his life. Ultimately, the way forward is death (Pluto) of the persona one has developed (Ascendant) to make way for a new one to be born.

FAMILY

Steve has said on multiple occasions that his relationship with his father was tense and distant (the family always referred to his father by his first name and not as Dad), even hostile as Steve got older. Steve was surprised when friends of his father told him how funny, caring, and outgoing his dad was because he has said he rarely felt he saw this side of his father.

After his father seemed to grow increasingly antagonistic, especially toward his mother, which Steve witnessed through arguments overheard, he resolved that "only the most formal relationship would exist" between his father and him, a rift that continued until his dad's final years. He characterizes his mother as behaving submissively in an effort to avoid his father's temper but then whispering her true thoughts to Steve and urging him to keep the secret between them, which led him to believe for a great many years that it was "dangerous to express one's true opinion."

Much of this dynamic between Steve and both of his parents individually and what it might have taught Steve at a young age may come through in the square between the Moon and Pluto, as well as Venus opposing the stoic Capricorn South Node and making a wide conjunction with Saturn.

The Moon is a very primal astrological symbol—it is in play before we can talk or walk and represents the tone and style with which we receive (and give) nurture. While the Moon and the planets/sign in the fourth house represent family and home, they do not describe one's parents objectively. Instead, the Moon and fourth house can provide insight into the way the native, in this case Steve, sees and experiences his parents as caregivers and authorities.

There is a level of emotional intensity from the start with a Scorpio Moon, and a propensity for seeing and being alert to emotional undercurrents in the home and between family members, especially those that are darker and therefore hidden from children (though not always). Many times, prominent Scorpio such as this often turns a person into an unwitting confessional, a keeper of others' secrets even if the person doesn't seek them out.

The Pluto square adds a further edge, representing a wound (Pluto) to trust (Moon) at a fundamental level. In one way Steve may long for nurture and in another, reject it, not wanting to become dependent on it and then lose it, causing further pain. He saw his mother as many things, no doubt, but mentions her secretiveness with him, and his father's smoldering, swallowed anger like a powder keg ready to be ignited, both creating an intense underlying atmosphere in the home that would have put a crack in Steve's sense of emotional safety (Moon square Pluto), perhaps teaching him that keeping things hidden is the way to go.

Venus tucked in Cancer in the sequestered twelfth house and as far away from his South Node in Capricorn as it can get reveals just how far away the more tender expression of affection that he is quite capable of may have seemed, especially in early life when the pull of the South Node is quite strong. Venus in Cancer can be quite a romantic, emotional, loving, and kind influence, but in a self-protective chart, Cancer's shell can be quite thick, and in the twelfth house, it can be difficult to find a way to make it real and apparent. Recognizing and claiming that part of himself, and then being willing to reveal it in relationship to someone he trusts, would probably take many years.

Perhaps in part because of his distance from his father and in part simply his nature, Steve was seemingly always independent and self-reliant, including emotionally. This probably in no small part stemmed from his Capricorn, sixth house South Node—working hard, taking on responsibility at a young age, and being self-sufficient.

Although Steve gives his father credit for being "the generous one" of the family (financially), Steve himself seemed to be unsettled being in his debt, or in any debt at all, for that matter, and has said that as an adult, he's never bought anything on credit.

Overall, Steve's communication and interaction with family was infrequent and minimal. He has said that was most comfortable away from home and that he felt an overall "familial ineptness" that contributed to keeping family relationships distant. He avoided discussing his work with his father, who he felt withheld approval and offered only criticism. He began an effort to reconnect with his parents when he was in his late thirties and early forties (heading toward that North Node?) and notes that his father's feelings toward him began to become softer but that he believes the first time the words "I love you" were ever spoken between them was not until his father was in his eighties.

LOVE

Although Steve has had several significant romantic relationships and two marriages, his refusal to discuss his private life beyond rare, superficial remarks makes it difficult to see intimately into his romantic life, but a few facts coupled with a couple of anecdotes can offer a glimpse. Steve has mentioned a reluctance to have children and an ambivalent attitude toward marriage on more than one occasion. Although he has alluded to his time on the road in his eighteen-year stand-up career as being sprinkled with one-night stands and some brief "interludes with monogamy," he said in a 1980 interview for *Playboy*, "I couldn't go for the one-night thing anymore. I couldn't wake up with a stranger. That whole thing—it's depressing."

Out from under the duck-and-cover atmosphere of home long enough and with time and self-discovery, Venus and the North Node purpose can start to unfurl, with a long road ahead to reach full bloom. Restrictive and self-protective Saturn stands guard close by the Venus–North Node conjunction, and this, in addition to the dynamics of his Pluto-Moon square, make this Venus–North Node work particularly challenging. The North Node is not a goal you arrive at or a destination that can be reached, but a road sign you follow throughout life. Moving away from brief relationships in which intimacy cannot form beyond a certain point into longer and more complex ones may be not only a natural part of maturity but an important part of Steve's path toward the North Node through Venus.

One of the most telling revelations in his autobiography connects the stress and distance in his relationship with his father to his romantic life:

"Having cut myself off from him, and by association the rest of the family, I was incurring psychological debts that would come due years later in the guise of romantic misconnections and a wrong-headed quest for solitude."

And later, in a final conversation with his father, Steve says he felt "a chill of familiarity" when his father said on his deathbed that he wanted to cry "for all the love I received and couldn't return." Only Steve can say whether this familiarity he describes stems from recalling his childhood days or recognizing the truth of what his father said at work in Steve's own life, but it could certainly represent the challenge it has probably been to remove some of his emotional road blocks, especially in love.

CHAPTER 17

TROUBLESHOOTING
THE CHART

Even with skill, practice, and solid technique, there's often something in a natal chart that requires extra effort to understand. Here are a few common troublesome situations and some suggestions on how to resolve the confusion that can arise with them.

RESOLVING CONTRADICTIONS

Perhaps you've seen something like this from a computerized natal chart report: "You are outgoing and expressive" and a few lines later, "You are a solitary type and like to keep to yourself." Well, which is it? You may have a natal chart with Mars in Cancer in the private twelfth house, which seems to give the impression of a quiet, behind-the-scenes type of person, but with a Leo Ascendant, which is supposed to be outgoing, expressive, and dominant. Computer-generated reports aren't typically able to handle the nuances of conflicting astrological influences, but you can.

Sometimes it may be situational, such as someone being shy in groups but social in one-on-one situations. Though the traits of "shy" and "social" seem to conflict, it can be natural to find parts of our personalities partitioned in this way. In most cases, however, you can get more depth and nuance if you consider the forces underneath the conflict instead of simply resorting to "sometimes you're this, other times you're the complete opposite."

We all have conflicting urges inside of ourselves that battle it out for dominance, and those things are reflected in a natal chart, often by the challenging aspects such as squares or oppositions. If you think that two parts of a chart don't make any sense when you try to imagine them inside of one person, you are probably beginning to understand how that person feels with those conflicts inside of them! Try accepting that these two influences, though in conflict, are both valid. What could they each need? How might this internal conflict take shape in a real person or an everyday circumstance?

THE BIG OVERPOWERS THE SMALL

Sometimes when there are conflicting planetary need combinations reflected in the chart, one might show up in the person's life as more dominant and overrun the less dominant combination. This might be because one planetary configuration is more socially acceptable, is more convenient, or is seen by that person as more admirable, and so that need gets met more easily and more often than the other. The less dominant need or behavior won't be eradicated, but it may be subverted. If this is the case, it can be a good opportunity to call the person's attention to it and help them recognize how to get that need fulfilled and the importance of giving that part of them an equal voice.

Consider someone with the Sun and Moon in Capricorn and a Cancer Ascendant. A simplified statement about these three influences might be that they would have a strong streak of practicality, groundedness, and an orientation toward productivity and efficiency (Capricorn). They would also prefer to approach life (Ascendant) with caution and care to maintain a sense of security as they interact with the world (Cancer). They might be less inclined to do things that are a wasteful use of their time and resources, or things that are risky, even if they are fun, because they don't meet these primary needs. But if this person had Jupiter in Aries, then the part of them that wants to grow and explore their potential (Jupiter) is more fed by experimentation and risk (Aries), which isn't as comfortable for the Capricorn + Cancer part of the person. Experiments often don't produce usable results, or they involve more failures than successes, and risk involves the potential for getting hurt, two things this person would be more inclined to avoid.

So while these two needs are inside one person, we only have so much energy to devote toward living, and prioritizing the dominant Capricorn + Cancer needs over the lone Jupiter in Aries need will keep this person satisfied more of the time. Therefore, this person is vulnerable to letting the dominant need outweigh the less dominant one. The Jupiter in Aries need may have a harder time finding satisfying expression. Perhaps it comes out only when risk is inconsequential or small or when there's a safe and controlled outlet for it. This may be a reasonable way for them to work out this conflict, and it's up to you to consider the many ways that this conflict may express itself, this way being one of them.

Conflicting influences in a chart can show up in a variety of ways. Essentially, any time what you know about one configuration clashes with what you know about another, you have a conflict. More specifically, planets in signs and houses that square or oppose each other can directly indicate a conflict. A chart with a great deal of planets placed in one element and little of another may also indicate conflicting internal needs. Your own confusion in trying to understand the influences is the best indicator that here is a knot to be untangled in the natal chart, both in your understanding as an astrologer and in the person who belongs to the chart!

UNCONVENTIONAL COMBINATIONS

The combinations of planet-sign-house with another planet-sign-house within a natal chart can be confusing when they seem to contradict each other, but sometimes it only takes a planet in a disparate sign or house to grind the flow of chart interpretation to a halt. There are no set combinations that are more difficult than others, because everyone has their strong and weak spots of understanding, but often combinations like Saturn in Aries or Uranus in Capricorn can be confusing because they can seem like trying to combine oil and water. This confusion can also happen in situations where a sign's ruling planet is in its opposite sign, such as Mars in Libra or Neptune in Virgo. Yet another confusing possibility can be signs in their opposite houses or in a disparate house, such as Aries in the seventh house or even Capricorn in the fifth house.

You can start to unravel any one of these apparent contradictions with a similar method. Remember that although the astrological alphabet tells us that certain planet-sign-house combinations share similarities and therefore are ruled by that planet, it does not mean their individual meanings are identical. You must deconstruct the astrological alphabet. Jupiter rules Sagittarius, and Sagittarius, being the ninth sign, is naturally aligned with the ninth house, but Jupiter is not Sagittarius is not the ninth house.

Check your assumptions about the definitions you've attributed to the planet, sign, and house configuration that's giving you trouble. Are there any keywords you've misattributed? For example, the ninth house represents the act of engaging with big systems of thought, such as philosophy or religion, and seeing big patterns of meaning. It also represents higher education in general and travel. These are the activities one does in the ninth house, but the style in which they're done is not necessarily Sagittarian. The Sagittarian style applied to the ninth house would emphasize education through experiential means, and might travel in an adventurous style, like camping or backpacking or hitchhiking in exotic locations. However, a different sign, such as Libra, would apply itself to the ninth house by emphasizing a style of objectivity and balance in thought, a more intellectual approach to learning, and perhaps an interest in the arts, law, or relationship topics when educating themselves. They also might travel for a different reason, such as wanting to expose themselves to the finer things of life, visiting museums or traveling to romantic locations.

PLANETS ON THE CUSP

Recall that *cusp* is the term used to define the division between one sign and the next, and one house and the next, in an astrological chart. Many people know this term because they have heard they were born "on the cusp," which means they were born close to the point in time when the Sun is about to cross into a new sign or has just crossed into a new sign. To be born on the cusp embodies a much narrower time frame than most people typically realize. Someone might say they were born on the cusp if they were born two or three days before or after the Sun's shift into a new sign, but in reality, the sign divisions are quite clear. To be born on the cusp of a sign is more about the *actual moment* when the Sun moves into the new sign, where the "disc" of the Sun is actually straddling the cusp of two signs. If you were born with the Sun in the last degree of Capricorn, you are still solidly a Capricorn, even though a day or even hours later the Sun moved into Aquarius.

Very few people are actually born on a sign cusp. That is not to say that we may not feel a certain duality in our personalities, or feel that we are represented by more than just Capricorn, for example. As you know by now, a natal chart is composed of many different combinations of symbols, and those combinations combine with other combinations that speak to a person's complexity and uniqueness. Many people use the "cusp" explanation to help them understand why they don't feel wholly and solely described by their sign. But there are more likely explanations than being born on the cusp when you take the entire natal chart into account instead of simply the Sun sign.

While sign cusps are clear, questions of planets on the cusp separating two houses still causes some debate among astrologers as to its importance.[30] If any planet lies close to the beginning or end of a

---

30. The reason for this may be twofold: one, because within the tropical system there is no debate about where sign boundaries begin and end, but there are multiple house systems, each calculated slightly differently, which is enough to change house cusps by a couple degrees from one to the next (the angles remain the same among most systems, however); and two, a planet may be in a sign for days or even years, but house cusp positions within those signs shift rapidly throughout a single day, so the difference between a planet being in one house or the next may be a matter of minutes.

house, it can bring up questions about how to interpret that planet because it lies close to a cusp—meaning, if that person had been born just a few minutes later or earlier, one or more planets in their natal chart may have been in an entirely different house. Therefore, while the planetary energy is set with its placement in a natal chart, it seems significant to some astrologers that it was in the midst of a change of house and might affect the planet's expression.

The question of what to do with planets "on the cusp" seems to be an eternal one in astrology, with almost as many opinions as there are astrologers. It is an issue that tends to incite more fretting than is warranted, but questions about the issue eventually come up, such as these: If a planet lies close to the cusp of a sign or house, is it interpreted in its current exact place, projected forward into the next sign or house, or considered to be a blend of both? And how close to the cusp of the next sign or house must a planet be to be considered "on the cusp"?

The reasoning behind one's decision to either interpret a cuspal planet as is or "push" it into the cusp it borders is often arbitrary. There is no inherent reason that compels an astrologer to consider the issue of cusp a problem, although many will have a fervent opinion one way or the other. Unless you feel specifically drawn to one line of reasoning or the other, the most straightforward thing to do is to take the chart at face value and interpret every planet in the sign and house in which it technically appears, even if it's close to a cusp. Wherever you land on this issue, it helps to follow a consistent rule, especially in the beginning of your astrological journey. As you gain skill, you can try experimenting and see what seems to produce the most consistent meaning.

OUT-OF-SIGN ASPECTS

Each sign has a set relationship to every other sign in the zodiac. Taurus immediately follows Aries, and that never changes. Aries is always square Cancer and opposite Libra. Therefore, any planets in these signs will reflect that relationship. A planet at 14° Aries will be square to another planet at 14° Cancer, never conjunct, trine, or opposed, because Aries and Cancer are in an eternal square to each other.

However, most aspects are not exact. There is often an orb of a small number of degrees between one planet and another. A planet at 11° Aries is still considered to be squaring a planet at 14° Cancer, with an orb allowance of 3°. Occasionally this orb allowance will make it possible that planets in an aspect to each other, such as a square, are actually in signs that typically sextile or trine each other. This happens when one of the planets involved is at the end of a sign and the other planet is at the beginning of a sign. If Mercury was placed at 28° Aries and Jupiter was found at 1° Leo, these planets would be in signs that are in a permanent trine relationship to each other, but the degrees of these planets' placements in these signs are technically squaring each other mathematically, being roughly 90° apart. When in doubt about an aspect, count the degrees between them, following the shortest distance from one planet to the other.

To resolve the confusion of an out-of-sign aspect, think creatively about what these signs have in common and what is different about them. If the planets are in a challenging aspect to each another, such as a square or opposition, consider how these two signs (which normally have some common ground) may conflict. In the case of a flowing aspect between two planets, such as a trine or sextile, think about how those signs, perhaps normally in conflict with each other, might find common ground.

Every sign can have differences or points of compatibility with another sign. For example, even though Libra and Sagittarius are signs that are in a permanent, flowing sextile relationship to each other, they have obvious differences, such as Sagittarius's desire to leap in instinctually to an experience compared to Libra's natural (in)decision process. Conversely, Sagittarius and Pisces are in a permanent, challenging square relationship to each other, but they both share an open and optimistic energy.

CHAPTER 18
TIPS AND TRICKS
OF CHART INTERPRETATION

If you continue to study and practice astrology, you'll acquire a lifetime of tips and tricks that you've discovered along the way to help you draw the most out of a natal chart. Here's a few to get you started.

LOCATE THE DOMINANT PLANET/PLANET COMBO

Many interpretation techniques have already been outlined with the aim of helping you find the theme in a natal chart. While these and other techniques can help you create a foundation for chart interpretation, an additional tip that you may discover on your own or uncover while utilizing one of these themes is a dominant planet. The "follow the ruler" method outlined previously is one way to uncover a chart's ruling planet, which can have a dominating effect over a natal chart. However, a dominant planet may appear in a natal chart in a number of ways, even if it is not the chart ruler.

A certain planetary influence sometimes seems to echo throughout the chart, either directly because it's involved in many aspects or through rulership (such as a strong Neptune coupled with a large Piscean influence). A planet conjunct the Ascendant or a planet involved in a large number of aspects in the natal chart (especially if that list includes the Sun and Moon) so that it influences many other natal planets are examples of how a dominant planet may present. Not every chart will display this circumstance, and even so, it may exist not as part of but in addition to the chart's theme, so this tip will not be applicable in every natal chart. If all, or at least many, roads lead back to a planet, sign, house, or combination through rulerships, it can yield an eye-opening insight and is worth checking into.

TRY A LITTLE FINE-TUNING

Two concepts, *retrograde* and *interception*, can help you fine-tune the expression of a planet in a natal chart. They are subtle influences, but if present, they can provide additional information as to how a planet operates in a natal chart.

Introduction to Retrogrades

Earth orbits the Sun along with the other planets like cars driving along the freeway next to each other in their individual lanes. Because of the varying orbit lengths of each planet and their respective distances from the Sun, planets overtake each other in their orbits, sometimes seeming to come from behind to pass us and sometimes falling behind as we pass. When Earth overtakes another planet in its orbit, it appears from our viewpoint that the planet we are passing is moving backward, when actually we are simply moving in front of it. This is called *apparent retrograde motion* and is significant in understanding the motion of the planets as well as interpreting them in a natal chart.

Visually, planets will appear to slow down, stop, and then reverse direction for a period before slowing down, stopping, and going in direction motion again. If we trace the orbit of a planet during its retrograde period, drawing a line as it moves through the sky backward and forward, it does not just switch back and forth on the same plane but appears to make a backward "loop," just as a rollercoaster car may traverse an upside-down loop in its track. Again, this is just its *apparent* motion, as planets do not really reverse their orbit, but this loop is an apt metaphor for the effect attributed to natal retrograde planets. The expression of the planet's energy may seem to be indirect, or delayed, before manifesting outwardly, as if the process had to make an internal loop first. Some astrologers consider a retrograde planet, especially if it is one of the inner planets (Mercury, Venus, and Mars), to be significant and will consider how it affects the planet's expression in the natal chart.

Because of their positions in the solar system, the Sun and Moon are never retrograde, and the outer planets (Uranus, Neptune, and Pluto) are retrograde for long periods of time throughout each year.

Introduction to Interception

There are twelve signs and twelve houses. Nice and neat, right? Yet, signs and houses don't often match up that neatly; it is most common for a house cusp to begin somewhere in the middle of a sign and end in the middle of the next sign. Still, this fact generally allows for each house to begin in a different sign, twelve for each, all around the chart.

The exception is an idea known as *interception*. Interceptions are more common in birthplaces of extreme latitude. Due to the fact that the houses are not equally sized, sometimes a house will seem to swallow an entire sign (figure 10); that is, a house cusp will begin in one sign and not end until *two* signs later, such as the second house beginning in Cancer and the third house not beginning until Virgo, swallowing Leo up entirely within the second house. Since every sign is an equal 30° wide, an interception occurs when a house is particularly large, spanning more than 30° of the natal wheel. The reverse can also happen, where two house cusps fall within the same sign. This happens if a house is particularly narrow, spanning less than 30°.

Because the natal wheel is a fixed 360° circle, these circumstances typically occur together, the wide houses filling up some of the space that the narrow houses then have to relinquish. In addition, what happens on one side of the natal wheel will happen on the other side, reflected as in a mirror. Not only will a wide house (engulfing a sign) and a narrow house occur together, but they will occur on the other side of the chart in the opposite place. If one sign is intercepted, so will its opposite sign be. If two house cusps begin within the borders of one sign, the opposite two house cusps will begin in the opposite sign.

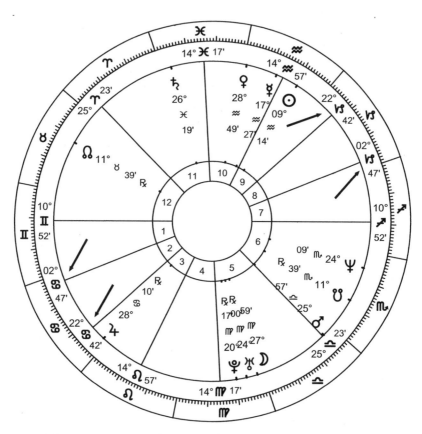

Figure 10: Intercepted Houses: The Signs Cancer and Capricorn Fully Surround the Second and Eighth Houses

Signs that are swallowed entirely within a house are called intercepted signs (figure 11); therefore, any planets in those intercepted signs are also affected and referred to as intercepted planets.

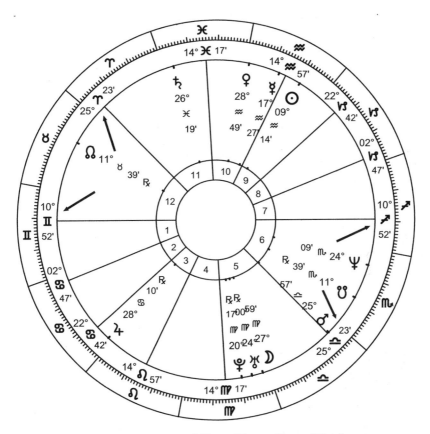

Figure 11: Intercepted Signs: Houses Six and Twelve
Fully Surround the Signs Scorpio and Taurus

House cusps are thought to be sensitive points in the chart, where the expression of the sign energy on the cusp of that chart can express itself most directly. That is why planets close to house cusps, and especially the four angles, are often considered significant. If a planet falls within a sign that is intercepted, it has no house cusp through which it can act. That intercepted sign is, in essence, a little more hidden and therefore so is the planet's ability to express in an overt way. One might compare it to trying to hear someone talk through a thin blanket—you can hear it, but it may be slightly more muffled than usual.

Astrologers vary widely in their opinions about the importance of interceptions. Like planets in retrograde, the effect of planets intercepted is slight, an additional fine-tuning to add to the sum interpretation of the planet-sign-house combination. Astrologer Chris McRae refers to the effect of intercepted signs or planets as being subject to "intensification due to internalization," with the idea being that because no house cusp serves as an outlet, its effect on our lives plays out in a more inwardly expressed and developed way.

UTILIZE WHOLE SIGN ASPECTS

Aspects are meant to help you understand how well different planet-sign-house combinations get along with each other, so you can begin to see the bigger narrative at work in a natal chart. Although an aspect between two planets is determined by the specific numbers, whole sign aspects can be relevant in certain circumstances and are based on the natural positions of the signs. A whole sign aspect occurs when two planets are in signs that have a fixed relationship with each other, even if the exact orb of the degree placement of those planets is otherwise very wide.

The signs are always in a fixed relationship with each other: Taurus always comes after Aries, Sagittarius is always three signs before Pisces, etc. Aries, for example, will always be in a trine to the signs Leo and Sagittarius, but always squaring the signs Cancer and Capricorn, and always opposed Libra. Therefore, Aries is always in some agreement with Leo and Sagittarius styles, and always in some level of tension with Cancer, Capricorn, and Libra in the way its energy is expressed. When planets are placed in these signs, they may not technically be in aspect with each other if the orb between them is too large. However, the way each planet operates through its sign may still share a level of agreement or tension with another planet placed in a sign that naturally trines or squares (or opposes) it.

When blending planetary combinations together in a natal chart, this understanding can be helpful in seeing how the various energies cooperate (or don't) with each other. Even if there is no strict numerical aspect between two planets, gaining a holistic understanding of how those two planets function within the same person is still your goal, and whole sign aspects can sometimes help with that.

FIND AN ASPECT'S COMMON ELEMENT OR MODALITY

Aspects between two planets or even aspect configurations involving more planets can be understood by analyzing each component on its own, breaking the aspecting planets down to their essence by analyzing the pieces and letting that analysis build on what you discover at each step. However, one additional technique can serve to unify your understanding of an aspect. Unless you have the special circumstance of an out-of-sign aspect, planets in aspect with each other share a duality, a modality, or an element, traced through their respective signs. Obviously, planets in conjunction will share all three because they are in the same location. Beyond this, the most significant to note is a shared modality or element.

Planets aspecting each other in a square or opposition, as well as the aspect patterns T-square or grand cross, share a common modality; they will be dominantly cardinal, fixed, or mutable by sign placement. Planets trining each other, including the grand trine aspect pattern, share a common element—fire, earth, air, or water. Planets sextiling each other share a common duality through their sign placement, both being either projective or receptive.

The modality-sharing challenging aspects can reveal some ways in which these aspects manage the inherent conflict, in addition to the specifics of each planet involved. Cardinal-themed aspects can reveal a tendency to get up and start something in order to manage the tension between the conflicting planetary needs. Fixed-themed aspects may reveal an ability to endure the tension immovably, sometimes to a fault, with nothing changing and the conflicting needs just digging their heels in at the figurative negotiating table. The mutable-themed aspects show a propensity toward movement, as with the cardinal theme, but with the aim to wriggle out of the conflict or dodge its effects with restless energy bouncing back and forth in a repetitive cycle.

With the element-sharing aspects, a tight bond is formed between planets that are found to cooperate easily in a particular chart due to the trine energy. These planets use the tried-and-true method of the element to continue approaching every situation they touch in the same manner. Fire-element trines will operate by building enthusiasm and feast off their mutual creative or instinctual drives. Earth-element trines will cooperate with a practical approach and concrete applications of their methods. Air-element trines will seek out information and use it to stimulate and communicate new ideas. Water-element trines will use their intuitive senses to assess the meaning of any given situation and, subsequently, their emotional response to it.

This underlying commonality can help you solidify your understanding of the link between planets in aspect with each other, and entire books and concepts have been written that build on this topic.[31] You will still need to go through the process of analyzing the individual planets in their sign and house, and then understand easily (or not) how they interact with each other, but utilizing this tip can help you further integrate their meanings.

HIGHLIGHT THE OVERLAP

When analyzing a planet-sign-house combination in a natal chart, there might be a dozen or more concepts and combinations that you could come up with. It can be helpful to lay out all the possibilities, but it can also be overwhelming to know which possibilities most likely apply. For instance, if someone has a planet in the ninth house, you can learn something about their education, their travel, or their philosophies (the underlying principles behind what they think is the right way to live). However, you can judge what the most significant things to know might be. For example, it might be more meaningful

---

31. Astrologer Noel Tyl's concept of the grand trine as "a closed-circuit of self-sufficiency" that manifests through its shared element and Tracy Marks' book *How to Handle Your T-Square* are two examples.

to take some time exploring a person's fundamental viewpoints and beliefs than to speculate on their favorite vacation spot (unless they are asking you where they should vacation next summer!).

The context of the chart will help you pull out the most meaningful statements in each planet-sign-house combination as you go. In the previous example, travel was somewhat arbitrarily deemed less important than one's philosophical views. However, if the rest of the context of the chart emphasizes a strong need for travel and the importance of its impact on the person or how meaningful of a catalyst it could be for the person (such as a predominance of Sagittarius or a lack of planets in signs or houses that require routine), you could realize that the travel component of the ninth house planet might be more meaningful than just a vacation spot suggestion.

This is why it's important to be familiar with the broad spectrum of meanings of each planet, sign, or house, but also to realize that you will not draw on the entirety of each spectrum when you are interpreting a natal chart. As you interpret the rest of the chart, draw out the keywords and concepts that are most relevant within the context of the chart. In a mentally or intellectually oriented chart context, where we see a lot of planets in air signs/houses or a strong Mercury placement, for example, it would make more sense that the person would use any planets in Gemini predominantly to facilitate learning, perhaps orienting them toward being a bookworm or an eternal student. In a more socially oriented chart, you might see any planets in Gemini leaning more toward the communicative side of this sign, perhaps orienting the person toward being a big talker or a tutor or a writer. All of these traits are part of the full spectrum of the Gemini experience, but what a person *actualizes* in real life has a lot to do with context.

This approach is based on the idea of overlap. If you have a variety of planet-sign-house combos and you've outlined the possible spectrums of meaning for each one, look for where those spectrums overlap. As you combine all the planets in signs and houses with the other planets and signs in houses in a natal chart, you look for over-lap, repetition, and reinforcement.

The natal chart represents countless potential combinations and, as such, reflects a human being's infinite potential. But potential is not actualization. Just because we might become anything we wish doesn't mean we can become *everything* we wish; we simply don't have the infinite lifespan or resources to do so. Likewise, each sign represents an archetype, a general field of experience that has count-less manifestations. However, a complex human with multiple natal chart combinations does not embody the totality of that archetype in their behavior. They partake of that archetype but are not a perfect representation of the pure, wholesale experience of that sign. What they pull from each archetype will not only be pieces of the whole archetype, they will be the *relevant* pieces, and what's relevant in each archetype will change with each natal chart, as the archetypes mingle together in that chart.

THINK SYMBOLICALLY

To keep your interpretation relevant and avoid overwhelm, you need to strategically narrow your interpretations until you're left with the essence. As stated in the previous paragraphs, people don't actual-ize every possibility of every planet, sign, or house in every moment. However, you also want to avoid being *too* narrow in what you ex-tract from an archetype into your interpretation. You're looking for that sweet spot! The idea is to narrow the spectrum to the potentials that are probably most important, while understanding that people grow and change in how they express those potentials. One way to do that is to avoid being too *literal* in your interpretation, becoming fix-ated on just one idea or one potential manifestation of an astrological symbol.

Any interpretation of a planet in a sign or a planet in a house will have more than one possible outcome. When you consider Mercury, and put it in a sign, and then put it in a house, you are specifying and defining the way that Mercury will express itself, thereby refining and narrowing the possible outcomes. However, there are still multiple ways that Mercury will express itself within that range, and it's not just a matter of guessing which one will manifest, but understanding that several of them probably will. Further, trying to guess all the forms of expression any planet-sign-house combo could take is pointless and impossible. Will everyone with Mercury in Virgo in the tenth house be an accountant? Of course not. Mercury in Virgo in the tenth house can pick a number of ways to utilize the urge to communicate (Mercury) in an analytical and precise manner (Virgo) in the public realm or in accordance with their career goals (tenth house). Do not try to guess whether person X will be an accountant or person Y will have a fondness for collecting pristine first-edition novels. That's for the individual to explore and decide and that's free will: multiple outcomes to display and utilize the core planetary energy. Instead of engaging in guessing games, focus on the heart of the matter: the one or two root causes that may bring about numerous effects. Insight into these root needs and causes will not only increase your accuracy but also be of the most value to an individual whose natal chart you interpret.

KEYWORDS: ROOT OR BRANCH?

So now you understand that keywords that are common examples or metaphors for a planet, sign, or house may not apply *literally* in every chart. Pluto rules crime and the underworld, but while everyone has Pluto in their chart, we're not all gangsters. If you get stuck on a keyword, try considering whether it communicates example or essence. Does it take you down to the root of its meaning or is it just one possibility that branches out from that root? Generally, the more complex and multifaceted a keyword's meaning is, the more likely it's a root. *Communication* and *learning* are essential root keywords for Gemini, but a degree in journalism, a love of crossword puzzles, enjoyment of television talk shows, or membership in a book club are only potential branches on the Gemini tree. They may not all be apparent in a Gemini's life, but they all stem from the roots that sustain every Gemini.

DON'T FORCE THE THEME

Finding a natal chart theme can feel like you've hit the jackpot, and it's tempting to make every planetary island conform to it, but this will not always work out. Sometimes you may have a major theme and a subtheme, or two themes that play out against each other. Other times you may have a lone planet that seems to refuse every attempt to link it with the theme you've discovered. At this point, it can be useful to rethink or reframe your conclusions to see if maybe you've missed something important, but it can happen that this planet wants to stay isolated. It may be that the isolation is actually part of the theme (or a second, contradicting theme) that represents a part of the person that they have a hard time feeding or integrating into the rest of their lives, as reflected in the isolation of the planet in the natal chart. For example, if the rest of the chart seems to illustrate travel and adventure but a Taurus Moon in the fourth house suggests a homebody love of routine and security, this is indeed contradictory and can point to challenges this person has in trying to meet all their own needs and the conflicts that may arise. Chart components that stand outside of or are in direct conflict with your theme can be just as useful as the ones that contribute to it.

CONTRAST AND COMPARE

Much of an astrologer's work is in continuing to deepen their understanding of the basic archetypes of planet, sign, and house. If you are having trouble understanding the essential meaning of a sign or a house or just want to deepen your understanding, contrasting it with its opposite can give you some perspective. You've already read about the houses and signs in great length; use the following condensed, essential meanings to help you solidify your understanding.

Aries vs. Libra

Aries doesn't hesitate. It acts directly and powerfully, passionately going after what it wants. Competitive and bold, it's every man for himself, for better or worse. Aries is driven, self-motivated, and confident but also prone to impulsiveness, hotheadedness, and black-and-white thinking.

Aries is the fighter and Libra is the peacemaker, focused on ensuring that everyone gets a turn and has their say while avoiding unnecessary conflict. Skilled at compromise, Libra is gracious and fair-minded. Libra sees everything in shades of gray—not absolute but varied and complex. It is this ability to see a perspective other than their own that makes them so socially aware but also prone to chronic indecision and hesitation.

Taurus vs. Scorpio

Taurus is sustained by a calm, peaceful, and stable existence. It knows the value of taking things slowly and enjoying life as it comes. There is stillness at the heart of Taurus that makes it seem deeply rooted and unflappable. Taurus revels in the simple and straightforward, embracing the motto "no muss, no fuss." Taurus prefers to avoid drama and will often stubbornly avoid change in favor of the safety of the known.

Scorpio feels most alive when it's living not on solid, open ground but on the edge of life. It thrives on complexity and intensity, and while others may crumble or freeze in crisis, Scorpio flourishes. Scorpio craves the catharsis of renewal that change promises, sometimes seeking it out purposefully but prone to drumming up drama where none would otherwise be found. Scorpio is skilled at seeing beneath the surface of situations or others' behavior down to the bare and sometimes uncomfortable truth and may therefore have difficulty accepting things at face value, suspicious of that which seems to be pure or simple.

Gemini vs. Sagittarius

While Gemini and Sagittarius both have a lust for learning and experience, their methods differ. Gemini asks questions and wants its questions answered but is delighted when those answers lead to even more questions. A never-ending mirror ball of multiple perspectives ensures that its curiosity is rarely sated, but it will move on quickly when bored.

Sagittarius wants to uncover and experience meaning, not just by collecting a handful of abstract facts to file away but through personal experiences. It thrives on living an experience to know truly what something is all about. It has a penchant for putting ideas together to see a unifying conclusion but sometimes jumps to the wrong conclusions if it glosses over important specifics.

Cancer vs. Capricorn

Capricorn prioritizes the goal first, then attends to (emotional) needs, whereas Cancer prioritizes the emotional needs and takes care of what needs to be done afterward. To Cancer, the world can wait but the heart won't, and mustn't. Capricorn's long-range view makes it difficult to rest in the moment, knowing that what isn't done today will be twice as difficult tomorrow, because it's the world that won't wait. To Capricorn, results are the only thing that matter; to Cancer, it's not just the result but how you get there that makes all the difference.

Leo vs. Aquarius

This sign duo shares common ground in the desire for self-expression but through opposing means. Leo's warmth and expressiveness shine when it's given a chance to show its stuff and draws others in by its playfulness. Aquarius seeks to clarify its sense of self by differentiation and separation so that it can express its true self with authenticity. While Leo's method involves engagement and inclusivity to draw out its best, Aquarius's method relies on detachment so it is free to be its best.

Virgo vs. Pisces

Virgo utilizes clear definitions and boundaries in order to understand, contain, and control its world. It categorizes and organizes, acting with intention and purpose. While Pisces wilts under pressure and expectation, Virgo thrives on it. Virgo must focus and concentrate its energy, whereas Pisces' energy is naturally dispersed and open. Virgo can lose sight of the big picture in favor of the details, and Pisces is always so tuned in to the bigger picture that it may suffer from overwhelm.

Pisces is not about control but surrender. It is not about exercising control to perfect itself but to surrender to the whole of itself and life's experiences because it knows the beauty of perfect imperfections. Pisces operates on compassion, empathy, and imagination, whereas Virgo operates on discernment, logic, and critical thinking.

First House vs. Seventh House: Self and Others

In the first house, we do things that help us discover or reinforce our sense of self, so we serve only our self and our needs. We may not have much perspective on ourselves because we are working from within. In the seventh house, we consider how what we want mixes with another's needs, compromising and resolving conflict where necessary in order to continue sharing some part of our lives with them. In the seventh house we see our self through another's eyes, and whether or not we like what we see, we can get some perspective on ourselves even though our partner isn't always right and has their own blind spots.

Second House vs. Eighth House: Personal and Shared Resources

In the second house, everything rides on us: what we are capable of, the resources we create or acquire through our own efforts, and the decisions we make about using them. In the eighth house, we pool our resources with another, supporting and/or being supported by them, and in this sharing we become both stronger and more vulnerable. Both houses share an underlying thread of survival, with the second house survival matters being more practical and eighth house survival matters being more existential or emotional.

Third House vs. Ninth House: Information Gathering and Distilling

While the terrain of both these houses incorporates learning, the third house activities center on the immediacy of what we are observing, learning, or relaying. We react to what we observe on a moment-to-moment basis and it changes our perception constantly. The ninth house activities take us out of the immediate and rapidly changing world of perception and into the terrain of big systems of knowledge and its long, established traditions that seek to organize knowledge into meaning. Generally, in the ninth house, the information has been distilled and organized, and meaningful connections have been made.

Fourth House vs. Tenth House: Private and Public

In the fourth house, the terrain is focused on where we begin and where we come from, whether it's our birth into our family of origin or beginning each day at home before we step out into the world. There is an aura of privacy, shelter, and clan when we engage in fourth house activities. In the tenth house, it is not about where we've come from but what we are making of ourselves in the world, and our public engagement with it. We are known and seen through the roles we fulfill in the world, and are focused not on the world within but on bringing what we cultivate in that world within to the world outside.

Fifth House vs. Eleventh House: Now and Then, Me and Them

The activities of the fifth house draw us into the present moment, where the world falls away and we are caught up. The activities of the eleventh house draw us out, into the future, into the possibilities, into the crowd. While the fifth house activities have us on our own private stage, the activities of the eleventh house draw us into the audience, becoming a voice in the whole chorus in order to achieve a goal or to maintain a sense of community.

Sixth House vs. Twelfth House: the Material and Immaterial World

It gets pretty real and mundane in the sixth house. Nothing is less glamorous than taking out the trash or feeding the cat, punching a time clock or brushing our teeth, but these activities and hundreds like them make up the activities of the sixth house. It's where the real-world work gets done and our perspective narrows to the task at hand. We are often never more *in* and *of* the world than when we embody the sixth house.

In the twelfth house, we are focused not on the material but the spiritual, the eternal, the transcendent. The activities of the twelfth house encourage a larger perspective and may lead us, if only temporarily, out of the concerns of the everyday world for a time. Our consciousness expands beyond the small tasks at hand to the broad expanse of life itself.

WRITE YOUR OWN BOOK

At the primary level, an astrology chart is a series of formulas. Insert tab (planet) into slot (sign) with bolt (house). The formula will spit out a string of keywords, but you know by now that keywords are not the final product; they are there to stimulate your thought process as you dig down to the essence of meaning. They are finalized, fixed branches of the living, archetypal roots. The way to understand a sign's keywords or some planetary combination is to take it out of the conceptual and down-to-earth through examples and something relatable. The longer you study astrology, the more examples, stories, quotes, and other precise nuggets of meaning you'll accumulate.

As you become more familiar with the archetypes, they will come alive for you, in you, and through you. This is a rich process that will happen over time, and the longer you practice astrology, the richer your knowledge will become through experience. You'll be able to put your own spin on the possibilities of a sign, planet, house, or aspect, and that is how astrology will continue to flourish. In the beginning of your studies, you may try to emulate the voices of your teachers, following their examples and using their words until you, yourself, become the teacher.

Is there something you read somewhere that really drove home the essence of Leo to you? Something someone said that really served as a prime example of a flesh-and-blood experience of living the third house? A quote of the day that struck you as something Venus herself might say? These insights are priceless gems that can be gathered and brought out again when you need them. We all have a different set of learning experiences and perspectives that color how we understand something. Life speaks to us all through books, movies, myths, songs, comics, relationships, triumphs, joys, sorrows, and more. Everything you are, every hobby and interest, skill and experience, can be brought to bear on your unique understanding and application of astrology because astrology is life. When you find something that really represents an astrological symbol *to you*, it'll stick with you longer and more deeply than any concept or keyword will.

Get a blank book and set apart sections for the signs, planets, houses, aspects, interpretation techniques, and any other astrological component you like. Write down the ideas and stories that have impressed upon you the heart of the meaning of a particular symbol, in addition to the basic definitions as you understand them. Over time, gather all the sayings, ideas, examples, and metaphors that illustrate an astrological concept with a simple, singular, grounded, and relatable example. After a while, you'll have your own astrology book, tailor-made for you, to jumpstart your creativity whenever you're stuck trying to understand something in a chart. Here are some ideas to get you started on your book:

Think about your favorite movies. What central themes did they present? Can you relate that to a certain sign or planet? Try this with your favorite book, fairy tale, and so on.

What profession might a certain sign like *and, more importantly, why?*

How would you personify a sign into a simple character? What iconic character, living or dead, real or imaginary, do you think is the embodiment of each sign?

Create or collect any cheat sheets or tables such as keyword lists, an astrological glyph decoder for the signs and planets, groupings of elements and modalities and the signs in each, and any other handy-dandy information summaries. Look for local or online astrology classes or informative websites that might give you at-a-glance information to incorporate into your book. These could also be great ways to network and learn from others.

Paste or copy into your book your own natal chart, as well as the charts of those you find particularly fascinating and/or of close friends and family, so you'll always have them ready when an idea strikes you.

Collect a few meaningful quotes or sayings that you think speak to the essence of an astrological symbol.

Take your book everywhere with you so you'll be ready to add to it if inspiration strikes!

GLOSSARY

Some terms in this glossary have not been discussed in this book but have been included to offer additional concepts to spark your curiosity and further your astrological study.

affinity: When two or more factors in a chart are linked in a harmonious way, such as planets placed in complementary signs.

angles: The four directions in a chart, marked by the beginning cusp of the first, fourth, seventh, and tenth houses as calculated by four points where the horizon or meridian intersect the ecliptic at the time and place of birth.

angular: A planet may be referred to as angular if it is in one of the four angular houses (first, fourth, seventh, or tenth) and/or conjunct one of the four angles.

applying: A term used to designate when an aspect is pre-exactitude. Also called *approaching*.

archetype: An idea or concept that resides in the collective unconscious, which is universally present in each individual's subconscious without the person having necessarily learned it consciously; a primal symbol.

Ascendant (see also *rising sign*): The first of the four angles of the chart that mark the four directions in most house systems. The

Ascendant is the precise point at which a particular degree of a zodiac sign intersects with the ecliptic at the moment of birth, as differentiated from the *rising sign*, which refers to the entire sign in which the Ascendant is contained. The terms rising sign and Ascendant are often used interchangeably for convenience.

aspect: The angular relationship between two planets or points as measured in arc (degrees apart) in a chart.

aspect pattern: An aspect involving more than two planets, each in specific relationship to each other and often crossing over the entire chart.

asteroid: Planetary-like objects (sometimes called planetoids) found primarily in the asteroid belt located between Mars and Jupiter that maintain orbit around the Sun as a planet does. Asteroids are part of a larger group called *minor planets*, which includes dwarf planets (such as Ceres and the reclassified designation of Pluto as of 2006), centaurs (bodies in orbit between Jupiter and Neptune), and trans-Neptunian objects (those orbiting beyond Neptune, which, yes, also includes Pluto). Some astrologers incorporate asteroids into an astrological chart and seek to interpret their meaning in the same manner as the planets. Popularly used asteroids in astrology include (among others) Ceres, Juno, Pallas Athena, and Vesta. Pluto is still considered a planet in most astrological references as far as its relevance.

astrology: The study of the heavens as they relate symbolically to events and people on Earth.

astrology, types of: Many different astrological systems and uses have been imagined over time. Here are a few:

> *Chinese astrology:* A system altogether different from Western/tropical astrology. Twelve signs make up the zodiac of this system, and are not connected to constellations along the ecliptic. They are Rat, Ox, Tiger, Rabbit, Dragon, Snake, Horse, Goat, Monkey, Rooster, Dog, and Pig. One's birth

year, month, day, and hour, referred to as the Four Pillars, has a correspondence with one of the twelve animals, with the maximum possibility of four different animals representing an individual's character or destiny.

electional astrology: The use of astrology to determine the most favorable moment and place to "birth" something, such as a business, a marriage, or even a child.

horary astrology: The use of astrology to determine the answer to a specific question by casting a chart for the exact time and place of the question as it is asked.

Jyotish astrology (also referred to as Hindu, Indian, and Vedic astrology): Another system that differs from Western astrology. Jyotish employs the same twelve signs but defines them according to *sidereal* coordinates. It also incorporates a further division of the sky into twenty-seven sections, called lunar mansions, and utilizes sixteen elements.

Mayan astrology: An astrological system differing from Western in that it utilizes twenty signs—some animals, some objects, and some concepts or events such as death or wind. Mayan astrology also uses directions instead of elements and a 260-day yearly calendar called the Tzolkin.

medical astrology: The use of astrology to analyze one's physical health from an individual's natal chart. Each sign (and, in some applications, each planet too) corresponds with a few specific areas of the body.

mundane astrology: The use of astrology to analyze world affairs and events, including political analyses. The astrology of places.

natal astrology: The use of astrology to study the makeup of an individual from many angles, including psychological, spiritual, emotional, and biographical.

sidereal astrology: A method of defining the zodiac sign boundaries. The use of the zodiac of twelve signs based on the fixed stars of the constellations that lie along the ecliptic rather than the designated sections of sky that begin with the point of the vernal equinox (tropical).

tropical astrology: A system so called for its method of defining the zodiac sign boundaries. The tropical astrology use of the zodiac of twelve signs based on the declination of the Sun as it moves between the tropics of Cancer and Capricorn, as differentiated from the alignment of the constellations of the same names (sidereal).

astronomy: The study of the universe and celestial objects, including analysis of their positions, movements, composition, and origin.

arc: The measurement around the circumference of a circle. The length of a given arc is a measurement of a portion of a circle.

axis: An imaginary line drawn through the center of the earth (or any planet) between the poles, about which the planet rotates or "spins."

benefic: An ancient term that refers specifically to a planet or aspect that is seen as beneficial, good, or favorable, typically Venus or Jupiter.

celestial sphere: As Earth is surrounded by infinite space, the celestial sphere is an imaginary sphere meant to represent the universe surrounding Earth in every direction, with Earth at the center.

chart: In astrology, the two-dimensional representation ("map") of the heavens at a moment in time.

constellation: A defined area of the celestial sphere containing a set of stars, or star pattern, that has been given a name, which varies according to cultures and time period.

contraparallel (see also *declination*): A less well-known aspect between two or more planets that is based on their *declination*, their latitudinal distance from the celestial equator. When two planets are found in the same degree (typically with a 1° orb allowance) on opposite sides of the celestial equator (one north and one south), they are contraparallel to each other. This aspect is often interpreted as a weaker opposition.

cusp: The boundary that separates one sign or house from the next.

debility (see also *dignity*): Refers to a planet located in a sign that is considered its fall or detriment.

decan/decanate: The division of each of the twelve signs into three equal parts, measuring 10 degrees each.

declination: The distance of a planet or *point* from the celestial equator, north or south, as measured by degrees, minutes, and seconds of arc.

degree (see also *arc*): A unit of measurement. A circle is measured in 360 even portions, each one called a degree.

delineate: A term used in astrology to refer to the chart interpretation process, more specifically to interpreting the combining of any two chart components, such as a planet in a sign or an aspect between two planets.

Descendant: The third of the four angles of the chart that mark the four directions in most house systems. The Descendant is the precise point at which a particular degree of a zodiac sign intersects with the ecliptic at the moment of birth on the western side.

dignity: A term used to measure the strength or prominence of a planet by its placement in a chart. When a planet is placed in a sign that is considered beneficial to the expression of the planet according to ancient designations, that planet is in *essential* dignity. There are five essential dignities: domicile (vs. detriment), exaltation (vs. fall), triplicity, terms, and face (decanate). A planet in *accidental* dignity refers to how prominent that planet is because of how it is placed in the context of the whole chart. A planet's influence may be greater in a chart because of a number of reasons, including (but not limited to) being placed in a prominent location (such as in a house containing one of the four angles) or having great neighbors, such as in a favorable aspect to a benefic planet.

direct: A term used to describe the apparent forward motion of a planet in its orbital path, as opposed to retrograde, which is apparent backward motion.

dispositor: A planet that rules the sign on the cusp of any house or planetary placement in a chart. For example, Taurus on the second house cusp would defer to Venus, because Venus rules Taurus. Mars in the sign of Taurus in a natal chart would also defer to Venus for the same reason. The word dispositor comes from the Latin word meaning "to put in different places." A planet that rules the sign on a house cusp or that rules the sign any other planet is in is said to move or carry the energy forward around the chart.

duality: A category in which the twelve signs are divided into two groups: projective and receptive, also commonly called masculine and feminine or positive and negative.

eclipse: The temporary occurrence of a planetary body obscuring another planetary body, such as the Sun's light obscured by the Moon when viewed from Earth or the reflected light from the Moon when the earth lies between the Sun and Moon. This phenomenon can only occur in total when all three bodies align at the same (total eclipse) or near the same (partial eclipse) *declination*. The blocked planetary body can be obscured either by another planetary body moving in front of it (from our perspective on Earth) or by passing through another planetary body's shadow. A solar eclipse, when the Sun's light is blocked, occurs when the position of the Moon is such that it stands between the earth and the Sun, blocking our view of the Sun (an *occultation*). A lunar eclipse, when the sunlight that reflects off the Moon is blocked, happens when the position of the earth is such that it stands between the Moon and Sun, with the shadow of the earth falling over the Moon.

ecliptic: The apparent path of the Sun as it appears, from the viewpoint of Earth, to travel across the celestial sphere over the course of a year.

element: In astrology, the classification of each sign and house into four elemental categories: fire, earth, air, or water. Three signs and three houses are assigned to each of four elements and share certain qualities with others in their elemental group.

ephemeris: A set of tables listing the positions of the planets (including the Sun and Moon and sometimes the North Node of the Moon and select asteroids). Each planet's position is given in degrees, minutes, and sometimes seconds of the sign the planet is in at the same time each day, once a day over a period of months or years. Standard ephemerides list a planet's position once a day, at either noon each day or midnight each day, for a period of fifty years. Astrologers use this data to track the position, apparent direction, and average speed of a planet as it moves through the signs in its orbital path along the ecliptic. This data is also used to calculate an astrology chart and is programmed into chart calculation computer programs.

equinox: The moment, occurring twice each year, when the length of the day and night are approximately equal. More technically, when the Sun is at one of the two points where the ecliptic and celestial equator intersect. The equinox points mark the beginning of the signs Aries and Libra.

fixed star: A star that does not appear to move in relation to the other celestial bodies, such as asteroids, comets, and planets. The word planet comes from the Greek phrase that means "wandering star."

geocentric (see also _heliocentric_): An astronomical reference to the earth as the center of the solar system or something viewed from the position of the earth.

glyphs: A set of symbols used as a kind of shorthand to represent the planets, signs, and aspects.

great circle: A plane that slices through the center of a sphere, such as the earth and surrounding celestial sphere, dividing it.

heliocentric (see also *geocentric*): An astronomical reference to the Sun as the center or the solar system or something viewed from the position of the Sun (*helios* = Sun).

hemisphere: Half of a sphere, dividing the earth and celestial sphere into north and south hemispheres and east and west hemispheres.

horizon: In common usage, the visible boundary separating the earth and sky. This is the *apparent* horizon, however; the true or *rational* horizon passes through the center of the earth.

horoscope: In common, popular reference, a term referring to brief personality descriptions or predictions for a person according to the sign position of the Sun at their birth. More accurately, this term refers to one's personal and entire natal astrology chart.

house: One of twelve sections that divide a natal chart, calculated according to the rules of an established *house system*. Each house represents a category of experiences, activities, and behaviors that everyone encounters in life.

house system: A set of principles and mathematical calculations by which the house cusp positions are calculated in an astrological chart, including but not limited to the Placidus, Porphyry, Koch, and Whole house systems.

***Imum Coeli* (see *Nadir*)**

inferior (vs. superior): Planets that are closer to the Sun than the earth (Mercury and Venus) are inferior planets. This term is not a value judgment but refers to their *inside* position in the solar system. The term inferior is most often used in the phrase *inferior conjunction*, which refers to a conjunction of planets that is occurring on the same side of the Sun as the earth.

ingress: In astrology, this term most often refers to the moment a planet enters a sign. It can also refer to a heavenly body crossing in front of another heavenly body (such as Mercury crossing in front of the Sun or the occurrence of a solar or lunar eclipse) from one's viewpoint.

interception: A birthplace of extreme north or south latitude can create an interception, which happens when a given house in an astrology chart is wider than 30 degrees, engulfing its sign within that house's borders entirely. Alternately, a given house that is narrower than 30 degrees can be engulfed within the nearest sign's boundaries. This results in two house cusps occurring in the same sign, or a house cusp skipping a sign entirely.

keyword: Astrologically, a keyword is a word that is used frequently to describe a characteristic, trait, or behavior of an astrological symbol such as a planet, sign, or house.

latitude: On Earth, distance as measured north or south of the equator. *Celestial* latitude is distance measured north or south from the ecliptic.

longitude: On Earth, distance as measured east or west from the prime meridian. *Celestial* longitude is distance measured eastward from the vernal equinox point (where the celestial equator and ecliptic intersect).

luminary: A term sometimes used to describe the Sun or Moon.

major aspects (see *Ptolemaic aspects*)

malefic: An ancient term that refers specifically to a planet or aspect that is seen as harmful, bad, or unfavorable, commonly Mars and Saturn.

***Medium Coeli* (see *Midheaven*)**

Midheaven: A Latin phrase that means "middle of the sky," the Midheaven is the point where the ecliptic and the meridian cross in the visible sky above the birthplace and is associated with the tenth house in an astrology chart.

midpoint: The shortest distance around the circle of the natal chart between two planets or points.

minor aspect: An angle between two or more planets in an astrology chart that is not defined as a major (or Ptolemaic) aspect, including but not limited to the quincunx, sesquisquadrate, and semisextile.

modality: Refers to three categories—cardinal, fixed, and mutable— that divide the signs into groups according to broad characteristics they share. Also sometimes called qualities or quadruplicities.

mutual reception: Two planets that reside in each other's sign of rulership, such as the Sun in Aries and Mars in Leo.

Nadir: Defined as the "lowest point," the Nadir is associated with the fourth house in an astrology chart. Astrologically, it refers to the point where the ecliptic and meridian meet beneath the earth in relation to the birthplace. Astronomically, it is the point directly beneath the observer and directly opposite the zenith.

natal chart: A circular representation of the celestial sphere with the location of planets, sign and house divisions, and calculated points depicted at the time and place of birth.

nativity: A term used to reference a natal chart.

node: Astrologically, a point in the celestial sphere where a planet crosses the ecliptic. Two calculation methods of nodes are in popular use: the *mean* node uses a calculation that averages out the "wobble" in the earth's rotation (see *precession of the equinoxes*); the *true* node uses a calculation that accounts for this wobble.

orb: The allowable distance between two planets that are in aspect but are not exact. For example, two planets that are three degrees apart from each other would form a conjunction, with an orb of 3°.

orbit: Astronomically, the path of a planetary body around another, such as the planets around the Sun, or the Moon around the earth.

out-of-bounds: A planet that travels outside of the bounds of the ecliptic, north or south, as it orbits.

parallel (see also *declination*): A less well-known aspect between two or more planets that is based on their *declination*, their latitudinal distance from the celestial equator. When two planets are found in the same degree (typically with a 1° orb allowance) and on the same side of the equator (both north or both south), they are parallel to each other. This aspect is typically interpreted as a weaker conjunction.

peregrine: From the Latin word meaning "foreign," this term primarily and originally refers to a planet that has no *dignity* in its placement in a chart—it is not in a sign it rules nor in a sign in which it is exalted, etc. Astrologer Noel Tyl has used the term in reference to planets that do not participate in one of the five Ptolemaic aspects.

phases, lunar: Designations assigned to the portions of the Moon that are illuminated by the Sun's light (as seen from Earth), which change cyclically according to the Moon's orbit. The phase designations are somewhat arbitrary, as the Moon's light cycle could theoretically be divided into any number of parts of the whole, but the most common phase system in Western astrology is the eight-phase system. The eight-phase system comprises the following stages: new, waxing crescent, first quarter, waxing gibbous, full, waning gibbous (sometimes called *disseminating*), last or third quarter, and waning crescent (sometimes called *balsamic*). The term *waxing* is applied to designate when the illumination of the Moon is increasing toward full, and *waning* when decreasing toward new.

phases, planetary: The lunar phase designations are mainly applied to the lunar light cycle but are also applied in slightly different ways to planetary positions. Just as the lunar phases are determined by the relative position of the Moon to the Sun (as viewed from Earth), so each planet has a position relative to every other planet. Any given planet has a phasal relationship with any other planet, even if it is not one of the designated aspects. The phase between planets is determined by starting from one planet's position and counting degrees onward in a clockwise motion from that planet to another planet.

planet: From a Greek phrase meaning "wandering star." In casual reference astrologically, the term also includes the Sun and Moon.

planet, inner: Astrologically, a term that refers to the planets Mercury, Venus, and Mars, also sometimes called *personal planets*. The Sun and Moon may also be included.

planet, outer: A term that refers to the three planets that lie outside of the seven visible planets: Uranus, Neptune, and Pluto. These three are also sometimes called *transpersonal planets*, because of their exceptional distance from the center of the solar system, or *modern planets*, because they were discovered long after the practice of astrology was established. They may also be referred to as *invisible* planets, as opposed to the seven *visible* planets.

planet, visible: A term referring to the "original" seven planets (including the Sun and Moon) before the inclusion of Uranus, Neptune, and Pluto.

planet, social: A term that refers to the two "middle" planets, Jupiter and Saturn.

point: A casual term to refer to any significant astrological component that is not represented by a physical body, such as the nodes.

polarity: Signs that are located on the opposite side of the zodiac circle are said to be polarities.

precession of the equinoxes: A nontechnical term used to refer to the continuous change in the orientation of the earth's axis relative to the celestial sphere. If the earth's axis is imagined to extend out into the celestial sphere, it would point to a certain location. The place in the heavens to which this extended axis "points" changes slowly over time in a repeated pattern that takes approximately 26,000 years to complete. Like a toy top that has begun to wobble slightly, the earth also "wobbles," and its axis subsequently traces a small imaginary circle in the heavens. Also called *axial precession*.

Ptolemaic aspects: A term usually used in reference to a group of aspects: the conjunction, sextile, square, trine, and opposition. Also called *major* aspects. The term refers to Claudius Ptolemy, a second-century astrologer/astronomer who described these aspects in his influential work *Tetrabiblos*.

quadrant: A fourth of a circle. The natal chart is divided into four quadrants, with three houses forming each quadrant. The first quadrant comprises houses 1–3, the second quadrant comprises houses 4–6, etc.

rectification: A process or set of processes to determine the likely time of birth by comparing significant events in the biography to the motion of the planets at the time of those events.

retrograde: The appearance of a planet moving backward through its orbital path as viewed from Earth. The more accurate term for this is *apparent* retrograde motion, since the planets do not actually change direction but only appear to.

rising sign (see also *Ascendant*): The sign that was rising over the eastern horizon at the time of birth is known as the rising sign, which contains the Ascendant.

ruler, chart: The planet that rules the sign of the Ascendant and/or a planet that is located in close proximity to the Ascendant.

ruler, planetary: The planet that is said to express itself most seamlessly through a certain sign and therefore "at home" in that sign is said to be its ruler. The original assignment of planet-sign rulerships included only the visible planets and was constructed not strictly according to affinity but assigned according to a pattern, fanning out from the luminaries.

separating: A term used to designate an aspect that is post-exactitude—that is, as the planets move farther away from each other, they are separating from each other, with a continually widening orb or arc between them.

sign: One of twelve sections that circle the edge of a natal chart, correlating with the 30° section of sky that lies along the band of the *zodiac*. Each sign represents certain archetypal traits and characteristics.

station: The state of a planet when it appears to stop in its orbit before changing directions.

stellium: A group of three or more planets in close conjunction with each other, all in the same sign or house.

Sun sign: A term used to refer to the sign in which the Sun was found at the time of birth. This is often simplified in popular use to simply "sign," as in "what's your sign?"

zenith: The point directly above the observer in the celestial sphere.

zodiac: A circle, or narrow band, that lies along the ecliptic (the apparent path of the Sun) and is divided into twelve equal sections (signs).

RECOMMENDED READING AND RESOURCES

STUDYING THE NATAL CHART

Arroyo, Stephen. *Astrology, Karma, and Transformation: The Inner Dimensions of the Birth Chart.* Second revised and expanded edition. Petaluma, CA: CRCS Publications, 1992.

———. *Astrology, Psychology, and the Four Elements: An Energy Approach to Astrology and Its Use in the Counseling Arts.* Petaluma, CA: CRCS Publications, 1975.

———. *Chart Interpretation Handbook: Guidelines for Understanding the Essentials of the Birth Chart.* Petaluma, CA: CRCS Publications, 1990.

Forrest, Jodie. *The Ascendant.* Borrego Springs, CA: Seven Paws Press, 2007.

Forrest, Steven. *The Book of Pluto: Finding Wisdom in Darkness with Astrology.* Second edition. Borrego Springs, CA: Seven Paws Press, 2012.

———. *The Inner Sky: How to Make Wiser Choices for a More Fulfilling Life.* Borrego Springs, CA: Seven Paws Press, 1997.

———. *Yesterday's Sky.* Borrego Springs, CA: Seven Paws Press, 2008.

Green, Jeff. *Pluto: The Evolutionary Journey of the Soul, Volume 1*. St. Paul, MN: Llewellyn Publications, 1985.

Herring, Amy. *Astrology of the Moon: An Illuminating Journey Through the Signs and Houses*. Woodbury, MN: Llewellyn Publications, 2010.

Jones, Mark. *Healing the Soul: Pluto, Uranus, and the Lunar Nodes*. Portland, OR: Raven Dreams Press, 2011.

Marks, Tracy. *Planetary Aspects: An Astrological Guide to Managing Your T-Square*. Revised and expanded edition. Lake Worth, FL: Ibis Press, 2014.

Oken, Alan. *Rulers of the Horoscope: Finding Your Way Through the Labyrinth*. Newburyport, MA: Red Wheel Weiser, 2008.

FURTHER TECHNIQUES

Forrest, Steven. *The Changing Sky: A Practical Guide to Predictive Astrology*. Second edition. Borrego Springs, CA: Seven Paws Press, 2008.

Sullivan, Erin. *The Astrology of Midlife and Aging*. New York: Tarcher, 2005.

SPECIALIZED TOPICS

Burk, Kevin. *Astrology Math Made Easy*. Woburn, MA: Serendipity Press, 2005.

Coppock, Austin. *36 Faces: The History, Astrology, and Magic of the Decans*. Hercules, CA: Three Hands Press, 2014.

George, Demetra, and Douglas Bloch. *Asteroid Goddesses*. Lake Worth, FL: Ibis Press, 2003.

March, Marion D., and Joan McEvers. *The Only Way to Learn Astrology, Volume 2: Math & Interpretation Techniques*. Third edition. Epping, NH: Starcrafts Publishing, 2009.

McRae, Chris. *Understanding Interceptions: A Key to Unlocking the Door*. Tempe, AZ: American Federation of Astrologers, 2000.

HISTORY OF ASTROLOGY

Bobrick, Benson. *The Fated Sky: Astrology in History*. New York: Simon & Schuster, 2006.

Campion, Nicholas. *A History of Western Astrology, Volume I: The Ancient and Classical Worlds*. New York: Continuum, 2009.

———. *A History of Western Astrology, Volume II: The Medieval and Modern Worlds*. New York: Continuum, 2009.

Holden, James Herschel. *A History of Horoscopic Astrology*. Second edition. Tempe, AZ: American Federation of Astrologers, 1996.

Tarnas, Richard. *Cosmos and Psyche: Intimations of a New World View*. New York: Penguin, 2006.

BEYOND ASTROLOGY

Jung, Carl. "The Stages of Life." In *The Collected Works of C. G. Jung, Volume 8*. Princeton, NJ: Princeton University Press, 2010.

———. *The Portable Jung*. Edited by Joseph Campbell. New York: Penguin, 1976.

Martin, Steve. *Born Standing Up: A Comic's Life*. New York: Scribner, 2008.

WEB RESOURCES AND FURTHER READING

www.astro.com is an excellent resource for free chart calculation. They also have an astrological forum, a large library of articles, and a clickable chart feature and astrological reports. Their 9,000-year ephemeris is exceptionally helpful for advanced studies.

www.heavenlytruth.com is Amy's professional website, which hosts a large library of astrology articles. Beginning astrology video learning and classes are available. Lecture schedule and consultation information can also be found here.

www.cdc.gov/nchs/w2w.htm gives a listing of links by state (United States only) that can help you obtain a copy of your birth certificate if you do not have one.

www.findastrologer.com/astrology-organizations/local-astrology
-organizations can help you network, network, network. Find
established astrology groups in your area, and if none exist, start
your own and list it here.

http://astro.unl.edu/animationsLinks.html#ca_coordsmotion has a
large number of animations that will show you a variety of simu-
lations and maps to help you visualize the celestial sphere and
astronomical phenomena such as the seasons shifting, eclipses,
and more.

GET A COPY OF YOUR CHART

From the Author

If you'd like a free PDF copy of your natal chart, write to me through my website HeavenlyTruth.com with your name and complete, exact birth data and I'll email you a free copy!

On the Web

There are many websites that will calculate your natal chart for free, but they are not all created equally. A chart calculation program is only as good as the human programming it. Daylight saving time conversions, birthplaces that are unknown or have changed names, and more can complicate the matter and potentially produce an incorrect chart. Books can provide basic ready-to-go information on what signs the planets were in on certain days, but one has to take into account the time of day (and in what time zone) a planet moved from one sign to the other. There are also the houses to calculate, which are different for each chart, and the Ascendant. Some books give you a table to use to look up your Ascendant, but they are often incorrect (I thought I was the wrong rising sign for over a year when I first started studying astrology because of this!). So be careful and consider the source. It's always a good idea to confirm a natal chart calculation by using more than one source to calculate it and comparing the two.

Software

Professional software is typically the most preferred option to use for calculating your birth chart, but the cost is often prohibitive for new students or hobbyists. Again, beware of free or low-cost software. Professional programs are more likely to have accurate data because the effort and research has been put in by qualified programmers *and* astrologers. You tend to get what you pay for with this resource.

Some of the top software programs used by professionals and serious hobbyists are Solar Fire, Win*Star, Kepler, Janus, and Time Passages.

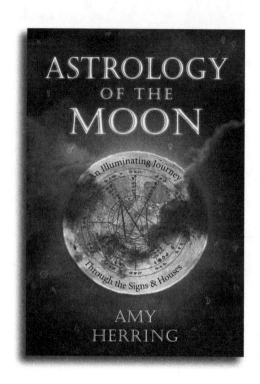

ASTROLOGY
OF THE
MOON

An Illuminating Journey

Through the Signs & Houses

AMY
HERRING

Astrology of the Moon
An Illuminating Journey Through the Signs and Houses
Amy Herring

Your moon sign represents your emotional nature and lights the way toward profound spiritual growth. With *Astrology of the Moon*, you can identify your core emotional needs, learn to fulfill them, and make the best choices for a more rewarding, spiritually enriched life.

Focusing on the natal and progressed moon relationship, this information-packed guide explains the Moon's powerful energetic potential in relation to the signs, houses, planets, and aspects. In an easy-to-use "cookbook" format, Herring lays out your emotional needs in the areas of love, family life, your career, and more, with practical ways to meet these essential needs so you can create happiness at every stage of life.

978-0-7387-1896-5, 312 pp., 6 x 9   **$21.95**
